LEARNED SOCIETIES AND
ENGLISH LITERARY SCHOLARSHIP

LEARNED SOCIETIES AND
ENGLISH LITERARY SCHOLARSHIP

IN GREAT BRITAIN AND THE UNITED STATES

BY

HARRISON ROSS STEEVES

AMS PRESS

NEW YORK

Reprinted from the edition of 1913, New York
First AMS EDITION published 1970
Manufactured in the United States of America

Library of Congress Catalogue Card Number: 70-112943
SBN: 404-06238-5

AMS PRESS, INC.
NEW YORK, N.Y. 10003

TO

JOHN FRANCIS STEEVES

AND

IMOGENE UPSON STEEVES

PREFACE

The following chapters were written as a dissertation for the doctorate in the Department of English, Columbia University. The work was originally planned as a bibliography, with a brief introduction covering the substance of the present volume; but with the growth of the introductory material, it became apparent that this alone would be sufficient to satisfy the special requirement. The volume is therefore plainly limited in its scope, and more or less arbitrarily planned and presented.

The writer is under obligation to Professor George Philip Krapp, Professor William Peterfield Trent, and Professor Harry Morgan Ayres, of the Department of English at Columbia, all of whom have read the manuscript and given him generous and valuable help. He owes much also to the personal kindness of Mr. Frederic W. Erb, of the Columbia Library, and Mr. C. W. Kennedy, of the British Museum, and to the courtesy of the officials of the Library of Congress and the libraries at Yale and Cornell.

CONTENTS

INTRODUCTION

It is certain that one of the most important features of modern scholarship—as, indeed, of every progressive intellectual interest of to-day—is organization. The force of specialization in modern investigative methods, which is a distinct outgrowth of collective effort, is of course too apparent to require comment. Probably few of us, however, who have mentally noted the general efficiency of the literary societies of to-day have stopped actually to measure the quantity and quality of their contributions to criticism and literary history. Originally devised to concentrate individual interests in the common purposes of study, they became eventually to a large extent the purveyors of patronage for scholarship, increasing its remuneration, moral as well as material, and hence its efficiency; and in the last half century they have created a public interest in the products of conscientious research which has literally opened the storehouse of literary antiquity. It does not seem too much to say that the greater part of the scholarly accomplishments in the field of literature during the last century was due to the activities of the learned societies. Scarcely a noted student of that period could wholly separate his success from that of the societies with which he was connected. Such bodies have made generally accessible a quantity and kind of material that could not under other conditions have reached a supporting public in anything like the same limited time. What is perhaps almost as important in the end, co-operation in these societies has given definition to method and conscience in scholarly pursuits.

The society of to-day, however, is not the result of a day's growth. The reliable and monumental products of a modern text publication society owe much of their value to the recognition of the hasty, erring, and at times unconscientious scholarship. of a mid-century specialists' society; and these societies in turn represented a generally marked advance in motive and accuracy of scholarship over the aristocratic book clubs of the early part of the century. Before all of these, of course, were the inevitable beginnings in private meetings among small numbers of students, with no defined scholarly policy, and no notion of general publication.

The beginnings of organized literary study, in fact, antedate any records of a self-styled literary society. It is not necessary to assume that the development of the society idea as applied to literary investigation has been constantly progressive and uninterrupted. As a matter of fact, there is really no precedent or tradition for such established cooperation before the beginning of the nineteenth century, though there are some interesting and at times important earlier instances of society activity, wholly isolated, which represent the incentives of the first generally recognized movements. The history of this important phase of nineteenth century scholarship has not been, so far, connectedly presented. Hence the following volume, which will, it is hoped, indicate with an approach to finality the historical growth of these movements and their influences upon the scholarship of their day and our own.

LEARNED SOCIETIES AND ENGLISH LITERARY SCHOLARSHIP

CHAPTER I

THE FIELD

Organized literary scholarship in England, like practically all phases of Renaissance intellectual activity, was a relatively late development. Indefinite as the immediate purposes of the academies of Renaissance Italy may at times seem to us, there can be no question as to the substantial value of such bodies in the development of current culture. In England, however, we find no traces of an amateur literary organization until almost the last quarter of the sixteenth century, at the moment when Italian academies were at the zenith of their popularity and effectiveness; and even then such organizations neither invited nor possessed public prominence. For this reason it is difficult to trace a continuous tradition of this sort through our most important literary period. The movement, exotic in itself, and unsupported by the general humanistic enthusiasm which gave life to the Italian academies, died almost in its birth and left no important effects to succeeding ages. What activity and interest we find in learned societies and academies, then, from the early seventeenth to the late eighteenth century, can generally be considered a reflection of such activities and interests in Continental Europe; and the uniform failure of all such projects throughout almost two centuries can be attributed to a lack of responsible native enthusiasm in such movements. The function of societies of this kind during this period was in the main critical, and aspired to profound effect upon the destinies of the vernacular language and literature. For this reason the lack of vitality in academy movements in England is probably connected more or less directly with the practical failure of the well defined classical critical traditions and the theories of vernacular *illustration* then current on the Continent. At any rate, the two facts may be regarded as co-incident evidences of the popular temper of English literary scholarship at the time. With the greater utility and the sharper definition of purpose in the learned societies of the nineteenth century, England comes well to the front; but before this time, we have only occasional and elusive traces of interest in the society idea.

From the earliest period of their existence, the activity of so-called learned societies in the cultivation of English literary traditions, either creative or historical, is affected by a diversity of conceptions as to the function, scope, and methods of organized philological scholarship. These acknowledged differences in attitude and in forms of activity make it necessary to define the fields of interest of the many English literary learned societies. Definition and division on these grounds is not difficult, and is not necessarily arbitrary. A glance at the various early organized movements in the general direction of philological criticism and research shows three fairly well marked types of society.

The first type, first in importance in its time because of its critical authority in Italy and France, is what is generally known as the "academy," the purpose of which is to establish canons of literary taste, and to facilitate and correct the growth of the vernacular. Such an established academy has never really existed in England. Even the actual incorporation of the British Academy in 1902, after suggestion and pressure from the Council of the Royal Society,[1] though it aimed in part to represent philological scholarship in England at the meetings of the International Association of Academies, could do no more in this direction than to revive the acknowledgment that there never has been, and probably never can be, an authoritative academy of English language and letters. The many efforts to found such an academy, however, extending over a century of critical scholarship from Bolton to Swift, form interesting history.[2]

The second type of philological society that I have chosen to distinguish from organizations of connected interests is in its general attitude rather closely allied with the first, but differs from it importantly in the fact that its aim is primarily creative, not objectively critical. There is, as far as I know, no class name given to this type; without compromising the dignity of these usually small unions of literary men, we might call them "authors' clubs." The first important society of this kind in England was of course the Areopagus, formed by Dyer, Greville, Harvey, Spenser and Sidney in 1579.[3] Other examples readily suggest themselves, as the Martinus Scriblerus Club, and Tennyson's Apostles. In this kind of organization the interest in literature is essentially personal—the interest of the artist in his own product, completed or projected. The field of literary study is the present, not the past. The obvious purpose of such a society is to outline policies of creative work; the concerns of the society are the plans of the individuals who form it; and however these interests may extend themselves

---

[1] *Proceedings of the British Academy*, 1903–1904, vii–ix.

[2] The recurrence of these efforts is traced by Mr. B. S. Monroe in his article, *An English Academy*, in *Modern Philology*, VIII, 107–122 (1910).

[3] Jefferson B. Fletcher, *Areopagus and Pleiade, Journal of English and Germanic Philology*, II, 429–453 (1898).

into generalized theory, the bond of association is always that of the projected contact of the creative artist with his readers.

Differing markedly from these two kinds of literary organization is what is generally called the "learned society" of letters. Here the objects are not creative, not individual, not didactic; they are historical and objective; they touch the past of literature, not the present or the future; in a word, they imply scholarship, not *a priori* critical theory or the notions of literary artists. The object of such societies is to preserve literary monuments, to use them for the illumination of the national background, to cultivate historical knowledge, to concentrate it by discussion, to diffuse it through publication. All the interests that I have indicated are not necessarily to be found in all the societies of this type; but as a point of certain distinction it is probably fair to say that few or none of the peculiar interests of the literary society are to be found in the academies or the authors' clubs. It is with the literary society, or the learned society of letters, that I propose to deal.

CHAPTER II

THE ELIZABETHAN SOCIETY OF ANTIQUARIES

The most ancient of our literary societies—and probably the most ancient of all English learned societies—was the Assembly of the Antiquaries, founded by Matthew Parker, Archbishop of Canterbury, in 1572.[1] The history of this foundation has been presented in large part by a number of extended references to the society. Thomas Smith's life of Sir Robert Cotton, prefixed to his catalogue of the Cottonian Library and afterwards reprinted in a collection of biographies,[2] seems to be the fountain-head of historical information on the subject. From this account Hearne secured the material for his *Collection of Curious Discourses*,[3] which in turn was utilized by Richard Gough, the author of the introduction to the first volume of the *Archaeologia*.[4] Prof. Flügel's recent contribution to the history of the body is a reprint, with brief comment, of the prospectus for the incorporation of the society, probably presented in 1589.[5] This prospectus is fully digested in Smith's

[1] Henry Spelman, *English Works*, 2d ed., 1727; Part b, 69–70.

[2] Thomas Smith, *Vita D. Roberti Cottoni;* in Gryphius's *Vitae Selectae Quorundam Eruditissimorum ac Illustrium Virorum*, 434–536, Vratislaviae, 1711.

[3] Thomas Hearne, *A collection of curious Discourses*, I, *iii-*viii, xi–xvii, lvii-lxi, II, 324–326, 421–449 (2d ed., 1775).

[4] [Richard Gough], *An historical account of the Origin and Establishment of the Society of Antiquaries; Archaeologia*, I, i–xxi (1777). This article, the authorship of which was unknown even to Joseph Hunter, who reworked the early history of the Society of Antiquaries in *Archaeologia* XXXII, is ascribed to Richard Gough by Nichols, in his *Literary Anecdotes of the Eighteenth Century*, VI, 297 (1812).

[5] Ewald Flügel, *Die älteste englische Akademie; Anglia*, XXXII, 261–268 (1909).

account of the society, and was printed substantially as a whole by Hearne. In reworking Smith's memoir of the society, Hearne expanded the historical matter to some extent, and printed many of the papers read before the society, expressing his debt to Smith's materials, where Smith had merely printed a representative number by titles. We see, then, that the bulk of the historical material was brought out by Smith, with some additions by Hearne. Smith, however, seems unfortunately to have been forgotten by most of those who have had occasion since Hearne's time to write upon the society.[6]

In all the historical accounts of this assembly its importance in the general field of English scholarship has been obscured by the narrowness of the special interests of the writers upon the subject. All save Professor Flügel are antiquaries pure and simple; and his purpose is confined to pointing out the scheme for the society's incorporation as the earliest plan for the organization of an English academy.[7] From the fact that most of the historical material relating to the society was originally brought out by antiquaries, we can feel reasonably certain that the nature of their interest in the body dominated their judgment of what was specially

[6] An independent sketch of this society appeared in William Oldys's *Life of Sir Walter Ralegh*, prefixed to his edition of Ralegh's *History of the World*, 1736 (I, cxxx–cxxxi). There are special reasons for considering this article separately; see *post.*, 32, note.

[7] Mr. Monroe (*op. cit.*, 107) states that the society was actually chartered in 1589; but I can not find evidence, in the face of Smith's express denial, to support this conclusion. Richard Carew, a member, writing to Sir Robert Cotton in 1605, shortly after the dissolution of the society, says: ''I heard by my Brother, that in the late Queenes tyme it was lykelie to have received an establishment and extraordynarie favour from sundrie great personages'' (*Original Letters of Eminent Literary Men*, Camden Society, 1843; 99). This passage seems to indicate clearly that the society never secured legal recognition.

important in its history. The selected papers published by Hearne are all concerned with architectural and numismatic antiquities and miscellaneous evidences of social and political organization; philological inquiries, though represented at times, are meager and only incidental. The restricted aims of the writers who have treated the activities of the society at greater or less length have tended, therefore, to confine our impressions of its general importance. It seems, however, that we can not measure the full historical value of this organization by standards of judgment and interest as limited as those which have so far been applied. It is worth noting, in this connection, that no account down to the present writing has dealt adequately with one significant clue to the nature of the society's concerns, and a most important test of its organic efficiency: that is, the effect which the personnel of the society must inevitably have had upon its activities. Furthermore, in an effort to trace the history of literary scholarship in this period we must not omit to recognize two well defined facts: that literary history then was only a vaguely distinguished phase of antiquarian study, and that this fact itself is due to the natural failure to separate *belles lettres* from the literature of knowledge. It is hopeless for us to expect to find at this time clear literary conceptions of a race and a period which were only at that moment being brought within the field of investigative study. We have, it must be granted, no positive evidence of the existence of literary interests in this society; we have, however, no evidence which denies the possibility of such interests. Considering, then, the obviously partial—and literally partial —historical remains which have descended to us, we must fall back upon what inferences are to be drawn from the evidence of its personnel.

Archbishop Parker, the founder of the society, was an

ardently industrious antiquarian, and, as his biographer,
Strype, puts it, "a mighty collector of books." His interest
in English antiquity was of more than ordinarily practical
value because it was measured by his intellectual responsibility to the church of which he was the appointed head.
His chief concern with ancient English literature seems to
have been to justify, by reference to old authorities on
church history and ceremonial, the Anglican establishment.
But his interest in secular history also was broad and generous; and above all, he must be remembered for his timely
and practical recognition of the urgent necessity of collecting ancient manuscripts, even though for narrower reasons
than may move us to-day. An idea of how gravely immi-
nent was the practical annihilation of quantities of manuscript records after the closing of the monasteries may be
gained from Bishop Bale's characteristically vigorous but
convincing picture of their advancing fate.[8] It is interesting to find that Parker was Bale's correspondent upon this
very subject,[9] and that he endeavored for some years after
Bale's death to purchase his collections for permanent
preservation, probably actually securing them in the end.[10]
Parker's own collections of manuscripts were exceedingly
extensive, and critically made. His ecclesiastical duties, as
well as the mere magnitude of his ambition as a collector,
prevented him from assembling personally the bulk of his
library; but he employed for this purpose a number of
travelling agents, including John Stow, William Lambarde,

[8] *The Laboryouse Journey & serche of John Leylande, for Englandes Antiquitees, with declaracyons enlarged: by Johan Bale*, 1549,
Preface.

[9] *A Letter from Bishop Bale to Archbishop Parker, communicated
by H. R. Luard; Cambridge Antiquarian Communications*, III, 157–
173 (1879).

[10] *Correspondence of Matthew Parker, D.D.*, Ed. John Bruce and
Thomas Thomason Perowne, 198, 287 (1853).

and Stephen Batman, the last of whom alone is said to have gathered for the Archbishop 6700 volumes.[11] Twenty-five volumes of historical manuscripts were presented by Parker in 1574 to the Cambridge University library;[12] the greater part of the library, however, was bequeathed by him to Corpus Christi, Cambridge, his own college.[13]

This learned antiquary's extraordinary importance as a library builder, however, scarcely exceeds his note as a powerful and intelligent patron of early English literary scholarship. It is unnecessary to quote contemporary eulogia on this point; suffice it to say that practically every antiquarian writer of his day had reason to express his indebtedness to Parker not alone for his collections, but for his encouragement and personal interest in work under way. His own household was from time to time opened to the students of his period, and he extended vitally necessary aid to the scholarly labors of Foxe, Lambarde, and his own secretary Joscelyn.[14]

It was presumably with John Joscelyn's assistance that he issued the first Anglo-Saxon text in Anglo-Saxon types, cut by his order for his printer, John Day.[15] This volume was *A Testimonie of Antiqvitie, shewing the auncient fayth in the Church of England touching the sacrament of the body and bloude of the Lord,* published according to Strype's "guess" in 1566, and according to Wanley in

[11] John Strype, *The Life and Acts of Matthew Parker,* II, 497-8, 517 (1821). The untiring activity of Parker in hunting down literary relics can be seen in numerous notices by Strype: I, 419, 466-7, 509, 511, 522-5, II, 497-500, 515-20.

[12] *Ibid.,* II, 410-11.

[13] The remarkable historical value of this collection in the field of early English literature may be judged from Dr. Montague Rhodes James's *The Sources of Archbishop Parker's Collection of MSS at Corpus Christi College, Cambridge* (1899).

[14] Strype, *op. cit.,* II, 500, 502-3, 514-9.

[15] *Ibid.,* II, 514.

1567.[16] Whether Parker was or was not the responsible
editor of this work—and there are critical opinions that
Joscelyn, or even Foxe, was principally instrumental in
publishing it[17]—there can be no doubt that the Archbishop's
connection with the publication was one of commanding
supervision. The volume includes in its contents Aelfric's
Paschal Homily, two epistles of Aelfric, the Creed, the
Lord's Prayer, and some scriptural passages, all in the old
tongue, and employed to support Anglican views on the
doctrine of transubstantiation.

Parker's subsequent publications of the materials of early
English history were the *Flores Historiarum,* wrongly
assigned by his predecessors to a "Matthew of Westminster,"[18] in 1567–70; Matthew Paris's *Chronica Majora,*
1571; Asser's life of Alfred, *Aelfredi Regis Res Gestae,*
1574;[19] and Thomas Walsingham's *Historia Anglicana,*

[16] *Ibid.,* I, 472; Humphrey Wanley, *Antiquae literaturae septentrionalis Liber alter, seu Catalogus historico-criticus,* 326 (1705).
It is worth noting that Strype (II, 448) observes that some pieces of
ancient documentary evidence in Parker's *Defence of Priests' Mar-
riages,* 1562, were "set down in the Saxon tongue." This may de-
prive the *Testimonie* of its claim to be the first printed Anglo-Saxon
work.

[17] See R. M. White's preface to his edition of the *Ormulum,* I,
viii–ix, note (1878).

[18] Sir Frederic Madden has established the fact that the greater
portion of the *Flores Historiarum* is an abridgment of Matthew
Paris's *Chronica Majora,* probably prepared under Paris's direction.
See *Matthaei Parisiensis Historia Anglorum,* ed. Sir Frederic Madden, 3 v., 1866–9; I, xx–xxviii. Though Parker's edition of 1570,
issued after the discovery of manuscripts which showed the edition of
1567 to be incomplete, did not correct the error in ascription, Parker
evidently recognized the error by the following year (*op. cit.,* xxxii).
The mistake, however, was generally prevalent until Madden pointed
it out anew.

[19] The Asser, although a Latin text, was printed in Parker's Anglo-
Saxon types for the purpose of encouraging acquaintance with the
character in which the Anglo-Saxon monuments were for the most
part written.

1574.[20]   Parker's claim to special recognition for these
services to learning is simply that of having set an example.
It is very well known that his texts are not at all faithful to
his manuscripts, and this in spite of his direct assertion in
the preface to Asser's *Alfred* that he "never added anything of his own, nor diminished from the copy; but expressed, to a word, everything as he found them in the
originals."[21]   Modern criticism has not been inclined to
generosity toward Parker's faults as an editor, though it
should be admitted by his critics that Elizabethan conceptions of textual sacredness were by no means as well defined
as they are to-day.[22]

[20] Mr. Sidney Lee in his biography of John Stow, *Dict. Nat. Biog.*,
LV, 4, assumes that Stow himself was the responsible editor of
Parker's texts of the *Flores Historiarum*, Matthew Paris, and Thomas
of Walsingham.   His opinion, I believe, may be traced to a misin-
terpretation of Stow's statement that among the manuscripts which
Parker printed were those mentioned, "all which he received of my
hands" (*Annales or generall Chronicle of England, continued and
augmented by Edmond Howes*, 1615; 679).   Both Strype and Sir
Frederic Madden have interpreted this phrase more reasonably as
indicating merely that Parker used Stow's manuscripts.

[21] Strype's translation from Parker, II, 501.

[22] The inaccuracy of Parker's texts has been pointed out from a
period almost within reach of his own lifetime.   Not one of his texts
is wholly free from blame; and most of them have been submitted to
scathing criticism.   See Thomae Walsingham, *Historia Anglicana*,
ed. Thomas Riley, 1864, I, ix–xii; Matthaei Parisiensis, *Historia
Anglorum*, ed. Sir Frederic Madden, 1866–9, I, xix–xxxvii; Matthaei
Parisiensis, *Chronica Majora*, ed. Henry Richards Luard, 1872–83,
II, xxii–xxviii; Asser's *Life of Alfred*, ed. William Henry Stevenson, 1904, xvii–xxi.   These references enable us without doubt to
estimate fairly the value of Parker's editorial work: in the light of
modern scholarship, his texts are practically useless.   The fact is
indisputable, but it is far from determining with finality Parker's
importance as a scholar; for as against the evidence of his texts, in
itself so strongly condemnatory, we have these points to consider.   In
the first place, it has not been demonstrated that he was personally

An old English publication for which the Archbishop was less directly responsible than for the works already referred to was the Anglo-Saxon version of the Gospels put forth by John Foxe in 1571. Foxe states in his preface that it was at Parker's instance and at his cost that the publication was undertaken.

Upon William Camden, one of the original members of the society, it is, of course, unnecessary to enlarge. Though responsible for his texts; it has been ever since Parker's time a matter of dispute whether he was the actual overseer of these publications. As to Asser's *Alfred* we have more or less definite and reliable evidence: Hearne, whose opinion and whose command of literary tradition are, when his prejudices are not involved, generally to be depended upon, says without qualification that Joscelyn was responsible for the editing of this volume (*Remarks and Collections*, VII, 240). On the question of Parker's responsibility we have no evidence touching his issues of the *Flores Historiarum* and Paris's *Chronica Majora;* but what is apparently true of the Asser is quite conceivably true of all the other publications which appeared under his auspices. Further than this, no evidence other than the attribution of these works to the editorship of Parker remains to convince us that he was actually capable of performing the textual work on them; Joscelyn and Lambarde, on the other hand, have left substantial memorials of their scholarly attainments. Miss E. T. Bradley makes the general claim in behalf of Joscelyn that Parker in all probability received credit for much of his secretary's editorial work (*Dict. Nat. Biog.*, XXX, 205), and both Madden and Stevenson seem disposed at least to admit the plausibility of this view (Matthaei Parisiensis, *Historia Anglorum*, I, xxxvi–xxxvii; Asser's *Alfred*, xvii). These facts may explain Parker's asseveration of his fidelity to his manuscript, reverently echoed by Strype (*Life and Acts of Parker*, II, 501). If we may assume that Parker was not spared sufficient leisure from his ecclesiastical and political duties to supervise the preparation of his texts, he may well have been ignorant of what his editors, not bred in a tradition of scholarly ethics, and almost certainly incapable of understanding the weight of their offence, were actually doing with the texts. In any event, there is apparently sufficient doubt in the whole matter to make it dangerous to pronounce an unqualified judgment of Parker's guilt.

his interest in literature for its own sake was certainly less than for its service to his historical and antiquarian labors, still the mere extent of his correspondence with learned men of letters and the weight of his incidental services to literary and linguistic scholarship give him unquestioned importance in the domain of philological study. His most specific claim to recognition as a student of letters lies in the publication in 1602-3 of his collection of six early English-Latin chroniclers.[23] This publication, dedicated to Fulke Greville, who had secured for Camden his appointment as Clarenceux King of Arms, though valuable for its time, was hastily done, the erratic text of Parker's former publications, for example, having apparently been followed without any attempt at corrected readings.[24] The work is not merely open to criticism on this ground, however, for it may be remembered that it was in this edition of Asser's life of Alfred that the notorious interpolation concerning the foundation of Oxford before the time of Alfred appeared, the substance of which had already been used by Camden in the fifth edition (1600) of his *Britannia*.[25] In spite of the great unreliability of Camden's work as an editor, however, we must concede to him, as to Parker, credit for his pioneer labors. Camden's interest in the

[23] *Anglica, Normannica, Hibernica, Cambrica, a veteribus scripta: . . . plerique nunc primum in lucem editi, ex bibliotheca Guilielmi Camdeni*, Francofurti, 1603.

[24] *Asser's Life of King Alfred together with the Annals of Saint Neots*, edited by William Henry Stevenson, 1904, xxii.

[25] For the history of the controversy as to the authenticity of this passage see James Parker, *The Early History of Oxford*, 1885, 39–45, and Asser's *Life of Alfred*, ed. William Henry Stevenson, 1904, xxiii–xxviii. Whether or not Camden was the actual author of the passage—and there seems adequate reason to believe that it may have been forged by "Long Henry" Savile (*op. cit.*, and *Dict. Nat. Biog.*, L, 369–70)—there seems to be little doubt that Camden's use of the passage was purposely misleading, if not altogether dishonest.

society was obviously, and unlike Parker's, purely antiquarian. Indeed, it might not be too much to assume that
the ardor and the engaging personality of Camden did
much to determine the trend of the tastes of the later members, and hence to color the interests of the society as a
body.

William Lambarde's connection with the society was due
very evidently to his association with Archbishop Parker.
He was one of the earliest accomplished scholars in Anglo-
Saxon, having studied the language with Laurence Nowell,
probably the pioneer in the field.[26] His general contributions to linguistic scholarship are acknowledged to have
been great, though his labors of this kind are obscured by
the fact that they are usually incidental to a wider interest
in English antiquity. His antiquarian works were his
Ἀρχαιονομία, published in 1568, a digest of Anglo-Saxon
laws, and his *Perambulation of Kent,* 1576, the first printed
county history.

Sir Robert Bruce Cotton joined the group in 1590, after
the range of its interests had been, we may assume, definitely
circumscribed. It has been suggested by Mr. Sidney Lee[27]
that Cotton's antiquarian interests may have been aroused
during his years at Westminster School, where Camden was
at that time master. Cotton's importance to literary
scholarship rests chiefly in his formation of the remarkable
library which has for more than two centuries been in the
possession of the English nation. This library made him
practically indispensable to the historians and literary students of his day, and it probably constituted the attraction
that toward the close of Elizabeth's reign made his home
the meeting place of the society.[28] His extraordinary gen-

26 Anthony à Wood, *Athenae Oxonienses,* edited by Philip Bliss,
1813–20, I, 426.

27 *Dict. Nat. Biog.,* XII, 308.

28 Richard Carew, *The Survey of Cornwall,* 1723, xiii.

erosity in putting his materials at the disposal of the scholars of his day and his general interest in literary work are seen in an illuminating series of letters from Verstegen, Speed, Camden, Usher, Selden, and others.[29] Cotton himself never produced a work which did justice to his unusual erudition, though an exceptional breadth of intellectual interest is seen in his concern for the occupations of his friends. The Cottonian Library is today, as it was in his own time, probably the most notable collection of original materials for national and literary history collected by a single individual.

John Stow, the annalist and publisher of Chaucer, and Francis Thynne, Lancaster Herald, and son of William Thynne, publisher of the first collected edition of Chaucer, were also members of the society. Stow's purely literary scholarship was not particularly notable, as, rightly or wrongly, he has taken the blame for introducing into his 1561 edition of Chaucer a quantity of non-Chaucerian material that was, whether he intended it or not, accepted by his contemporaries as really Chaucerian.[30] Be the case as it may, the edition is not now regarded as a remarkable one; so we may not be niggardly if we refuse him credit for anything beyond the mere labor of publication—which, after all, is a tangible credit in itself. As an annalist and historian, and incidentally to this, a continuator with Francis Thynne of Holinshed's *Chronicles,* his place in literary history possesses some additional importance. For our purposes, however, an item of interest possibly more significant than any of these is a reflection of his predilections as an antiquarian student of literature found in a

[29] *Original Letters of eminent literary Men,* 1843, 102–103, 107–113, 123–145.

[30] Prof. Skeat has discussed the questions relating to Stow's edition of Chaucer in his *Chaucerian and other Pieces,* 1897, ix–xiv, and in *The Chaucer Canon,* 1900, 117–126.

contemporary record. In 1568, complaint was made to
the Ecclesiastical Commission that "John Stow, tailor, the
same that was the laborious collector of the Historical
Antiquities of London and England," was, under pretence
of gathering materials for his labors, assembling a collection of papistical writings. Accordingly descent was made,
under Bishop Grindal's direction, upon Stow's house, and
a memorandum was prepared of the books found in his
possession which might justly merit suspicion. The omis-
sions from the inventory, however, are of considerably
greater interest than the inventory itself, for a significant
section is lumped in the phrase "a great sort of foolish
fabulous books of old print, as of Sir Degory Tryamour,
&c. a great parcel also of old written English chronicles."[31]
In other words, Stow was very evidently a Bannatyne, a
Collins, a Percy, or a Sir Walter Scott of his own century.
This is a point of interest that centers in him personally a
responsibility generally assumed by our nineteenth century
societies—the conservation of antiquarian and popular
literature. Another indication of his importance as a
collector and student of pure literature is his own, let us
suppose, true, assertion that he owned most of the manuscripts of Lydgate the list of which he gave Speght for his
1598 edition of Chaucer.[32]

Francis Thynne was, at least potentially, and for his day,
a really great Chaucerian scholar. He apparently in-
herited his love for Chaucer from his father. What makes
him specially interesting to us in this connection is his

[31] John Strype, *Life and Acts of Edmund Grindal*, 1821, 184–185,
516–519.

[32] Eleanor Prescott Hammond, *Chaucer, a bibliographical Manual*,
1908; 124. Miss Hammond quotes the heading of Stow's list: "A
Catalogue of translations and Poeticall deuises . . . done by Iohn
Lidgate monke of Bury, whereof some are extant in Print, the residue
in the custody of him that first caused this Siege of Thebes to be
added to these works of G. Chaucer."

critical essay occasioned by the faults of Speght's issue of Chaucer in 1598,[33] an edition, apparently, which anticipated one which Thynne himself was projecting, probably largely from the twenty-five odd Chaucerian manuscripts which he says his father had left him.[34] His displeasure seems also to have touched Stow at this time,[35] probably because Stow had given Speght material aid in the preparation of this new edition. Thynne's criticisms of Speght's edition, sour though they may be, are in the main apposite; and, as Furnivall pointed out,[36] in only four important instances in the essay can we find errors of magnitude either of fact or inference. Indeed, Thynne's historical, genealogical, and heraldic information is applied with at times surprising acuteness to the careless assumptions in Speght's biographical and interpretative material. At the end of this work Thynne announces that he himself contemplates a new edition of Chaucer,[37] to be worked over, we may be sure, with the same impartial critical sense that he displays in condemning the spurious attributions that are found in the editions published by his father.[38] The *Animaduersions* do, in fact, show convincing editorial aptitude on Thynne's part; and we must agree with Furnivall that if Thynne had actually carried out his intention, much of the necessary research on the poet in the eighteenth and nineteenth centuries might have been saved his subsequent editors. Speght, apparently under conviction, appears to have taken Thynne's corrections kindly, and was evidently

[33] Francis Thynne, *Animaduersions vppon the Annotacions and Corrections of some imperfections of impressiones of Chaucers workes. Edited by G. H. Kingsley. Revis'd edition by F. J. Furnivall.* Early English Text Society [and Chaucer Society], 186[7]5.

[34] *Op. cit.,* 11–12.

[35] *Ibid.,* ciii.

[36] *Ibid.,* cii.

[37] *Ibid.,* 75.

[38] *Ibid.,* 69.

3

inclined to solicit Thynne to undertake the edition he had had in prospect; but with the demand for a second edition, Speght appropriated Thynne's criticisms, and actually enlisted his personal assistance, producing a greatly improved edition in 1602.[39]

Sir Henry Spelman joined the Antiquaries in 1593, at about the beginning of what seems to have been their period of greatest activity and regularity. It seems, however, that he was not specially active in the society at this time, as no communication from him to the society is referred to by Hearne. Spelman himself recorded the discontinuance of the meetings of the society during this period,[40] but there can be no reasonable question as to the activity of the organization at this time, since Richard Carew apparently believed it to be in existence in 1605,[41] and the bulk of Hearne's *Discourses* covers the years 1599 to 1604. Certainly Spelman can not have been in touch with the society during the years when he considered its meetings in abeyance. The society did, however, cease its meetings about the year 1604; and the first and last appeal for its reorganization was made, it appears, by Spelman himself in 1614.[42] Spelman's interest in Anglo-Saxon studies led him to found the first university lectureship in this branch, which was established at Cambridge in 1639, after correspondence with Abraham Wheelocke, who became the first incumbent of the office.[43] The lectureship lapsed, it is generally assumed, because of the sequestration of the Spelman estates during the Revolution, but not until William Somner had secured its stipend, after Whee-

[39] *The Workes of ovr ancient and learned English Poet, Geffrey Chaucer, newly printed*, London, 1602, (''To the readers'').

[40] Spelman, *op. cit.*, 69.

[41] *Original Letters of eminent literary Men*, 1843; 98.

[42] Spelman, *op. cit.*, 69.

[43] *Original Letters of eminent literary Men*, 154–157, 161.

locke's death in 1653, to complete the publication of his Anglo-Saxon dictionary. Spelman's position as the most conspicuous patron of Anglo-Saxon scholarship in his century is noteworthy, and he was himself a very industrious and acute student in his favorite field.

Two other scholars of importance, we are told by Thomas Smith, and by no other authority on the subject, may be included in the catalogue of the society's members: John Selden, and William l'Isle of Wilbraham.[44] Selden's vast learning was directed twice to the furtherance of early English studies: in his publication of Eadmer's *Historia Novorum* in 1623, and in his collaboration in the editorial work upon Sir Roger Twysden's *Historiae Anglicanae Scriptores X* in 1653. For our purposes it is also worth noting that the historical illustrations to Drayton's *Polyolbion* were from Selden's hand. His edition of Eadmer, though satisfactory, has been superseded for the reason that the Cottonian manuscript from which Selden printed the work is clearly not its latest authoritative recension.[46] His considerable share in Twysden's *Scriptores* includes a critical preface, "Ad lectorem, Ioannes Seldenus, de scriptoribus hisce nunc primum editis," (i–xlviii), and probably general services recognized in Twysden's preface to the reader. Again in Selden too we find an interesting anticipation of the work of the collector of popular literature; for in his library, which reflects, throughout, extraordinary refinement of scholarly taste, we find a single curious volume of typical medieval popular

[44] Thomas Smith, *op. cit.*, 455–6, "De caeteris sociis, praecipue post annum hujus seculi quintum, admissis, nondum constat; licet de Gulielmo Lisle, Henrico Spelmanno, & Joanne Seldeno non dubitandum videtur; nec de aliis hariolari libet." It must be remembered that Selden could have been only twenty years old when the society discontinued its meetings in 1604.

[46] *Eadmeri Historia Novorum in Anglia,* Edited by Martin Rule, 1884; xiv.

literature, including "Richard Cuer de Lyon, Syr Bevis of Hampton, Syr Degore, Syr Tryamoure," and kindred titles.[47]

William l'Isle, a scholar recluse of acknowledged attainments in his day, did little that appealed to the public eye. His acquaintance, however, embraced the most conspicuous students of his time, both English and foreign. He reprinted, in the second edition of his *Treatise on the Old and New Testament*, 1623, the pre-Norman materials used by Parker in his *Testimonie of Antiquitie*. L'Isle contemplated an issue of Aelfric's scriptural translations and an Anglo-Saxon Psalter, but died in 1637, before his projects were realized.[48]

Other members of the society of less immediate interest to the literary antiquary were Richard Carew of Anthony, the Cornish glossarist, Sir John Davies, the poet, and William Hakewill, executor of the will of Sir Thomas Bodley.

The weighty influence of the members of this society upon the development of Anglo-Saxon scholarship is nowhere more aptly illustrated than in the direct and indirect connection of its members with early Anglo-Saxon lexicography. The date of the earliest efforts to compile a general vocabulary of Anglo-Saxon is obscured by the fact that none of the early dictionaries were published. There can be no doubt that the first, now preserved in the Bodleian Library, was by Laurence Nowell. This dictionary came into the hands of Lambarde, and it is plain, from a fore-word that Lambarde attached to it, that he contemplated publishing it. The note outlines an introductory chapter on the history of the English language, to be illus-

---

[47] William Dunn Macray, *Annals of the Bodleian Library, Oxford, A. D. 1598–A. D. 1867*, 1868; 86–87. Was this volume in Stow's possession? See *ante*, 14.

[48] H. F. Heath, in *Dict. Nat. Biog.*, XXXIII, 345.

trated by references from the period of the pre-Norman
laws and the Saxon Chronicle down to Gower and Chaucer,
"by the which, and such like it maye appeare, how, and by
what steppes our language is fallen from the old Inglishe,
and drawen nearer to the Frenche. This may well be light-
ened by shorte examples from theise bookes, and is meet to
be discovered when this Dictionarie shall be emprinted."[49]
The note is signed by Lambarde, with the date, 1570. It
may be significant that this date is six years before the
death of Nowell; the fact that the lexicon was in Lambarde's hands before Nowell's death may lend color to a
possible assumption, supported by the known intimate
association of Nowell and Lambarde in their studies, that
Lambarde himself had some share in the compilation.
Curiously enough, Hearne assigns the dictionary to Lambarde, not to Nowell,[50] but it seems clear that this is an
error due to his misunderstanding of the title of the
manuscript (Dictionarium Saxonico-Anglicum Laurentii
Noelli & ab Auctore Guil. Lambardo dono datum.), and the
note by Lambarde. Lambarde did, however, compile a
glossary for his Ἀρχαιονομία.

Joscelyn, Strype records, was "earnestly excited" by
Archbishop Parker "to digest his collections into a Lexicon
for the public; which he accordingly intended to do, but
was by death prevented."[51] A manuscript copy of this
dictionary in the Cottonian Library is entered by Wanley[52]
as "Codex chartaceus in Quarto per Joannem Josselinum &
Joannem Parkerum D[octoris] Matth[aei] fil[ius] (ut
videtur) scriptus."

[49] Humphrey Wanley, *Antiquae literaturae septentrionalis Liber
alter*, 1705; 102.

[50] *Remarks and Collections of Thomas Hearne*, edited by C. E.
Doble, III, 216–217 (1888).

[51] Strype, *Life and Acts of Matthew Parker*, II, 514 (1821).

[52] Wanley, *op. cit.*, 239.

Parker's lively interest in the publication of an Anglo-Saxon dictionary, however, was quite eclipsed by the much more active enthusiasm of Sir Henry Spelman, the moving spirit of the society in its waning years. Spelman's persistent interest in securing a dictionary of the old tongue was roused by his difficulties with the language in a projected work upon the foundations of English law. His interest in archaeological lexicography was, to be sure, grounded in his legal and historical studies, but was none the less effective for philological purposes. His biographer, William Carr,[53] says: "His glossary gives him a title to the name of inaugurator of philological science in England." This glossary[54] was begun at an early date. The first volume was published in 1626, and work upon the second volume was in progress until the closing years of Spelman's life; but this volume did not appear until 1664, twenty-three years after his death, when it was seen through the press by Sir William Dugdale.

As strongly as Spelman's publication of this work supports Mr. Carr's characterization of his importance in the field of English philology, his close connection with the publication of the first printed dictionary of Anglo-Saxon gives him a more special note. Johannes de Laet of Leyden, who was at that time engaged upon an Anglo-Saxon dictionary, addressed Sir Henry in 1638 upon that subject.[55] But Sir Henry, who was "not willing that it should be done by a stranger," replied to de Laet that he himself would endeavor to secure the compilation of a dictionary of old English, and "desired his conjectanea and association in the business." At the moment he was in correspondence with Abraham Wheelocke, soon to be the incum-

[53] Dict. Nat. Biog., LIII, 331.
[54] Archaelogus in Modum Glosarii ad Rem Antiquam Posteriorem, 2 v., 1626–1664.
[55] Original Letters of eminent literary Men, 154.

bent of the Spelman lectureship; he urged Wheelocke to assist in the publication of the dictionary.[56]   Wheelocke undertook the lexicon, probably as one of the obligations of his academic office; but again, in all probability, the author was "by death prevented." His fragment is entered by Wanley[57] as "Lexicon Saxonico-Latinum, maxima ex parte ex Bedae Historiae Ecclesiasticae versione Saxonica."

In the meantime, de Laet, probably discouraged by his own lack of facilities for the prosecution of his work, commended the completion of it to Sir Simonds d'Ewes, who in 1649 was importuned by Sir William Dugdale[58] to secure the assistance of William Somner in his work. As a matter of fact, a letter from d'Ewes to John Selden dated February 1648/9, and quoted in Hickes's *Thesaurus*,[59] seems to show that at this time d'Ewes's dictionary must have been completed, as he refers to it as covering two volumes ("duobus comprehenso tomis"), in which form it is preserved now among the Harleian manuscripts.[60]   In any event, whether d'Ewes might have profited by Somner's help or not, he did not ask it. Incidentally, it is worth while noting that Dugdale's advice to the Baronet is so vague that it may be interpreted as referring to the publication, and not to the compilation of the dictionary, which in the end never went to press.

It is to the credit of Sir Simonds's usually jealous temper that at about this time he himself offered assistance in Somner's labor upon a lexicon. Somner was indebted to him at least for a copy of Joscelyn's dictionary,[61] the loan

---

[56] *Op. cit.*, 154–155.

[57] Wanley, *op. cit.*, 303.

[58] *Original Letters of eminent literary Men*, 175.

[59] *Linguarum vet[erum] septentrionalium Thesaurus, Auctore Georgio Hickesio*, I, xliii (1705).

[60] Rev. Augustus Jessopp, in *Dict. Nat. Biog.*, XIV, 453.

[61] *William Somner, Dictionarium Saxonico-Latino-Anglicum* Oxonii, 1659 (Preface: *Ad Lectorem*).

antedating, naturally enough, d'Ewes's death in 1650. A fortunate circumstance enabled Somner to proceed with the publication of his lexicon, the first to appear in print. The Spelman lectureship, which was vacated by the death of Wheelocke in 1653, was so disposed that the stipend of the lecture (ten pounds annually) was, on the advice of Archbishop Usher, separated from the impropriate living and assigned to Somner for the publication of his work.[62] This appeared in 1659 under the title *Dictionarium Saxonico-Latino-Anglicum*.

There are extant references to other Anglo-Saxon vocabularies of this period, notably those of William l'Isle,[63] Sir William Dugdale,[64] Richard James (Sir Robert Cotton's librarian),[65] and William Camden.[66] Glossaries appeared also in various works on antiquity and in reprinted texts. The most noteworthy of the latter group is Somner's glossary to Twysden's *Scriptores*, 1652. All these, however, are generally regarded as lacking the historical interest that belongs to the others.

This brief resumé of the early history of Anglo-Saxon lexicography seems sufficient to show that at least ten dictionaries, in the main complete, had been compiled in the period prior to Somner's publication, probably half of which are of really high importance. Of these ten, three were produced by members of the society—Camden, Spelman, and l'Isle, and four of the remainder by scholars dependent upon members of the society for patronage or financial aid—Joscelyn, James, Wheelocke, and Somner.

A final, though casual, contemporary testimony to the

[62] White Kennett, *A Life of Mr. Somner*, 75–78. (Prefixed to Somner's *A Treatise of Gavelkind*, 2d ed., 1726.)

[63] *Original Letters of eminent literary Men*, 152.

[64] Wanley, *op. cit.*, 104.

[65] *Op. cit.*, 101.

[66] *Op. cit.*, 246.

strong impress of the society upon the philological history
of the late sixteenth and the early seventeenth centuries is
found in Graevius's reference to the great Anglo-Saxon
scholars from Leland to Langbaine.[67] He enumerates fourteen students of this period, barring Junius, five of whom,
Parker, Lambarde, Camden, Selden and Spelman, were
members of the society, and six others associated by inti-
macy, relationship, or patronage with those members:
Joscelyn, Nowell, Foxe, Sir John Spelman, Wheelocke, and
Somner. A concrete modern testimony to the predominant
importance of Parker and Spelman in our field is given
by Professor Wülcker:

Bisher [1605] war der Hauptgönner und Beförderer dieser
Studien Erzbischof Parker. Als dieser gestorben war, so dauerte
es längere Zeit, bis sich wieder ein Mann fand, der, nicht nur durch
seine Kenntnisse, sondern auch durch seine Geldmittel imstande
war, diese Bestrebungen gehörig zu unterstützen. Der Mittel-
punkt der nun folgenden angelsächsischen Studien waren die
Spelman's, Vater und Sohn.[68]

I believe that my outlines of the literary engagements of
these men—who constituted certainly the most conspicuous
part of the Assembly—justify definite conclusions as to the
scholarly importance of the society as a body. Archbishop
Parker's publications, most of them still recent at the
founding of the club, and some of them as yet unpublished,
were monumental in their importance to Anglo-Saxon and
Anglo-Latin literary scholarship. His tastes, which must
certainly have given color to the proceedings of the society
in its early years, were preeminently those of the literary
antiquary. One can find scarcely a trace of interest on his
part in historical remains other than manuscripts. He was

[67] *Francisci Junii, Etymologicum Anglicanum Praemittuntur Vita
Auctoris* [Auctore Johanne Georgio Graevio], (1743).

[68] Richard Wülcker, *Grundriss zur Geschichte der angelsächsischen
Litteratur*, 1885; 10.

in all probability not to be entertained by discussions on "The antiquity and forms of tenures," and "The antiquity of the name of 'Barones' in England," discourses which even Francis Thynne, with his more widely trained antiquarian predilections, found in 1591 to be "tedious and course."[69] At any rate, we can not avoid thinking that the Archbishop's interests must have affected the occupations of the society during the first few years of its existence; though it is wholly probable that if his presence and influence did stimulate interest in literary questions during the three years before his death, in 1575, this interest may have subsided greatly when the tastes of the newer (and in the main less gifted) members showed themselves to be more peculiarly antiquarian. Camden, probably the most generally known of all the members of the organization, was likewise a noteworthy publisher of literary materials and an influential student of the old English tongue, though his work took character mainly from his devotion to historical studies. Lambarde, l'Isle, and Richard Carew were all of them important early students of the language. Sir Robert Cotton is immortal in what is probably the most valuable manuscript collection of old English literary materials. John Stow was a notable student of historical literature, and an editor, though a very faulty one, of Chaucer. Francis Thynne, the son of the most reputable early editor of Chaucer, contemplated publishing the first edition of the poet which should attempt to deal seriously with spurious and doubtful attributions, and was prevented only by the anticipation of a part of his labor by Speght. Selden's scholarly intelligence, the soundest of his age, was devoted at least occasionally to our early historical literature. Henry Spelman, as the latest member of conspicuous note, continued the tradition of Anglo-Saxon scholarship through a

[69] Thynne, *op. cit.*, xciii–xciv.

period of intellectual dearth and founded the first university chair for Anglo-Saxon studies.

Here, then, are the most brilliant and influential members of the group. That we can survey their names, contemplate the vitality and the supreme utility of their interest in our old literature, and conceive that this society had no objective literary occupation, seems impossible. This body of scholars, united primarily for the purpose of antiquarian study, were incidentally so closely occupied with the importance of literature and literary investigation as a reflection of the life of the past that their proceedings as a society could not have been without effect upon their individual knowledge and judgment in the field of literature, and for this reason, part, at least, of the revival of interest in Anglo-Saxon literary antiquity, and much of the impetus of its continuance, was due directly to the fact of their organization. Here in all probability, then, we find the first instance in England of a society serving to an important degree the purposes of philological scholarship.

Materials for the history of the society are scant, elusive, and at times contradictory; but the following points seem clear. Spelman is authority for the date of foundation, 1572 or thereabouts. In the introduction to his *Discourse on the Law Terms* in Bishop Gibson's collected edition of his works,[70] he refers to the first meetings of the society as "about forty-two years since." The date of this discourse is generally accepted as 1614.[71] There is nothing to indicate the nature of the society's activities in its earlier years, however, Hearne's account recording no discussions prior to the year 1590. In 1589 the Antiquaries submitted a petition for incorporation, on terms that would legalize their organization and extend their influence, one of the principal

[70] *Op. cit.* [Part b], 69–70. The introductory note, "The Occasion of this Discourse," is not printed in the separate edition of 1684.

[71] Hearne, *Collection of Curious Discourses*, II, 331.

desiderata of establishment being the securing of facilities for the formation and maintenance of a permanent library. The petition was signed by Sir Robert Cotton, James Ley, and Sir John Doddridge.[72] Smith assigns the petition to the closing years of the sixteenth century ("seculo superiore exeunte"),[73] and intimates that the proposal was suspended in the Queen's judgment until her death. It is clear from an extant notice of meeting addressed to Stow, and published by Hearne,[74] that the gatherings in the later years of the society's activity were more or less formal, at least in the introduction of subjects for discussion. Spelman's statement that the society was dormant for about twenty years from 1594 to 1614 is not reconcilable with the fact that nearly all the recorded discussions of the members are dated within that period.[75] It is apparent, however, that shortly after James's accession the society fell under political suspicion, in spite of Sir Robert Cotton's efforts to interest the monarch in the society itself or in its plan for incorporation.[76] Gough gives definitely as the date of the society's suspension 1604 or the early part of 1605.[77] The final effort to resuscitate the society was made in 1614, when Cotton, Camden, Davies, Spelman, and others met to reorganize, taking care "not to meddle with matters of state or religion." They appointed a meeting one week later, for which Spelman prepared his Law Terms discourse. But, as Spelman relates, "Before our next Meeting, we had notice that his Majesty took a little Mislike of our Society; not being inform'd, that we had resolv'd to decline all

[72] Ewald Flügel, *Die älteste englische Akademie; Anglia*, XXXII, 261–268 (1909).

[73] Thomas Smith, *Vita Roberti Cottoni*, 453–4.

[74] *Op. cit.*, I, xv–xvii.

[75] *Ante*, 18.

[76] Thomas Smith, *op. cit.*, 454.

[77] *Op. cit.*, xvi.

Matters of State. Yet hereupon we forbare to meet again."[78] The effort, about 1616, to organize a body for somewhat similar purposes, urged in part by some of the members of the old society,[79] forms a new chapter in the history of society movements, and is, incidentally, of rather less interest to us because the purposes of the new "academy" were to be more miscellaneous and its literary connections less sharply defined.

Hearne names thirty-seven members of the society.[80] These are: Arthur Agarde, Lancelot Andrews, Bishop of Winchester, Robert Beale, Henry Bouchier, a Mr. Bowyer, Richard Broughton, William Camden, Richard Carew, a Mr. Cliffe, William Compton, Earl of Northampton, Walter Cope, Sir Robert Cotton, Sir John Davies, Sir William Dethick, Sir John Doddridge, [Thomas] Doyley, Sampson Erdeswicke, William Fleetwood, William Hakewill, Abraham Hartwell, Michael Heneage, Joseph Holland, William Lambarde, Sir Thomas Lake, Sir Francis Leigh, Sir James Ley, Arnold Oldisworth (not Michael Oldisworth, as Hearne gives the name, for Michael was born in 1591, only thirteen years before the paper assigned to him was read),[81] William Patten, [Sir John][82] Savile, Sir Henry Spelman, John Stow, James Strangeman, Thomas Talbot, Francis Thynne, Sir James Whitelock, Thomas Wiseman, and Robert Weston. Hearne does not, however, name Archbishop Parker, the organizer of the society,[83] or Archbishop Whitgift, a

[78] Spelman, *op. cit.*, 70.

[79] Joseph Hunter, *An account of the scheme for erecting a Royal Academy in England, in the reign of King James the First; Archaeologia*, XXXII, 132–149 (1847). *Post*, 36–39.

[80] *Op. cit.*, II, 421–449.

[81] Sidney Lee, *Dict. Nat. Biog.*, XLIII, 113.

[82] A. F. Pollard, *Dict. Nat. Biog.*, L, 372. Hearne was right in his belief that this Savile was neither Sir Henry, Thomas, nor "Long Henry."

[83] Gough, *op. cit.*, *Archaeologia*, I, v.

later president,[84] though Whitgift's title may refer to his patronage of the society rather than to his connection with it as an active officer.   Hearne also omits from his list Francis Tate, at one time secretary of the society,[85] though he prints a number of discourses by Tate at the meetings of the club.   Thomas Smith alone, as I have indicated,[86] names William l'Isle and John Selden.   Two modern biographers have included in the membership the historian John Speed,[87] but upon grounds of evidence, I presume, that have not fallen under my observation. The roll as variously recorded, then, by writers whom there is every reason to credit, gives forty-three members.   The very numbers of the society may account for the fact that none of its historians has given a list that corresponds exactly with any other.

But the further we go, the more interestingly this question of membership develops.   It is, of course, difficult to distinguish the list of members of the society for any specific narrow period of its activity; but some approximations seem possible, and these in turn bring up again the question whether the roll which we have so far is in itself complete. Of the thirty-seven members whose names are agreed upon by Hearne and Gough, the identity or the biographical records of nine are too indefinite to allow us to form any conclusion whatsoever as to the period of their connection with the society.   Of those remaining, six—Camden, Fleetwood,[88] Dethick,[89] Doyley and Lambarde, who were respec-

[84] *Ibid.*

[85] *Ibid.*

[86] See *ante*, 19.

[87] A. F. Pollard, in *Dict. Nat. Biog.*, LIII, 318, and Sidney Lee, in *Dict. Nat. Biog.*, XII, 308–309.

[88] Hearne, *op. cit.*, II, 434, says that Fleetwood was admitted a member after he became recorder of London; this was in 1571, so Fleetwood's membership must have dated from about the time of organization.

[89] *Ibid.*, II, 431.

tively the steward and the literary agent of Parker, and Robert Weston, if he was the Robert Weston, Chancellor of Ireland, who died in 1573—were in all likelihood members of the society in Parker's time. Five others—Carew, Cotton, Spelman, Hartwell and Andrews—we know joined the society after 1588; and six—Doddridge, Tate, Lake, Davies, Whitelock and Hakewill—whose birth dates range from 1555 to 1574, were too young at the date of foundation to have been members of the society then or shortly after. The remaining eleven may or may not have joined in the early period, and the fact that scholarly or official distinction came to many of them in later years warrants the assumption that not all were members in the years immediately following the society's organization. To recount, only six from these lists can be named with reasonable certainty as charter members; eleven were certainly not members during the first years; and about the remaining twenty we can draw no really accurate conclusions. Since, then, this list is made up in large part of later members of the society, the question naturally arises whether it includes all of the early members, say from 1572 to 1588. On this point, we must remember that Hearne, following Smith, does not give the name of Parker, that his interest is for the day in which Cotton, Carew, and Spelman were among the influential members, and that he records no activity of the society prior to 1589. Now the ultimate source of Hearne's information on the history of the society is the Cottonian manuscript from which Smith secured his material; and this, according to Gough,[90] is the record of the society's activities subsequent to 1591. Gough supports the evidence of this manuscript on questions pertaining to the history of the society by reference to manuscript materials left by Francis Tate, secretary of the society during the later period, and

[90] *Op. cit., Archaeologia,* I, vi.

to an Ashmolean manuscript which he mentions only casually. Tate was not a member of the early society, for he was only twelve years old when it was founded; for this reason, his list of members, especially if it had any direct connection with his secretarial duties, would probably include only his later associates in the body. There is nothing in the facts connected with the sources of Hearne's information, and Gough's, then, to make it appear that their catalogues comprehend the membership of the society for the entire period of its existence from 1572 to 1604, even though Gough, apparently from hasty inference, assumes this to be the case.[91]

There is, on the other hand, seeming evidence that these two lists do not cover the membership of the society during its first years. In another and later manuscript quoted by Gough, and attributed to a Mr. West,[92] which Gough uses for the historical data for his account of Edmund Bolton's project of 1616–7, but which he makes no effort to compare with the first mentioned manuscripts on points touching the history of the earlier society, we find a list of members of the old society which differs remarkably from that of Hearne. Here we have thirteen members named, with a broadly inclusive "etc.," only six of whom Hearne gives in his total of thirty-six—Lambert (Lambarde), Erdeswicke, Heneage, Thynne, Talbot, and Stow. The remaining seven of this list are "the late Earls of Shrewsbury and Northampton (not William Compton, who was made Earl of Northampton in 1618 and died in 1629, but probably Henry Howard, second son of the Earl of Surrey), Sir Gilbert

91 *Ibid.*, vi.

92 *Ibid.*, xv. This manuscript forms the basis of Oldys's brief sketch of the society in his *Life of Sir Walter Ralegh*, prefixed to his edition of Ralegh's *History of the World*, 1736 (I, cxxx–cxxxi, note). Oldys accepts the list of members which this manuscript gives apparently without a question as to its authenticity.

Dethick (the father of Sir William Dethick, whom Hearne names as a member), "Valence, Esq.," Sir Henry Fanshawe, "Benefield, Esq.," and T. Holland (not Joseph Holland, a member identified by Hearne). There are some considerations which throw doubt upon the authenticity of this list; notably the fact that errors in identification are suggested by the occurrence of an Earl of Northampton, a Dethick, and a Holland, where Hearne has given other individuals of these names. Again we must bear in mind the fact that the Cottonian records and the Tate list are probably contemporary with the society itself, while any manuscript connected with the Bolton project must be subsequent to the final dissolution of the society. But there does remain the significant fact that this list was certainly made while the memory of the old society was still fresh, and that the discrepancies between this list and Hearne's catalogue are sufficiently marked to demand careful consideration. As to the apparently important differences between the two sets of names, there is no reason why two Earls of Northampton and two Dethicks, father and son, might not have been members of the society; and the T. Holland for Joseph Holland loses some of its condemnatory force when we remember that Hearne himself is liable to errors in identification, since he certainly mistook Arnold Oldisworth for Michael Oldisworth.[93]

As to the chronological relationships of these various lists, all of the names in the West manuscript that Hearne identifies with the membership of the society are of the older generation of members, and none are named whom we know to have joined the society at a later date. The two other names on the West list that we can identify with practical certainty are those of Gilbert Dethick and Sir Henry Fanshawe, men of sufficient age to make it appear that they

[93] See *ante*, 29.

4

might have been members—if at all—during the early years. These facts seem to indicate that, granting the West manuscript whatever authority we may care to attach to it, we must regard it as referring to the early period of the old society's history; the Hearne list, which stands as the type of contemporary catalogues, seems to refer to the membership of the later years of the society's activity.

Surprises in the West manuscript, however, do not cease with the differences between this list of thirteen members and Hearne's list of thirty-six; for Gough, continuing his excerpts from the manuscript, says:[94] "To the deceased members the manuscript adds Sir Philip Sidney, Fitz Alan, last Earl of Arundel of that name," continuing with an enumeration of "members," to use his own term, which includes some of the most distinguished names of the period, among them Sir Walter Raleigh, Thomas Sackville Earl of Dorset, William Cecil Lord Burghley, the Herberts Earls of Pembroke, and Sir Henry Savile. So the question as to the authenticity of this manuscript becomes one of more moment than as affecting simply the question of the period covered by contemporary lists of members. If the West Manuscript is not vulnerable—and the lack of support from actually contemporary evidence must cause us to pause on this point—the society is vastly more significant from every aspect, literary, social, and political, than merely as a quiet gathering of serious scholars. Its influence, if Sidney, Sackville, Raleigh, and Cecil were actually members, must have been far greater than we have any reason to believe from extant historical accounts. With these names possibly associated with the history of the society, it acquires a speculative interest of a much broader kind—but still frankly, and possibly dangerously, speculative.

The antiquity and the uniqueness of the position of this society, and the tenuousness of historical facts concerning

[94] *Op. cit., Archaeologia*, I., xix–xxi.

it, have probably justified an inquiry into its existence and
the province of its occupations that is plainly out of proportion to its intrinsic historical value. The very isolation of
the body, and the fact that its motives and interests are
obscure, have been temptations to inquiry and surmise
that have probably yielded some tangible results, even
though these results are built upon probabilities rather
than facts.

The general inferences as to the scholarly importance of
the society may be briefly summarized. The dominating
personality of its earlier days was in all probability Archbishop Parker, whose interest in antiquity was satisfied
wholly, as far as we can discern, by literary studies. After
his death, Lambarde, Camden, Stow, and their associates
remained to preserve the society's traditions, but presumably with a transferal of their interests to the more typically
archaeological. With the advent of Cotton and Spelman,
and the beginning of probably the most active period in the
history of the society, the researches of the members, as
judged from their published work, drew more heavily upon
the literature of antiquity, recognizing its importance for
the study of the past, and thus aroused a greatly extended
interest in the general field of Anglo-Saxon and Anglo-
Norman literature. This interest developed a series of
textual publications and linguistic works which were not
always the direct products of these antiquaries, but for
which the scholarship and erudition of these members were
the sustaining forces. It is impossible to prove that the
society held a single literary meeting; but its personnel and
the individual literary activities of its members make it
difficult to believe that their antiquarian occupations barred
all collective interest in the materials of literature. In any
event, measuring the importance of the organization in this
field, we must concede it as a body an eminent place in the
traditions of English literary scholarship.

CHAPTER III

THE SEVENTEENTH CENTURY

The decease of the society which Parker, Camden, and Spelman had served over an intermittent period of forty-two years marks the decline of amateur literary organization in England for almost a century. The next effort to stimulate collective interest in literary and antiquarian studies, which immediately followed Spelman's final attempt to revive the old society, had in view a pompous honorary foundation under royal patronage; and with the failure of this scheme, organization for the ends of literary scholarship languished until the establishment of the present Society of Antiquaries in the early eighteenth century. Throughout the seventeenth century, then, over a period which covers the Anglo-Saxon revival of post-revolutionary days, and the still more important renascence of interest in the literature of English antiquity that was supported by the labors of Kennett, Gibson, Benson, Hickes, and Wanley, we find no record of formal or informal alliance on the part of literary scholars, though the age was rather remarkable for the good will and freedom from intellectual jealousy that prevailed among them. A few efforts which echo more or less clearly the ideas of Parker and Spelman are worthy, however, of remembrance, even if they serve only to demonstrate the lack of continuity in the society tradition.

The project of Edmund Bolton, historian and critic, to secure the favor of James I for a scheme intended to serve to some extent the general aims of the old society was first presented in 1616 or 1617.[1] Bolton's plan was to found an order of scholarship, with complex organization and elaborate pageantry, including decorations and special armorial bearings for the members, and gravely formal stated meetings. His proposal was urged specially through the agency of the Duke of Buckingham, whose influence at the court of James was then all-powerful. No action upon the plan was taken for some years, however, although the conception of such an august assembly flattered the monarchical vanity of the King to the point that "it finally pleased him . . . to enlarge the institution [*in posse*] itself with more grants and faculties than were desired."[2] The final plan, which was developed with the aid of numerous suggestions from James himself, outlined "The Academy Royal of King James" as an aristocratic foundation, the two ranking classes of which were to be composed of supernumerary court brilliants, and the third class of "Essentials, upon whom the weight of the work was to lie," who were to be gentlemen "either living in the light of things, or without any title of profession or art of life for lucre."[3] The principal public functions of the order were to be the superintendence of efficient translations of foreign secular works, and the issuance of authentic material for the history of the nation.[4] Its province was therefore more or less directly critical, though concerned more with questions of material and taste than with those of scholarship.

The list of "Essentials" includes many names of literary or scholarly eminence, with a generous adulteration of minor poets and personal friends of the projector. But important

[1] Joseph Hunter, *An account of the scheme for erecting a Royal Academy in England, in the Reign of King James the First; Archaeologia*, XXXII, 132–149, 1847; 136.

[2] *Ibid.*, 140.

[3] *Ibid.*

[4] *Ibid.*, 141.

men were really sufficiently numerous and sufficiently rep-
resentative to have made the foundation potentially great.
On Bolton's list of prospective members are found: Sir
William Alexander, Earl of Sterling, Sir Robert Aytoun,
Sir John Beaumont, Edmund Bolton, George Chapman, Sir
Robert Cotton, Sir Kenelm Digby, Sir Dudley Digges,
Michael Drayton, Ben Jonson, Inigo Jones, Endymion
Porter, John Selden, Sir Henry Spelman, Sir Henry Wot-
ton, and Patrick Young.[5]

It is clear from the stated objects and the personnel of
Bolton's proposed order that it was to serve the cultural
purposes of an academy, and principally, to stand as the
censor of national taste. Bolton succeeded in exciting the
King's interest in the idea until it appeared that all the
society lacked of establishment was his public sanction; for
James's final consultation with Bolton in 1624[6] seemed to
settle all the incidental questions as to the form and scope
of organization. But the King's procrastination was in the
end fatal to the scheme, for he died in the following year,
leaving the projectors to press anew with Charles their
appeal for royal sanction. In a markedly less cultured
court than that of James it is not surprising that the plan
eventually failed; in fact it is recorded that Charles was
prejudiced against the scheme before he came to the throne,
for when Bolton was endeavoring to secure the aid of James
in the project, Charles was heard to express his opinion
that it was "too good for the times."[7]

Charles's criticism of the proposed academy may not
have been wholly inapposite. His notion of "too good"
implies, we may assume, too pretentious rather than too
ideal. The form suggested for the body was certainly of a
sort to hamper rather than to aid the development of the

[5] *Ibid.*, 142–147.
[6] *Ibid.*, 140.
[7] *Ibid.*, 147–148.

literary resources of England of that day; and the ponderousness of the machinery of organization was without doubt too much for the ill-defined purposes it might have served. Charles's decision on this point is possibly more praiseworthy than his father's indecision—indeed, James's delayed favor may have been due to a practical distrust of what his pride induced him to foster, at least in appearance. It is interesting to consider, as we look back upon the idea, what effect the actual existence of the Academy Royal of King James might have had upon a growing classical influence in English literature, and indeed upon the whole course of national literature from that time on. But the point is scarcely relevant.

The projected Academy of King James was typical of a tendency in the critical program of the time that was more far-reaching in its effects than even Bolton himself was in all probability capable of recognizing. It is of course unnecessary to point out that if Bolton's scheme had been successfully established, an English academy, instead of the later French Academy, would have been the first national project of the kind to gain the authority of royal favor. It is worth while inquiring, however, whether the failure of this resplendent plan was merely an accident of fate— moving here in the guise of royal caprice—or whether the conditions of the times, political as well as intellectual, were right for such an establishment and could endow it with any prospect of continued usefulness. We must remember that if Bolton's effort was only an effort, it was at any rate well defined, serious, and dignified. The fact that so complete and promising a plan was a failure carries us into a consideration of the history of other attempts of a similar kind throughout the seventeenth century.

Up to the time of Bolton's plan the proposals for and activity in the formation of learned societies and academies had been wholly dilettante in character—and if prototypes of the academy idea in these earlier years need be sought, they may be found in the amateur status, and largely amateurish work, of the earlier Italian academies. We may recall that it was with precisely their spirit that Chapelain and his friends first held their private meetings in 1629, and that the larger importance of their body did not begin until political exigencies resulted in the establishment of the Académie Française by Richelieu in 1635.[8] Then its participation, with the panoply of authority, in a nation-wide controversy upon literary taste gave it a serious dignity and a critical finality which no body of the sort had ever before possessed. One of the obvious results of the transference of the machinery of French pseudo-classicism to England in the seventeenth century is found in reiterated proposals, from many of the leading English men of letters of the day, for the founding of an English academy of letters which should have the same weight of critical authority as the French Academy. Projects for such an academy were offered by Sprat, Dryden, Defoe, Addison, and Swift, and more casual recommendations were made by James Howell, Milton, the Earl of Roscommon, Pope, and Prior;[9] but these were without exception ineffective, although the idea was urged at intervals until the middle of the eighteenth century, when it was laid at rest, probably largely through the opposition of Dr. Johnson. In the absence of a special foundation for the improvement of the

[8] D. Maclaren Robertson, *A History of the French Academy*, [1910], 3–28.

[9] Mr. B. S. Monroe's article, *An English Academy* (*Modern Philology*, VIII, 107–122, 1910), treats in a thorough way the history of the various proposals for an English academy of letters during the seventeenth and eighteenth centuries. Dr. J. E. Spingarn's *Critical Essays of the Seventeenth Century* contains a compact but useful note on the subject; II, 337–8.

language, however, the Royal Society undertook, four years after its establishment in 1660, at least to acknowledge the want of an English academy by the appointment of a "Committee for Improving the English Tongue."[10] No record is extant of definite results attained by this committee, although it is certain that they held some formal meetings.[11]

That the existence and relative effectiveness of the French Academy failed to bring about the establishment of such an institution in England, especially in an age so strongly under the dominance of French critical ideas, seems matter for real wonder. The reasons which Matthew Arnold suggests for the existence of the French Academy and the absence of a similar body in England—briefly, that the characteristic of the English mind is individual energy, of the French, openness and intellectual flexibility[12]—account probably for the readiness of the English to dispense with a check upon intellectual freedom. But these reasons are not properly historical reasons; they explain a condition, rather than trace the origins of an historical fact. It is probably correct to say, in a general way, that the greater intellectual democracy of the English could not submit to such a tyranny of trained taste; but a more real reason for the failure of the academy idea in England is probably to be found in the intellectual conditions which determined the particular nature of scholarly comity throughout this century, and which gave birth to the Royal Society itself.

The Royal Society is as truly a coefficient of English intellectual interests in this period as the Académie Fran-

[10] Thomas Birch, *History of the Royal Society of London*, 1756-7; I, 499-500, II, 7.

[11] *Memoirs of John Evelyn*, edited by William Bray, 1827; IV, 144-9.

[12] Matthew Arnold, *The literary Influence of Academies;* In *Essays in Criticism*, 1895; 42-79.

caise is for France. Although at the first glance these two societies may seem to voice the same scholarly aims, no intellectual incentives could be more radically divergent than those which gave life to the two. The Academy owed its existence, under a nearly absolute political tyranny, to a demand for authority in matters of taste; the Royal Society responded to the growing outcry against everything savoring of scholastic authority, and stood as the expressed champion of the experimental philosophy of Bacon.

The tangible debt of the Royal Society to the "New Philosophy" of Bacon finds loyal expression in Cowley's *Ode to the Royal Society*.[13] Sprat states the debt more conservatively, but no less positively, in his *History;*[14] and it has in fact been admitted from the earliest years of the Society's existence that the initial impulse to organization for the purposes of experimental science is to be found in the philosophical writings of Bacon, particularly in the *Novum Organum* and the *New Atlantis*.[15]

But although the Royal Society was chartered for the "improvement of Natural Knowledge,"[16] its membership was by no means restricted to men of science. One of the intellectual ideals of the age was that of a universal prospect of knowledge, an ideal greatly expanded through the large results of experimental skepticism. The philosophical systems of Bacon and Descartes were, in their attitudes toward the field of knowledge, encyclopaedic; and the educational system of Comenius, which had great effect upon

[13] First published in Sprat's *History of the Royal Society of London*, 1667.

[14] *Op. cit.*, 35–36.

[15] Charles Richard Weld, *A History of the Royal Society*, 1848; I, 57–64.

[16] *Ibid.*, I, 126. The word "natural," it has been pointed out, was used as an antonym for supernatural, and implied for this reason the realm of knowledge that might be subjected to concrete tests. The word comprehends therefore the sense of experimental.

English thought at that time—largely through the influence of his friend Samuel Hartlib,[17] conceived the great scholarly desideratum of the age to be the establishment of a method of democratic interchange between the disciples of the various branches of learning. This new conception of intellectual comity probably determined to a large extent the miscellaneous complexion of the early membership of the Royal Society. Another point of significance in this connection is that the experimental philosophy of the seventeenth century had as comprehensive an effect upon all the provinces of intellectual interest in its day as the publication of the evolutionary theory had in the middle of the nineteenth century. It is not surprising, therefore, that along with philosophers, churchmen, and architects, the men of letters of the day were drawn into the Royal Society and into the special circle of interests which it represented.

Although the intellectual motives of the French Academy and of the Royal Society were in their essence not merely unrelated, but actually opposed, there was no sense of this in the minds of those who urged the foundation of an academy under the impression that it would further in the realm of language and literature the methods of the Royal Society in the field of science. We may recall that Sprat and Dryden, for example, supported the idea of an academy of language, whose purposes could be only *a priori*, arbitrary, and restrictive, in the belief that these purposes complied with the investigative methods of the Royal Society.

The fact of importance here is that historical scholarship

[17] H. Dircks, *A biographical Memoir of Samuel Hartlib*, London, 14–21, 42–43. Will S. Monroe, *Comenius and the Beginnings of educational Reform*, 1900; 51–57. Comenius's relationship to defined movements of scholarly organization in Germany is discussed at length in Ludwig Keller's *Comenius und die Akademien der Naturphilosophen des 17. Jahrhunderts; Monatshefte der Comenius-Gesellschaft*, IV, 1–28, 69–96, 133–84 (1895).

in literature suffered both from the distraction of the age with new avocational studies, and from the occupation of the critics of the time, in emulation of the French Academy, with constructive literary theories, at the expense of objective interest in the older literary field. This exploitation of the synthetic, as opposed to the historical, method seems significant of the spirit of the times; and it may be that the failure of an already awakened interest in the ancient and medieval literary history of the land may have been corollary to the general downfall of authority and tradition in the wider realm of philosophy. That scholarly interest in the older literature was waning throughout the greater part of this century seems to be wholly evident. Probably the typical attitude toward philological scholarship in this day is found in Sprat, who, while his scorn of early English literature[18] prevented his regarding it as fairly within the general philological domain, congratulates the scholars of his time on having exhausted the possibilities of philological study, and having before them, therefore, a clear field for experimental philosophy.[19]

So marked and important a change in the scholarly outlook between the day of Parker and the day of Sprat may be traced to a number of causes. Without doubt the decline of nationalism since the age of Elizabeth and the political and religious turmoil of the mid-century must have had a perceptibly deterrent effect upon the popular interest in literature;[20] and this must eventually have affected the special interests of scholars. But a more potent reason for

[18] Thomas Sprat, *History of the Royal Society of London,* 1667; 21, 42.

[19] *Ibid.,* 24–25.

[20] In the commendatory verses to William Somner's *Dictionarium Saxonico-Latino-Anglicum* . . . 1649, signed Johannes de Bosco, the discouraging outlook of literary and antiquarian scholarship during the period of the Civil War and the Commonwealth is pointed out.

the decline of the older literature from popular taste was the recession of the ancient matter and ideals of literature from the domain of vital contemporary interest, co-incident with a fecundity of novel and accomplished literary production throughout the Elizabethan period that completely filled the place of the popular literary product from Chaucer to Skelton.[21] The literary resources of the nation were probably multiplied many times in the fifty years following Parker's editorial activities. This fact alone was sufficient for the time being to kill the interest in literary antiquity which Parker had endeavored to foster.

We are of course familiar with the way in which the splendid literary consciousness of the Elizabethan age was transmuted into the exaggerated self-confidence of Augustan England. Whatever the forces that induced this revulsion in literary taste, the dominant aim of the day was to develop a classicism derived from the Continent and supported by arbitrary canons of taste. It seems characteristic of the history of all efforts at intensive cultivation of the

[21] A significant illustration of the abrupt decline in the general appreciation of middle English literature with the opening of the new century may be found in the relative frequency of reprints of Chaucer's works before and after the year 1602. Between the date of publication of William Thynne's first collected edition of Chaucer in 1532 and of the reprint of Speght's edition in 1602, a period of seventy years, six assumedly complete editions were printed. Only two more were produced down to the year 1721, when Urry brought out his new edition. More significant still are the dates of publication of the *Canterbury Tales*, which may obviously be taken as a more effective criterion of purely popular interest in Chaucerian literature. From Caxton's first edition of the *Canterbury Tales* in 1477–8 to Speght's collected edition of 1602 eleven issues were brought forth in one hundred and twenty-five years; from this date to 1775–8, when Tyrwhitt edited the *Canterbury Tales* alone, only three additional issues appeared in one hundred and seventy-six years—an average of one issue every eleven years during the first period, and of one in every forty-four years during the second.

vernacular that they imply a general lack of respect for the ancient vernacular literature; for the very belief in the future of the vulgar tongue carries with it a disrespect for its past. In addition to this, classical propaganda had always had little to do with antiquated vernacular literature, if for no other reason than that native literature in the making had never been considered part of a respectable cultural program. In any event, the classical tendency of the criticism of the time seems to supply another reason for the absence of interest in the older English literature. In England at least the condemnation of the older literature—and the classical perfectionists of the end of the century saw barbarism in the literary product of no more remote a period than the age of Elizabeth—was generally uncritical and generally prejudiced, but almost always ill informed. This lack of historical perspective assigned the supposed deficiencies of the Chaucerian period to barbaric unfamiliarity with critical principles and a lack of common knowledge of the language. But with the characteristic blindness of *a priori* theory, the seventeenth century failed to see its own overpowering critical incapacity in its ignorance of linguistic evolution and middle English prosody. The final word of the age on this point is found in the Preface to Dryden's *Fables;* here we see an otherwise perceptive and generous piece of criticism marred by a wholly unhistorical view of the subject.[22] Whatever the merits

[22] It is interesting to observe in the trend of critical opinion upon Chaucer's work throughout this century an effective criterion of the value of the assumedly historical criticism of the time on medieval English literature. Dr. J. E. Spingarn's *Critical Essays of the seventeenth Century*, 3 v., Oxford, 1908–9, presents a series of critical allusions which seem typical of the period.

Ben Jonson decries the use of Chaucer and Gower by students of untrained taste, ''lest falling too much in love with Antiquity, and not apprehending the weight, they grow rough and barren in language onely'' (I, 34). Edmund Bolton ''cannot advise the allowance of''

or faults of this age of criticism may have been, we must remember that here for once criticism did prescribe the literary taste of the day. So with the force of effective contemporary criticism arraigned against it, it is not surprising that interest in old and middle English literature in the day of Dryden was probably at its very lowest point of decline.

These largely correlated facts have been grouped without a pretence to finality. It would be absurd to insist that any given set of facts bear precisely the relations one to another that have been assigned to them here. After all, such facts can scarcely be explicitly classed as anything more than common evidences of a simple and natural reaction in literary feeling. But as to the part which scholarship plays in this reaction, it seems reasonably clear that it was affected by two causes which affected the popular appreciation of ancient English literature at the time: the weakening of English national culture, and the ever increasing remote-

Spenser's poems, "as for practick English, no more than I can do Jeff. Chaucer, Lydgate, Pierce Ploughman, or Laureat Skelton" (I, 109); Bolton's stricture upon the old literature is to be qualified, however, by the fact that he is dealing with the question of English for the historical writers of his own day. Peacham has an admirable word of praise for Chaucer, and seems to distinguish his capacities from those of Gower and Lydgate in a really efficient way (I, 132–3). Drayton's *Epistle to Reynolds* has a commendation rather labored in figure, but with a deprecation of the insufficiency of Chaucer's language for poetic expression (I, 135–6). Sprat's attitude of general scorn for medieval English has been referred to already, but it is worth noting specifically that he regards Chaucer's poetry as the only literature of its time worth reading twice (II, 113); but Sprat's praise of Chaucer has distinct limitation, for in an earlier passage of the *History of the Royal Society* (21) he commends the schoolmen "as we are wont to do Chaucer; we would confess, that they are admirable in comparison of the ignorance of their own Age." Rymer voices the characteristic sentiment of the latter end of the century: "But from our Language proceed to our Writers,

ness of the old literature from the field of immediate popular interests; and by two causes which touched it more
specifically: the eclipse of other intellectual pursuits in the
ascendancy of natural science, and the absorption of literary scholars in the critical abstractions of the day, both as
to language and as to literature. It is not surprising, therefore, that with so little in the national spirit and in the
scholarly occupations of the time to vitalize an interest in
the literary productions of a period then wholly out of
vogue, there should have been no organized group of
scholars to continue the traditions established by Parker
and Spelman.

Throughout so barren a period as this was for the productive student of the literature of English antiquity, the
few who were still concerned with the subject, and for
whom more remunerative occupations could afford the
necessary leisure, were supporting a languishing study
through textual editing and lexicography, and, quite as im-

and with the freedom of this Author, examine how unhappy the
greatest English Poets have been through their ignorance or negligence of these fundamental Rules and Laws of Aristotle. I shall
leave the Author of the Romance of the Rose (whom Sir Richard
Baker makes an Englishman) for the French to boast of, because he
writ in their Language. Nor shall I speak of Chaucer, in whose time
our Language, I presume, was not capable of any Heroick Character'' (II, 167).

Dryden treats Chaucer with more spontaneous judgment than most
of the critics of his day; in fact his Preface to the *Fables,* 1700, is
in many respects a monument of originality and critical honesty.
Yet he shares in the prejudice and the lack of perspective of his
time. He attempts expressly to confute Speght's judgment that
apparent deficiencies in rhythm were to be explained by differences
in the older pronunciation (*Works,* Ed. Scott and Saintsbury, XI,
224–5) and fatuously assumes that Chaucer ''must first be polished,
ere he shines.'' An echo of the narrowness of classical consistency
is heard in his: ''I deny not likewise, that, living in our early days
of poetry, he writes not always of a piece; but sometimes mingles
trivial things with those of greater moment'' (*ibid.,* 232).

portantly, through the medium of more properly antiquarian investigation. It might be broadly said, in fact,
that philological science in the latter half of the seventeenth
century was advanced more by incidental than by direct
contributions; and this continued to be measurably true
until the vogue of medieval literature was restored in the
middle of the eighteenth century as an incident of the
Romantic Reaction. The actual critical and scholarly activity of the age was, in fact, broad to an unprecedented
degree; but its deficiencies for the purposes of non-
utilitarian culture lay in the fact that its incentives and
ends were almost exclusively theological.[23] But although
churchmen and antiquaries still seemed to possess the
greater part of the current interest in Anglo-Saxon studies,
the most important and masterful work in the field was
accomplished by a foreigner, and a scholar of the most dis-
interested and devoted type, Franciscus Junius. It was
Junius, in fact, whose residence at Oxford during the closing years of his life enlisted the scholarly labors of some of
the most important students of his day, notably Marshall,
Nicolson, and Hickes. His great importance in the history
of Anglo-Saxon scholarship is not measured merely by the
value of his publications, his transcriptions, and his lexicography, but by the effect of his teaching and his personality upon the scholarly productions of the half-century
and more following his death.[24] This group of Oxford
scholars, united by their proximity and in a common aim,
though without any pretence of formal organization, main-

[23] See Prof. Foster Watson's chapter on *Scholars and Scholarship,
1600–60,* in the *Cambridge History of English Literature,* VII, 304–
324, 1911.

[24] The weight of Junius's influence upon the philological scholarship of the late seventeenth and the early eighteenth century appears
in Wülker's list of Anglo-Saxon publications for this period.
Grundriss zur Geschichte der angelsächsischen Literatur, 1885, 19–23.

5

tained a continued and increasing productivity until well into the new century, when the revival of antiquarian research, with the establishment of the Society of Antiquaries, provided a more tangible and more efficient foundation for scholarly development.

Meawhile the tendency toward concentration on the part of scholars and dilettanti marks the slow but effective growth of the idea of the learned society. Organization was probably less generally evident in England than on the Continent,[25] but a number of segregated instances mark the history of the movement. Projects and actual organizations for pedagogic, political, scientific, and merely social aims are found in every decade of the century; but none can be strictly identified—barring the Royal Society and one or two others of similar but less conspicuous purposes— as in the main parallel to the modern conception of special society activities.

The educational feature of Bolton's proposal for an academy was embodied in later pedagogical projects designed to serve the ends of a modern cultural training—usually for "gentlemen's sons." The most notable scheme of this kind was Sir Francis Kynaston's Musaeum Minervae, which was licensed by Charles I in 1635[26] and continued in existence until 1642. Balthasar Gerbier's academy was established in 1649 to continue the purposes of the Museum Minervae, but it was dissolved in 1651.[27] These foundations are of interest only as private projects of more liberal and utilitarian educational aims than the universities; they bear no relation to societies organized for the furtherance of scholarly interests. Comenius's pedagogical projects did, however, include a plan, incidental to his pansophic pro-

[25] Gothofredi Vockerodt, *Exercitationes Academicae*, Gothae, 1704, 15–124 *passim*.

[26] *Dict. Nat. Biog.*, XXXI, 355–6.

[27] *Dict. Nat. Biog.*, XXI, 227–229.

gram, which contemplated a "universal college"; and apparently this plan seemed for a time in 1642 to be on the eve of accomplishment in England itself, through the interest of Parliament in Comenius's educational theories.[28] This proposal, though suggested as a purely educational measure, is a very significant reflection of the expansion of the ideal of scholarly comity.

It has been noted[29] that the methods and organization of experimental science in the sixteenth century were anticipated, or rather definitely outlined, in the "Salomon's House" of Bacon's *New Atlantis*.[30] Bacon's plan—if so cursory and highly imaginative a picture may be called a plan—compassed not merely a fellowship of scientific scholars, but also "Novices and Apprentices, that the Succession of the former Employed Men does not faile";[31] in this provision we see the long prevalent inclination to combine the investigative with the pedagogic aim. Whether Thomas Bushell's declared intention of instituting a society upon the lines suggested by Bacon was an intention in good faith seems to be open to question.[32] Closely similar projects were offered, however, by Hartlib, Evelyn, and Cowley before the formal organization of the Royal Society. Hartlib's projected "Macaria"[33] was probably the first of the unproductive efforts to put into effect the scheme of a philosophical society on the lines of "Salomon's House." Hartlib cherished his plan patiently for twenty years, and

[28] Will S. Monroe, *Comenius and the Beginnings of educational Reform*, 1900; 53–56.

[29] *Ante*, 42.

[30] Francis Bacon, *The New Atlantis*, Edited by G. C. Moore Smith, 1900; 34–46.

[31] *Ibid.*, 45.

[32] *Ibid.*, xxviii–xxix.

[33] Samuel Hartlib, *A Description of the famous Kingdom of Macaria. In a Dialogue between a Schollar and a Traveller;* London, 1641.

seems to have actually instituted a society, called at first Macaria, and afterwards Antilia, in the hope that he would eventually secure the aid that might make his schemes capable of realization.[34] It is interesting to note in this connection that Hartlib was in communication with the members of the Oxford Philosophical Society, and with some of the important early members of the Royal Society itself, including Boyle, Evelyn, and Wren.[35] His advocacy of the idea of a philosophical foundation upon these lines was, however, too general and too visionary to enable us to regard him as an important factor in a development which was after all inherent in the intellectual quality of his generation. The chief importance of his ideas touching investigative science lay in his wholesome efforts to extend the experimental method to the domain of useful popular knowledge. Hartlib's name has incidental connection with Sir William Petty's *Advice of W. P. to Mr. Samuel Hartlib, for the Advancement of some particular Parts of Learning,* 1648.[36] In the way of preface to the exposition of his plan for a more utilitarian education for children and youths, Petty points out the necessity of assimilating and systematizing the knowledge derived from experiment and observation.

Evelyn's proposal is outlined in a letter written in 1659 to Robert Boyle;[37] he contemplates the foundation of a scholarly community on a reservation adapted to the purposes of experiment in the fields of what are called to-day pure and natural sciences. The foundation was to be en-

[34] H. Dircks, *A biographical Memoir of Samuel Hartlib,* London, n. d.; 15–19, 44–45. There are numerous allusions to Macaria throughout Hartlib's early correspondence with Dr. John Worthington, in *The Diary and Correspondence of Dr. John Worthington,* Chetham Society, v. I, 1847.

[35] Dircks, *op. cit.,* 17–21. C. R. Weld, *op. cit.,* I, 30–41.

[36] Reprinted in the *Harleian Miscellany,* 1808–11; VI, 143–158.

[37] Robert Boyle, *Works,* 1772, VI, 288–91.

dowed under rather strict disciplinary regulations, and to provide accommodation for six scholars. Evelyn himself undertook to fill three of the scholars' cells, and to contribute to the carrying out of the project almost a third of its initial costs, which he estimated at £1600. Cowley's plan, published in 1661 as *A Proposition for the Advancement of Experimental Philosophy*,[38] was very much more pretentious than Evelyn's. The proposal followed Bacon's conception of a philosophical college by embodying a pedagogical as well as an investigative purpose. Cowley's proposition is worked out with elaborate detail, and calls for an annual income of £4000 for the support of "Twenty Philosophers or Professors," "Sixteen young Scholars, Servants of the Professors," and a veritable army of assistants and menials. There are noteworthy echoes of the details of Salomon's House, as for instance, "a Gallery to walk in, adorned with the Pictures or Statues of all the Inventors of any thing useful to Humane Life," "a very high Tower for observation of Celestial Bodies," and "very deep Vaults made under ground, for Experiments most proper to such places." An interesting feature is provision for a public school for two hundred boys, to be trained from youth in the methods of experimental investigation.

But the faults of the various schemes which aimed to make scholars either recluses or pedagogues were probably too self-evident to carry any of these plans further than the point of careful elaboration. In addition, a more natural development in the direction of organized and collective research had been in progress since 1645, when the informal meetings of a group of experimental philosophers laid the foundations of what the future was to name the Royal Society.[39] This group became divided about 1648, by reason

[38] Abraham Cowley, *Essays, Plays and sundry Verses*, Edited by A. R. Waller, 1906; 243–258.

[39] Weld, *op. cit.*, I, 30–40.

of the removal of some of the leading members, into Bishop Wilkins's so-called Philosophical Society of Oxford, and a continuation in London, in which Boyle was active, of the former society, which seems to have borne the name of the "Invisible College." Either, or rather both, of these societies may be regarded as parent of the Royal Society, the existence of which is generally dated from the revival of the scientific meetings at the time of the Restoration, and which was chartered by Charles II in 1662. In view of the immediate popularity and scientific success of the Royal Society in its chosen field, it is matter of real wonder, that, as we have seen, its example met with no emulative interest in any other field of research for a period of almost fifty years after its organization. In fact, the only new society for experimental philosophy founded before the end of the century was the Philosophical Society of Ireland (the predecessor of the Royal Irish Academy), established upon the model of the Royal Society by Sir William Petty in 1683.[40]

Before leaving this period in the growth and application of learned society functions, it remains to review cursorily a few literary, political, and antiquarian gatherings which, because of the direction of their purposes or the literary importance of their members, deserve at least a passing note of recognition.

The earliest of these of which we have record is the well-known assemblage of churchmen and philosophers which met at Falkland's estate at Great Tew, about 1633.[41] Most

[40] Edmond Fitzmaurice, *Life of Sir William Petty*, 1895; 253.

[41] Lady Theresa Lewis's picture of this coterie (*Lives of the Friends and Contemporaries of Lord Chancellor Clarendon*, 1852, I, 9–11) is at once the most vivid and the most agreeable. She takes her material from both Clarendon and Wood, the latter of whom is probably indebted, as in many other instances, to Aubrey. See also J. A. R. Marriot's *Life and Times of Lucius Cary, Viscount Falkland*, 1907, 79–122.

of the members of this group held academic positions at Oxford, which was within convenient travelling distance. Among the most important of these were Charles Gataker, William Chillingworth, and George Sandys, the poet. This body of men has been referred to as anticipating the society activities of a later period;[42] but the fragmentary records of the gathering seem to show that they were held together solely by the community of their interests and occupations. The note of their unity seems to have been absolute freedom from collective responsibilities; and it is, indeed, not too much to say that intellectual solidarity in this case was maintained by a spiritual, rather than by a scholarly, earnestness, to which formal organization would have been only baneful.

About 1651 was established another body whose bond of union was as intangible and unutilitarian as that of Falkland's friends, but in this instance as much a sentimental as a spiritual bond. This was the so-called Society of Friendship of Katherine Philips.[43] It possesses a special interest for the student of literature in the fact that it was in response to The Matchless Orinda's request to compose a defence of the idealized friendship which was the cause and the end of their association that Jeremy Taylor, who was one of the number, wrote his *Discourse of the Nature and Offices of Friendship*, dedicated to Mrs. Philips. Here again, then, we find an organization of only the most casual literary importance.

Investigative or critical purposes, however, are apparently suggested in two intrinsically important records of the year 1659. Aubrey[44] and Pepys[45] have both left notes upon the

[42] Foster Watson, in *Cambridge History of English Literature*, VII, 305, 1911.

[43] Edmund Gosse, *Jeremy Taylor*, 1904; 138–140.

[44] John Aubrey, *Brief Lives*, edited by Andrew Clark, 1898; I, 289–291.

[45] *The Diary of Samuel Pepys*, edited by Henry B. Wheatley, 1893–9; I, 14 n., 20, 59.

"Rota," or "Club of Commonwealth Men," which, meeting first as a coffee-house gathering, attained eventually to recognition as a society. Aubrey records the manner of their meeting, and their purpose—to discuss questions of government as projected in Harrington's *Oceana*, and especially in the light of the current Parliamentary abuses. This club, of which the memorable Cyriack Skinner was chairman, and which was sustained by sufficient enthusiasm to support nightly meetings, was only short-lived, dissolving within a few months after its formation, "upon the unexpected turne upon generall Monke's comeing in." The other meeting recorded for this year is that of the "Antiquaries' feast," referred to in a memorandum in Ashmole's diary, July 2, 1659. Richard Gough, without a trace of justification, interprets this entry as evidence that the Society of Antiquaries which had dissolved in 1614 had "remained as it were in abeyance."[46] But Joseph Hunter suggests more convincingly that the Antiquaries of 1659 "can have been only a small private club."[47]

A reminiscence, in name at least, of Harrington's Rota is found in a pamphlet published in 1673, an attack upon Dryden's *Conquest of Granada*, under the title *The Censure of the Rota on Mr. Driden's Conquest of Granada*, which purports to be a record of the criticisms of the play gathered from the discussions of the "Athenian Virtuosi." The pamphlet opened a controversy in which three other publications appeared,[48] and which was noticed briefly by Dryden in his preface to *The Assignation*.[49] The names "Rota" and "Athenian Virtuosi" which appear in this

[46] *Op. cit., Archaeologia*, I, xxii, 1777.

[47] *Op. cit., Archaeologia*, XXXII, 148, 1847.

[48] Robert W. Lowe, *Bibliographical Account of English theatrical Literature*, 1888; 102.

[49] John Dryden, *Works*, edited by Scott and Saintsbury, 18 v., 1882–93; IV, 376.

controversy are clearly intended to convey the idea that
the criticism of the first pamphlet was backed by something
like collective opinion; but all contemporary references to
the dispute seem to accept it as a quarrel of individuals.
This inference is supported by the fact that the author of
the first pamphlet—all four were issued anonymously—is
known to have been Richard Leigh. It is, then, very doubtful whether the Athenian Virtuosi can be considered
seriously as a *bona-fide* society.[50]

The Athenian Society, which has sometimes been confused with the Athenian Virtuosi, was founded by John
Dunton, the London publisher, in 1691. Although the
History of the Athenian Society, published in the year of
organization, invites comparison of the aims of this society
with those of the Royal Society, the real purpose of foundation was to publish a periodical, which soon became popular
and which lived for the rather unusual period of six years—
the *Athenian Gazette,* afterwards called the *Athenian Mer-
cury.* All the evidence shows this society to have been a
wholly private project of Dunton's, established for his
purposes as printer and publisher and administered solely
by him. His fellow-members, who were during the period
of the *Gazette's* existence only three in number, acted
simply in the capacity of associate editors for Dunton's
publishing schemes. The name of the society continued in
Dunton's possession and use after the discontinuation of
the *Gazette,* certainly down to the year 1710. There is, we
see, then, no valid ground for considering the Athenian
Society at all comparable in its purposes or methods to the
class of society with which we are dealing.[51]

Daniel Defoe records for us the interesting fact that, at

[50] This subject I have discussed at considerable length in my
article *The Athenian Virtuosi and the Athenian Society; Modern
Language Review,* VII, 358–371, 1912.

[51] *Ibid.,* 363–371.

some time prior to the publication of his *Essay on Projects*, in 1698, he was a member of a "literary society," which concerned itself at least in part with the familiar plan for the improving of the tongue.[52] Whether Defoe meant by literary society a society devoted to the study of *belles-lettres* from any point of view is very much to be doubted; for this narrower definition of literature is in our language one of relatively recent acceptance. Until well into the nineteenth century, as a matter of fact, this term "literary society" was applied to any investigative society which encouraged so-called literary exercises, such as the reading of papers, or general publication.[53]

Evidence of the rapid popularization of the society idea in England during the closing years of this century and the first years of the eighteenth is seen in the wide expansion of local religious societies, such as the noted Society for the Propagation of Christian Knowledge.[54]

We have seen, then, that the history of experimental science in England during the seventeenth century is in the main the history of the opening of the continuous tradition of learned society activities in England. The Royal Society was the first permanent foundation of the learned society type, and the seriousness and effectiveness of its scholarly labors set the example for organization of a similar sort in other fields of study, although the force of example was slow to assert itself during the hundred years following the Royal Society's incorporation. In spite, therefore, of the

[52] Daniel Defoe, *Earlier Life and Chief Earlier Works*. Ed. Henry Morley, 1889, 124–5.

[53] On the history of the emergence of the modern sense of the word "literary," see Ewald Flügel's *Bacon's Historia Literaria, Anglia*, XXI, 259–288, 1899.

[54] Edward Chamberlayne, *Angliae Notitiae or the present State of England*. Continued by his son, John Chamberlayne, 21st ed., 1704, 331–336.

general recognition, by the end of the seventeenth century, of the usefulness of organization in the interests of scholarship, we can sum up the slow progress of the idea into general application in the opening words of Defoe's chapter on Academies:[55] "We have in England fewer of these than in any part of the world, at least where learning is in so much esteem."

[55] Daniel Defoe, *op. cit.*, 524.

CHAPTER IV

THE EIGHTEENTH CENTURY

We have seen that during the seventeenth century there was no impetus to collective engagement in historical scholarship in literature. In England, in fact, there was no effective collaboration even for the etymological study of the vernacular, which had first assumed importance in the discussions of Parker's Society,[1] and which, on the Continent, had constituted part of the labor of the French Academy, and practically the chief scholarly interest of the Fruchtbringende Gesellschaft.[2] There was throughout the century, however, a wholly natural tendency for antiquarian scholars to seek association or at least to carry on correspondence with men of their own inclinations. Thus in the early part of the century there was a more or less frequent interchange of ideas and measures of assistance between Cotton, Usher, Spelman, Camden, Casaubon, and their contemporaries;[3] and in the mid-century, as we have seen, between Spelman, Dugdale, Wheelocke and D'Ewes.[4] But the very narrowness of the current interest in antiquarian studies, and especially in the literature of English antiquity, made it almost inevitable that material advance in these studies should be effected through a more regular coordination among scholars than the century had as yet produced. The needed incentive was supplied largely in

---

[1] *Ante*, 7, 35.

[2] F. W. Barthold, *Geschichte der Fruchtbringenden Gesellschaft*, 111, 242–7 (1848).

[3] *Original Letters of eminent literary Men* . . . 1843, 102–164; *Gulielmi Camdeni et illustrium Virorum ad G. Camdenum Epistolae*, 1691, *passim*.

[4] *Ante*, 22–3; also Ellis's *Original Letters*, 153–161, 174–6.

the person of Junius, whose learning and personality concentrated about himself much of the activity in Anglo-
Saxon studies during the latter half of the century.[5] Later,
among Gibson, Hickes, Tanner, Kennet, and Nicolson there
was occasional correspondence on scholarly questions, relating principally to Anglo-Saxon desiderata and publications
in preparation.[6] But the fact that all of these last named
students of Old English were important and busy churchmen, who were prevented by ecclesiastical responsibilities
from meeting one another at all regularly, removed the
possibility of formal action for the furtherance of literary
scholarship.

Anything in the nature of an effective organization for
such purposes was therefore suspended until the early
eighteenth century, when the Oxford group of Anglo-Saxon
scholars had partly spent their productive power. The
new impetus to the study of old English literature and
antiquities was given by a number of scholars practically
self-educated in the old vernacular, some of them scarcely
touched by the tradition of culture. Such were Humphrey
Wanley, Thomas Hearne, John Bagford, George Ballard,
William Elstob, and Elizabeth Elstob, the last a protégée of
Ballard's, and one of the most truly erudite of the class of
learned ladies which Ballard made it his pleasure to defend.
Despite the educational disadvantages of these scholars,
their work was characterized by a fervor of interest and
activity which produced results quite as praiseworthy, and
in at least Wanley's case, quite as monumental, as any publications in the previous history of English literary studies.
Barring Hearne, whose vanity, jealousy, and ill temper
prevented his working harmoniously with his fellows, most

[5] *Ante*, 49, note.
[6] *Letters to and from William Nicolson*, [edited by] John Nichols,
1809, *passim;* [*"Letters from the Bodleian"*], 1813, *passim;* Ellis's
Original Letters, passim.

of these students were, like their predecessors, bound together by a useful common interest.

This general solidarity, however, was furthered at an early period by an actual organization which for the moment seemed to promise much for the immediate future of Anglo-Saxon study, but which because of an entire diversion of its interests to the field of monumental antiquities, such as seems to have occurred at an early date in Parker's society,[7] failed to perfect a program for the resuscitation of literary studies.

In 1707, we learn from notes made by Wanley himself,[8] John Talman, artist-antiquary, and John Bagford, literary antiquary and collector of the so-called "Bagford Ballads," agreed with Wanley to meet together for the discussion of antiquarian subjects. These meetings were informal, and increase in the numbers of the gathering was slow; but within two months eight members were assembling with more or less regularity. Among the first of the newer members were the distinguished Peter Le Neve, subsequently chosen as president of the society, and William Elstob, the Anglo-Saxon scholar, both of whom were introduced by Wanley. A typical evening's communications show the material for discussion on at least this one occasion to have been historical documents of practically no literary importance. There is real significance, however, in the bearing of the literary occupations of Bagford, Elstob, and particularly Wanley, upon the character of the society's discussions. Whether Wanley, who seems to have been the leader during the period of organization, intended the activities of the club to have been devoted largely to literary remains cannot be said with any degree of certainty; but considering his intense preoccupation with English palaeography

[7] *Ante*, 7, 35.

[8] Nichols, *Literary Anecdotes*, VI, 147–8.

and bibliography,[9] it seems inevitable that at least these easy informal meetings of the group must very frequently have touched literary antiquities. It is indeed quite certain that the province of the society's interest during this early period was supposed to include ancient English literature; for in a list of proposed publications which Richard Gough believes to have represented Wanley's own plans for the society's special field of study[10] we find a number of thoroughly significant entries. "Volumes of several old English historians, not yet printed" are mentioned as among the general desiderata; and in the list of "good books wanted" are found "A Glossary, including Somner, Spelman, Cowel. &c. and new words from charters, and other MSS; . . . A Compleat Anglo-Saxon Bible; another Bible of Wickliffe's time, with a comparative account of later editions and translations; a dictionary for fixing the English language, as the French and Italian; . . . a body of Saxon laws and homilies; a Cento Saxonicus, and a Brittania Saxonica, desired by Dr. Hickes; Of the use of musick, interludes, masques, and plays in England." Such a list of projected publications bespeaks for Wanley the distinction of having been the first, as far as history recounts, to have proposed a society for the publication of historical and literary texts, documents, and treatises. The realization of his plan, however, in a manner as systematic and as generally effective as he had anticipated, was to be deferred for more than a century.

It may readily be seen why Wanley's plans for publica-

[9] Wanley had already published in the *Philosophical Transactions* of the Royal Society, of which he was a member, a paper on the age of manuscripts, and had collaborated with Bagford in an essay on the history of printing. See the *Philosophical Transactions of the Royal Society, abridged by Charles Hutton, George Shaw, and Richard Pearson,* 1809; V, 227–237, 350–354.

[10] Richard Gough, *op. cit., Archaeologia,* I, xxix–xxxi.

tion were not then realized. In the first place, the small
number of the early members could not have prosecuted
so huge a task as Wanley's proposal outlines; in the second
place, the expense of publication of textual reprints and
books with engraved illustrations was then very high, and
sales, therefore, were difficult and slow. These two conditions, the history of modern printing societies has shown
us, are precisely those that collective publication is most
effective in meeting, given either a wealthy organization,
or an extended public interest in the society's aims; but
Wanley's group of associates were neither numerous nor
wealthy, and it can not be said that there was as yet anything like an extensive popular interest in antiquities,
though this was soon to develop with the growing importance of the work of the Society of Antiquaries.

Meanwhile Wanley's gathering seems to have progressed
along precisely the lines of Parker's "assembly," in con-
fining its attention generally to the legal, numismatic, and
monumental sides of antiquarianism. In 1717 the society
took definite steps toward an effective establishment, and
Le Neve was elected its first president. From this time on
its activity and influence became much greater; but although
it included in its membership down to the mid-century such
scholars as Rymer, John Warburton (whose name is insep-
arably associated with the manuscripts which his careless
servant cut up for humble culinary uses), George Ballard,
Sir John Clerk of Penecuik, Robert Stephens, Historiog-
rapher Royal, Edward Lye, Dr. John Ward, who presented
to the society in 1758 his *Four Essays upon the English
Language*,[11] and others largely interested in the historical
study of English literature, special attention to this field

[11] Edward William Brabrook, *Fellows of the Society of Antiquaries
who have held the Office of Director, Archaeologia*, LXII, 67 (1910).

seems to have been abandoned even before the formal organization in 1717.

The society was not actually incorporated until 1751.[12] As early as 1754 it was decided that some form of publication should be issued;[13] the first volume of *Archaeologia*, however, did not appear until 1770. From this time on articles of literary bearing appeared in the society's publication,[14] but with such infrequency as to emphasize the fact that this body, which in its inception had promised so well for the study of English letters, did not possess during the eighteenth century a very real importance in this field. Indeed, there seems ground to believe that shortly after the middle of the century the society took occasion to discourage efforts to gain recognition for Anglo-Saxon literary scholarship as one of its proper interests. Edward Rowe Mores wrote Ducarel in 1753 that the Society of Antiquaries had refused to undertake to print Junius's unpublished index to his edition of Caedmon, together with plates of drawings of the Caedmon manuscript.[15] It is not wholly clear from the substance of the letter, in fact, that Mores did not mean to say that the society really gave its refusal to a project for the publication of an entirely new text and translation of Caedmon; and it is apparently in this sense that Thorpe has construed Mores's letter.[16] It may be said to be practically certain, in any event, that since the society refused to lend its aid to the publication of these important Caedmon items, its decision implied a positive unwillingness to include among its functions the publication of materials for Anglo-Saxon textual scholarship.

[12] Gough, *op. cit.*, xxxix.
[13] Nichols, *Literary Anecdotes*, V, 392.
[14] *Post*, 91–2, 119–20.
[15] Nichols, *Literary Anecdotes*, V, 403–4.
[16] *Caedmon's Metrical Paraphrase of Parts of the Holy Scriptures in Anglo-Saxon*, London, 1832; vi.

6

That Wanley's advanced plan for a publishing society did not develop as he had intended is very much to be regretted. It seems probable that if the idea of collective publication had become established in the early eighteenth century, the interest in old literature and in manuscript materials so painstakingly cultivated by Ramsay, Percy, Ritson, and later scholars might have been much more rapidly diffused, with the result that much of the spolia- tion and disappearance of the materials of literary study might have been prevented. Hearne himself, who had little sympathy with the Society of Antiquaries, and little liking for many of its members, recognized the great oppor- tunity when he complained to James West that ''Societies should engage in some great Works, either never yet printed, or, if printed, are become either almost or quite as rare as MSS.''[17]

There can scarcely be a question that Joseph Stukeley, the first secretary of the Society after its establishment in 1717, and his close friends and associates, the influential members of the Antiquaries, who included Roger Gale, Maurice Johnson, Sir John Clerk, Samuel Knight and others, were interested almost exclusively in the archaeo- logical side of antiquities.[18] Stukeley himself is the very type of the antiquary of his day, much concerned with earthworks, burial-places, ruins and coins, and generally an efficient and industrious student of a subject that has

[17] Hearne, *Remarks and Collections,* VIII, 336 (1907). It is in- teresting to note in this connection that although Hearne was never a member of the Society of Antiquaries, but took every opportunity to ridicule the members and their affairs, he himself was a member of an informal club of antiquaries at Oxford (*Remarks and Col- lections,* VI, 216).

[18] See the voluminous correspondence of Stukeley and his friends in *Memoirs of William Stukeley, and the Correspondence of Wil- liam Stukeley, Roger and Samuel Gale, etc.,* 3 v., Surtees Society, 1882–7.

always attracted largely a dilettante following. It must be a matter of constant wonder that for such students the literary remains of the antiquity which they professed to reverence apparently had no charm. The reason is probably to be found in the fact that Anglo-Saxon studies were in those days nothing to the amateur if not taken seriously; and with all that can be said in praise of Stukeley and his associates, it must be confessed that their interest in antiquities was very amateurish. Stukeley's own opinion of the particular direction of antiquarian study that Wanley endeavored to encourage is to be seen in his exulting transcription of a passage in criticism of Hearne and his labors: "Every monkish tale & lye & miracle & ballad are rescued from their dust & worms, to proclaim the poverty of our forefathers, whose nakedness, it seems, their pious posterity take great pleasure to pry into; for of all those writings given us by the learned Oxford antiquary, there is not one that is not a disgrace to letters, most of them are so to common sense, & some even to human nature."[19]

Such was the catholicity of cultivated taste in the earlier half of this century that we find that many of the members of the Society of Antiquaries, and especially of this particular group, were also members of the Royal Society. It must be confessed, however, that Clerk, with his notion that the migrations of wild-fowl were accomplished with the aid of the diurnal motion of the earth,[20] and Stukeley, with a tenacious devotion to his hypothesis that earthquakes were the result of atmospheric conditions,[21] were not among the most responsible of the members of the Royal Society.

For the cause of learned societies in general Stukeley's circle did much of real importance. Their zeal in the

[19] Stukeley's *Memoirs and Correspondence*, I, 199.
[20] *Ibid.*, I, 247–258.
[21] *Ibid.*, I, 478, II, 379, 382–3.

service of society projects was so effective that they were responsible for the establishment of a number of lesser assemblies which maintained for many years an active correspondence with the Antiquaries of London. The most important of the societies organized by these evangelists of antiquarianism was the Gentlemen's Society of Spalding, which began its informal meetings in 1710, and effected a voluntary organization in 1712.[22] Of this society, some words later. The example set by the Spalding society was followed in the establishment of another Gentlemen's Society at Peterborough,[23] and in 1721 of a society of similar aims at Stamford, which Stukeley attempted to revive in 1745 under the name of the Brazennose Society.[24] In addition to these, Gough records the existence of a like body at Doncaster,[25] and Maurice Johnson, in a letter to Dr. Andrew Ducarel, mentions other societies of the same nature at Worcester, Wisbech, Lincoln, and Dublin.[26] Stukeley himself notes two "vertuoso meetings" which he established in London after the organization of the Society of Antiquaries, and "meetings" also at Market Overton and West Deeping.[27] Many of these assemblies were in all probability little more than small friendly gatherings of amateurs; but the more important societies had very reputable intellectual standing and numerous membership, those at Spalding and Peterborough including about one hundred members each, and carrying some really distinguished names on their rosters.

The Spalding society, which may be taken as the type of all of these organizations, originated, like the Antiquaries

[22] Nichols, *Literary Anecdotes*, VI, 5, 59.
[23] *Ibid.*, 4, 136–9.
[24] *Ibid.*, 4–5.
[25] *Ibid.*, 4.
[26] *Ibid.*, 144–5.
[27] Stukeley's *Memoirs and Correspondence*, I, 122–3.

of London, in an informal club, meeting in this case at a coffee-house, instead of a tavern, and subscribing to literary periodicals, the first of which was the *Tatler*.[28] The society recognized from its beginning a formal relation to the Society of Antiquaries, giving itself the name of a "cell" to the London society, and maintaining with it an uninterrupted correspondence over a period of forty years. The purposes of the Spalding society, however, were not exclusively antiquarian. Roger Gale wrote Maurice Johnson in 1735, "You have infinitely the advantage of our Antiquarian Society at London, which confines itself to that study and knowledge onely, whereas you take in, and very rightly too, the whole compasse of learning and philosophy, and so comprehend at once the ends and institution of both our London Societys."[29] Maurice Johnson wrote to Timothy Neve in 1745/6, "We deal in all arts and sciences, and exclude nothing from our conversation but politics, which would throw us all into confusion and disorder."[30] These quotations convey the sense of the "Rules and Orders" of the society, which were adopted in 1725.[31] The purposes of this society, then, are to be taken as miscellaneous.

The society took a rather active, though possibly not specially discriminating interest in contemporary literature. Pope, Addison, and Bentley were among its honorary members;[32] Gay was both a member and an occasional correspondent;[33] original poems were among the communications to the society throughout its existence, including

[28] Nichols, *op. cit.*, VI, 6.

[29] Stukeley's *Memoirs and Correspondence*, III, 129.

[30] Nichols, *op. cit.*, VI, 6–7.

[31] *Ibid.*, 29–32.

[32] *Ibid.*, VI, 106; William Moore, *The Gentlemen's Society at Spalding* (in *Memoirs of the Archaeological Institute of Great Britain and Ireland, Lincoln, July, 1848*, 82–)9 (1850)), 87.

[33] Nichols, *op. cit.*, 84–5.

manuscript poems by Prior and Pope,[34] and newly issued pieces by Parnell, Swift, Arbuthnot, and Eusden, and Gray's *Elegy;*[35] in addition, the society subscribed during its early period not only to the *Tatler,* but to the most important of the literary periodicals of the day, including the *Guardian* and the *Lover,*[36] and later the *Rambler.*[37]

This degree and kind of interest in literature is, however, what obviously might be expected of a "Gentlemen's Society" in any age. Whether the range of the society's interests may be assumed to have included the historical study of literature is more to be doubted, if we consider the personnel of the society and the spirit of the times. That literary history received at least occasional attention, however, seems to be indicated in a few scattered records of the society. In 1725, for example, the society voted to "take in" the *Bibliotheca Literaria* and *Memoirs of Literature.*[38] The "Gentlemen's Library at Spaldwin" appears also in the list of subscribers to Junius's *Etymologicum Anglicanum* in 1743. That at least one member possessed a live interest in English literary history may be seen in Beaupré Bell's intention, expressed in 1733/4, to publish an edition of Chaucer, to which end he had at that time collated a number of manuscripts.[39] But such instances as these can not be made to serve as evidence that the society as a whole felt any collective responsibility for the study of English literature. Barring, therefore, an occasional proof of incidental or individual interest in this field, it is probably safe to assume that, as Roger Gale expressed it, "the whole compasse of learning and phi-

[34] *Ibid.,* 67–8.
[35] Moore, *op. cit.,* 84–5.
[36] Nichols, *op. cit.,* VI, 62.
[37] Moore, *op. cit.,* 88.
[38] Nichols, *op. cit.,* VI, 32.
[39] Stukeley's *Memoirs and Correspondence,* II, 22.

losophy'' which the society chose as its province comprehended in reality no more than the special and restricted ''ends and institutions'' of the Society of Antiquaries and the Royal Society.

What is apparently true of the Gentlemen's Society of Spalding is in all probability true of the Stamford, the Peterborough, and the other local societies. Although they may have possessed an occasional and casual interest in literature as a branch of antiquarian study, their records convey to us no intimation of a vital and consistent interest in this field for its own sake.

Although an organization of no special importance to literary studies, the Society of the Dilettanti must be mentioned in passing as the first of the book clubs, a class of organizations which became very popular during the first half of the nineteenth century, and which without doubt was the most powerful single influence upon the growth of collective scholarship during this later period. The Dilettanti were, as their name may imply, a small group of wealthy and aristocratic travellers who combined the ambition of transmitting to England the culture of classical times with the solidly practical idea of dining well at more or less frequent intervals. The members were not renowned for scholarly attainments; but their position enabled them to exercise a not unwise patronage of real workers in their field. The Society was from the beginning small and exclusive, and did not pretend to exist for philanthropic purposes. It was founded in 1734 (possibly as early as 1732),[40] and accomplished little for the diffusion of the culture it nominally supported within its own circle until almost thirty years later. Then it undertook to contribute to the expense of publication of Stuart and Revett's *Antiquities of Athens,*

[40] *History of the Society of the Dilettanti,* compiled by Lionel Cust, and edited by Sidney Colvin, 1898; 4–5.

which appeared in 1762.[41]   The first work actually published by the Society was its *Ionian Antiquities,* the first
volume of which was issued in 1769, and the fourth in 1882.
In the issue of Payne Knight's *Account of the Worship of
Priapus,* 1786, which was not distributed beyond the actual
membership of the society except as signed presentation
copies,[42] we find foreshadowed the much deprecated custom
of the printing clubs of the nineteenth century of placing
strict limits upon the circulation of their issues.   In this first
instance, however, there were of course special reasons for
such a restriction which could not hold good for the books
of the Roxburghe Club and its successors.   The subsequent
activities of the Dilettanti Society, which still continues in
existence, have no significance for our purposes; but the
importance of the society as the forerunner of all our
modern organizations of this well known type cannot be
disregarded.

In Scotland during the greater part of the eighteenth
century an interest in societies on the part of cultivated
men, especially in the university towns, was one of the most
characteristic marks of the intellectual activity of the
period.   We have seen[43] that the Royal Society grew out of
a private gathering of experimental philosophers, that the
Society of Antiquaries was merely the more formal continuation of private meetings in the Bear Tavern,[44] and that
the Spalding Gentlemen's Society, with probably most of
the other local societies of its time, was begun in a similar
irregular fashion.   In the main, however, it is impossible
to trace from the English coffee-house clubs, and other informal gatherings which were so marked a feature of social
life in the seventeenth and eighteenth centuries, any very

[41] *Ibid.,* 79–81.
[42] *Ibid.,* 122–3.
[43] *Ante,* 53–4.
[44] See also Nichols, *Literary Anecdotes,* VI, 147.

general effect upon scholarly organization, much as we should naturally be led to expect such an effect. The notable exception seems to have been Johnson's literary club, to which we shall return; but in considering even this conspicuous instance, we must remember that this club grew out of established literary associations, and that its slight potential effect upon literary scholarship owed little to the mere fact of its existence. It is apparently true, then, that the few academic bodies which carried the whole vitality of the learned society movement in England through the eighteenth century had their origins in something closely akin to club gatherings. But the special development of English club life throughout this century had seemingly no connection with the learned society movement, since these clubs themselves were a divergent growth, and their character was in all cases almost purely social and not seriously intellectual. It would be impossible to assume, for example, that the frequenters of Button's or Will's regarded their casual meetings as anything but pure relaxation. In Scotland, however, the case was quite different; for here we find the social—even convivial—gatherings of the time developing into associations for the discussion, or more properly for the actual study, of the most profound subjects, and with an intellectual conscience that would have done credit to the Royal Society. Indeed, a comparison of the whole body of members of some of the mid-century Scottish societies, small and private as they were, with the larger and more widely important Royal and Antiquarian Societies of London would force us to admit that in actual intellectual impressiveness the Scotsmen were by no means the inferiors.

The first of these clubs of which we have record was the Rankenian Club at Edinburgh, named from its place of meeting, and dating from about 1716.[45] Dugald Stewart tells us that this club, which was composed in part of students at the University, corresponded with Bishop Berkeley on various questions connected with his idealistic philosophical views.[46] This society continued a more or less regular existence down to the year 1774.

A society for classical studies was established in Edinburgh within two years of the first stated meetings of the Rankenian Club. Thomas Ruddiman was one of the founders of this body, and the distinguished Lord Kames became a member at an early date.[47] This society, although nominally given over to deliberations on classical subjects, in all probability had a more general literary program, including the aim of improvement in composition and speaking, which seems to have been a common object among all such societies in Scotland during this period.

The most important, and, with its descendants, the most permanent, of these organizations, however, originated in Edinburgh in 1731 as a strictly medical society; and as such it published in its earliest years five volumes of transactions. In 1739, at the suggestion of Professor Maclaurin, one of its secretaries, the plan of the society was enlarged to include philosophical and literary subjects—''literary'' comprehending, as it almost invariably did throughout the eighteenth century, every interest without the domains of theology, philosophy, and science.[48] With its new fields of activity the society became known as the Philosophical Society of Edinburgh. Judging from the three volumes of

---

[45] Alexander Fraser Tytler, *Memoirs of Henry Home of Kames,* 2d ed., 1814; I, 243, III, 75–7.

[46] Dugald Stewart, *Collected Works,* 1854–8; I, 350–1.

[47] George Chalmers, *Life of Thomas Ruddiman,* 1794; 83–4.

[48] For the entire early history of this society see the anonymous *History of the Society* in *Transactions of the Royal Society of Edinburgh,* I, 3–22, 1788.

Essays and Observations[49] which were issued by the society in 1754, 1756, and 1771, the interests of the body were still predominantly in the sphere of medical science; but a few of the essays deal with physical subjects. There is no really literary paper in the three volumes. That the literary side of the society's program was not merely nominal, however, may be seen in the fact that Sir John Clerk of Penecuik read before the society in 1742 "An Inquiry into the Ancient Languages of Great Britain."[50] This paper possesses of course a special interest as an early society communication preserved for us *in toto*. The only paper definitely attempting to cover the historical position of the English language which was before this time prepared for a learned society and is still preserved even in abstract, was Edward Lhwyd's "Observations on Ancient Languages," read before the Royal Society in 1698.[51] As between the two papers there is perhaps little to choose. Lhwyd's appears from its abstract to have been meagre, trivial, and unscholarly. Clerk's deserves genuine commendation for its relative freedom from the *a priori* judgments and superstitious prejudices of former writers in regard to the antiquity and linguistic relationships of the English tongue.[52] But on the score of general merits it must be said that Clerk was radically and blindly wrong in his interpretation of clear historical evidence. Considering what Junius and a dozen native scholars such as Camden and Hickes had

[49] *Essays and Observations, read before a Society in Edinburgh,* 3 v., 1754–71.

[50] *Memoirs of Sir John Clerk of Penecuik,* edited by John M. Gray, 1892; 165. The entire paper was communicated by Clerk to Roger Gale in the same year, and is reprinted in Stukeley's *Memoirs and Correspondence,* I, 339–357.

[51] *Philosophical Transactions of the Royal Society abridged,* 1809; IV, 300–1.

[52] On this point see Lhwyd's *Observations,* and *Letters to and from William Nicolson,* 79–80, 114.

accomplished in "placing" the English tongue with reference to related linguistic stocks, it is remarkable that such ineptitude as is exhibited in the ill-informed and erratic productions of Lhwyd and Clerk should be the only documents left to us to represent the quality of the interest of the learned bodies of the day in their own vernacular. Nothing can serve as clearer evidence of the general indifference of the men of learning of that time to anything like a fundamental study of English philology.

The existence of the Edinburgh Philosophical Society was interrupted during and after the rebellion of 1745. When the society was revived in 1752 David Hume became one of its two secretaries.[53]   After the publication of the first two volumes of the *Essays and Observations,* the society seems to have dropped again into desuetude; but under the presidency of Lord Kames it enjoyed a period of prosperity until 1782.   In this year a project was offered by Principal Robertson to reorganize the society upon the more public and useful academy plan.   Accordingly the Royal Society of Edinburgh was incorporated by royal charter in the following year, and the members of the Philosophical Society were entered as members of the new institution.[54] The charter of the new society defines its purposes as extending not merely to the theoretical and useful sciences, but to archaeology, philology, and literature.[55]   For the furtherance of this plan the organization was divided into two classes, the Physical, and the Literary, and it is interesting to note that in the early years of the society the literary members outnumbered those of the other class.[56]   Among the members of the Literary Class were Kames, Hume,

[53] *Transactions of the Royal Society of Edinburgh,* I, 6.

[54] *Ibid.,* 10.

[55] *Ibid.,* 8.

[56] [James David] Forbes, *Opening Address, 1862;* in *Proceedings of the Royal Society of Edinburgh,* V, 10 (1866).

Tytler, Beattie, Reid, Burke, and Adam Smith.[57] There seems to have been a deliberate intention on the part of the society to "feature" the literary department; for no society had as yet appropriated literature as its field of scholarship. But the plans of the organizers met with relatively little success. The papers of the Literary Class printed in the first volume of the society's *Transactions* comprise articles on history, political science, and Greek philology, eight in all. The literary articles in the second volume were seven in number, covering in all but one title subjects from comparative philology, and Greek, Latin, German, and English literature. In the third and fourth volumes, however, which represented the activities of the society from 1789 to 1797, there were in the literary class three and two papers respectively, only one of the five touching the field of literature in our modern sense. The literary papers were no longer printed under a separate caption in the volumes following the fourth, although philological papers were printed at the rate of one a volume from the fifth to the tenth volume, ending in 1830. The Literary Class of the society continued a nominal existence for some years after its papers ceased to be separately printed; but towards the end of the eighteenth century its meetings became very infrequent, the time formerly devoted to them soon being given over more and more to scientific communications. The minute-book of the Literary Class closed in the year 1808.[58] From time to time, however, literary papers were read at the regular meetings of the society, but without being separated from the scientific papers. The election of Sir Walter Scott to the presidency in 1820 must be regarded as an effort to revive the literary communications in the society; but Scott, although he conscientiously presided at the meetings, contributed no

[57] *Ibid.*, 11.
[58] *Ibid.*, 12.

papers, and evidently was unable to rescusitate the flag-
ging interests of the literary members. The Literary Class
of the society was therefore finally abolished in 1827.[59]
Principal Forbes has taken pains to point out that the
failure of what is for us the more important division of the
society was not due to the encroachments of scientific
research, but to the cessation of the literary communications. Whether this is to be explained by indifference on
the part of the members of the Literary Class, or by their
recognition that the scientific studies of the day provided
a better ground for investigation than philology in its
then existing state, in any event it is to be noted that
an experiment in a new field which was at least temporarily
successful met its final failure in a period when literary
societies generally in England, and even in Scotland, were
beginning to achieve their distinguished successes.

Notwithstanding the eventual frustration of the literary
plans of the Royal Society of Edinburgh, we must concede
it the honor of having been the first publishing society of
Great Britain to have furthered consistently over a period
of some years an interest in philological studies. That this
interest was restricted in the main to classical philology
may be explained in part by the fact that the literary
members were recruited largely from the faculty of Edinburgh University, and partly by the fact that nothing like
a broad interest in the antiquity of English and Scottish
literature was possible to any but collectors or special students of literature before the period of general republication of literary materials which began with the opening of
the nineteenth century.

In 1780, two years before it was proposed that the Edinburgh Philosophical Society should be absorbed into the
Royal Society of Edinburgh, David Steuart Erskine, Earl

[59] *Ibid.*, 12.

of Buchan, had taken steps toward the formation of an antiquarian society in the same city.[60] This society was established at the end of the year as the Society of the Antiquaries of Scotland.[61] When the organization petitioned two years later for a royal charter, it encountered the opposition of the University and of the Curators of the Advocates' Library.[62] The objection of the University is probably to be explained by the fact that at this very moment the Philosophical Society, which represented generally the Faculty of the University, had petitioned the Lord Advocate to be included in the projected Royal Society of Edinburgh,[63] although the nominal ground of complaint was that there was not room in Scotland for two societies of this kind. Events seem to prove that this widespread objection to the foundation of another academic body in the northern capital was well grounded; for the history of the Scottish Antiquaries during the last decade of the eighteenth century and the first twenty years of the nineteenth was one of painful indolence and constant pecuniary embarrassment. Indeed, the society was twice within this period on the border of dissolution.[64] The original members of the Antiquaries of Scotland included, in addition to the Earl of Buchan, William Smellie, Kames,

[60] For correspondence with George Paton relative to the establishment of this society see *Letters from Thomas Percy and Others to George Paton*, 1830, 169–74.

[61] William Smellie, *An historical Account of the Society of the Antiquaries of Scotland*, in *Transactions of the Society of the Antiquaries of Scotland*, I, iii–xxxiii, 1792.

[62] Robert Kerr, *Memoirs of William Smellie*, 1811; II, 35–44.

[63] *Ibid.*, 37.

[64] Samuel Hibbert and David Laing, *Account of the progress of the Society of the Antiquaries of Scotland, from 1784 to 1830;* in *Archaeologia Scotica*, III, app., v–xxxi, 1831; and David Laing, *Anniversary address on the state of the Society of Antiquaries of Scotland, from 1831 to 1860;* in *Archaeologia Scotica*, V, 1–36, 1890.

Tytler, Blair, Boswell, and George Paton. The charter of the society[65] does not name literature as one of the provinces of its activity, but it empowers the incorporated body to collect books and manuscripts. The intense patriotism of the Scotsmen of this period, however, made it inevitable that their language and literature should constitute at least an occasional subject for investigation or discussion. Accordingly we find among the early communications a biography of John Barclay, the author of *Argenis,* by Lord Hailes, Tytler's dissertation on the life and writings of James I (subsequently published in his edition of James's *Poetical Works,* 1783), a paper by Pinkerton on textual publications of Scots poetry, a bibliography of native authors by Donald Mackintosh, and numerous special papers on etymologies, Gaelic philology and literature, and especially the Ossian controversy, in which, naturally enough, most of the members of the society were inclined to the acceptance of Macpherson's declarations.[66] In the early nineteenth century the literary activities of the body gave way before archaeological investigations; and although James Chalmers, the Skenes, Donald Gregory, and most notably, David Laing, occasionally communicated items of real importance to students of literature, the Society of Antiquaries of Scotland, like the Royal Society of Edinburgh, in time came to restrict itself practically to the province of interest represented by its distinguished senior in London.

Meanwhile, from the middle of the eighteenth century on, the important Scotch cities fostered a number of intellectual societies of great importance. Such societies were almost

[65] *Transactions of the Society of the Antiquaries of Scotland,* I, x–xii, 1792.

[66] *List of communications read at the meetings of the Society of the Antiquaries of Scotland, MDCCLXXX–MDCCCXXX;* in *Archaeologia Scotica,* III, app. 149–96, 1831.

without exception restricted in numbers; and the very fact
that their membership was not honorary removed from
their proceedings the superfluous checks of formality and
gratuitous reverence for personages. With more than one
of these are associated the names of Principal Robertson,
Adam Smith, Thomas Reid, and David Hume. The earliest
was the Glasgow Literary Club, constituted probably before
1750, and principally from among the scholars and the
ministers of the city which gave the club its name.[67] The
only members of more than local celebrity were Adam
Smith, during the period of the club's activity successively
Professor of Logic and of Moral Philosophy at Glasgow,
Hume, Reid, John Callander, and the Foulis brothers,
whose press was then beginning to gain for the small city
considerable note.[68] A local celebrity was Dr. James Moor,
whose work in classical philology is probably still to be
commended by classical students. Partly because of the
dominance of professorial dignity in the body, and partly
because of the quality of Scotch culture at the time, the
communications to the club were largely classical and philosophical. Moor seems to have been the moving spirit of the
society at the time of its greatest vitality; he contributed
some of the first essays read before them, three of which,
not specially relevant to our investigation, were published
by the Foulises in 1759.[69] Two other papers by Moor
which possess for us a more immediate interest are recorded
simply by title: these are, "Remarks on Dr. Warburton's
critical notes on Mr. Pope," read in 1765, and "Some
observations on the genius of English verse," read in

[67] William James Duncan, *Notices and Documents illustrative of
the literary History of Glasgow*, Maitland Club, 1831; 15–17, 131–5.
[68] *Ibid.*, 132–4.
[69] James Moor, *Essays read to a Literary Society at their weekly
Meetings . . . at Glasgow*, 1759.

7

1769.[70] Dr. Archibald Arthur, many years later the occu-
pant for a single year of the chair of Moral Philosophy
previously held by Adam Smith and Thomas Reid, was a
frequent contributor to the club, largely on philological
and aesthetic topics, and his interest in both subjects was
apparently chiefly pedagogical. His addresses before the
society, including a critique, *Concerning Mr. Burke's
theory of beauty,* were collected and published in 1830.[71]
The contributions of the Foulis brothers were usually on
questions in philosophical and theological casuistry. That
Adam Smith's communications to the society were at least
in part relative to literary study may be inferred from the
fact that especially during his early years he was an unusually profound and alert student of letters.[72] It is
further recorded that he "read those essays on taste, composition, and the history of philosophy, which he had previously delivered while a lecturer on rhetoric at Edinburgh";[73] and judging from an allusion by Dugald
Stewart, it is evident that he read before the society on
one occasion something in the nature of a program of
criticism.[74] From this brief review of the kind and quality
of this single side of the club's activities, it will be seen
that it possessed a genuine importance in its field. Indeed,
in view of the fact that the Philosophical Society of
Edinburgh even after its reorganization in 1739[75] limited

[70] *Notices and Documents,* 131.

[71] Archibald Arthur, *Discourses on theological and literary Subjects,* 1803.

[72] Dugald Stewart, *Account of the Life and Writings of Adam
Smith;* in *Essays on philosophical Subjects by . . . Adam Smith,*
1795; xiii–xiv, xvi.

[73] *Notices and Documents,* 16. Dugald Stewart (*op. cit.,* lxxxvii–
lxxxviii) believes that these essays were among those which Smith destroyed immediately before his death.

[74] *Op. cit.,* lxxx.

[75] *Ante,* 74–5.

its interests very largely to medical and physical science, it may very well be questioned whether the Glasgow Literary Club should not be considered as in actuality the first of our modern philological societies. It is certain in any event that although the society did not itself publish any of its deliberations, and hence should not be called a publishing society, it can not be said that any similar organization which preceded it was devoted so actively and continuously to extensive philological studies.

While Adam Smith was still at Glasgow he appeared as one of the constituent members of the Select Society of Edinburgh, established in 1754. "This society," says Dugald Stewart,[76] "subsisted in vigour for six or seven years, and produced debates, such as have not often been heard in modern assemblies;—debates, where the dignity of the speakers was not lowered by the intrigues of policy, or the intemperance of faction; and where the most splendid talents that have ever adorned this country were roused to their best exertions, by the liberal and ennobling discussions of literature and philosophy." Among the members of this body were Allan Ramsay, son of the poet, Robertson, Hume, Kames, and John Home, author of the tragedy *Douglas,* the production of which in 1757 created a turmoil among the Scottish clergy. The proceedings of this society were apparently more formal than those of the Literary Club at Glasgow; and this was probably due to the fact that the membership was quickly increased to more than one hundred and thirty.[77] There is some apparent significance in the observation that Hume, who

[76] Dugald Stewart, *Account of the Life and Writings of William Robertson,* 1801; 15–16.

[77] *Ibid.,* 212. A list of the members of the society is given in the appendix of Stewart's *Life of Robertson,* 214–220. Henry Grey Graham (*Scottish Men of Letters in the Eighteenth Century,* 111) puts the membership at three hundred.

was not usually indisposed to talk, and Smith, who had taken so prominent a part in the meetings of the Glasgow club, when at the meetings of the Select Society "never opened their lips."[78]   The only subjects of discussion barred by the rules of the organization were "such as regard revealed religion, or which might give occasion to vent any principles of Jacobitism."[79]   The conduct of the meetings was regulated by strict rules of debate; indeed, the prime object of the gathering, to improve the members in public speaking, in all probability made the proceedings anything but spontaneous.   Of a list of typical subjects discussed at the meetings a few bear upon very general literary topics; but the majority are of a political or an economic nature.[80]   The society endeavored also to encourage an outside interest in investigative literary work, as in 1756 it offered medals for "the best history of the Roman, and afterwards of the Saxon conquests and settlements . . . in Cumberland and Northumberland," for "the best account of the rise and progress of commerce, arts, and manufactures, in North Britain," and for "the most reasonable scheme for maintaining and employing the poor."[81]   An incidental venture of some of the members was a periodical book review, only two numbers of which appeared in 1755 and 1756.   The title of this publication is oddly but properly enough the *Edinburgh Review;* but it is of course not to. be confused with the periodical founded by Sydney Smith.[82]   A fact of more than ordinary interest

[78] *Ibid.*, 213.

[79] John Lord Campbell, *The Lives of the Lord Chancellors of England,* VI, 31 (1847).

[80] *Ibid.*, 32–3.

[81] *Scots Magazine*, XIX, 49, 1757.

[82] An entry in the *British Museum Catalogue of Printed Books* (*Periodical Publications,* 1899, 322) reads: "*The Edinburgh Magazine and Review. By a Society of Gentlemen [Adam Smith, David Hume, and others],* 5 vol., Edinburgh [1773–] 76." This is a clear

in the history of the Select Society is that through the good
services of John Home the first transcripts of Macpherson's
Ossian were placed before the society in 1759. Blair, by
virtue of his membership, became interested in the young
tutor and his alleged translations; and it was principally
at Blair's instance that in the following year the *Fragments of Ancient Poetry* were published.[83] The demise of
the Select Society was brought about by a curious plan "to
speak as well as to write the English language," in which
the society, practically as a body, participated. Thomas
Sheridan, father of the dramatist, and itinerant teacher
of elocution, having descended upon Edinburgh in 1761,
succeeded in inducing the society to undertake "the Her-
culean task of annihilating the Scottish tongue, and substituting the English language and pronunciation in its
place."[84] This scheme became the social fad of the
hour, and attracted many prominent residents in addition to the members of the Select Society. These
enthusiasts proceeded to the organization of "The Society
for promoting the Reading and Speaking of the English Language in Scotland"; but in spite of the eminence of many of the projectors, the plan met with a
general ridicule which brought it to an ignominious end;
and with the decay of the fad, the Select Society itself
ceased to be.[85] One effect of enduring importance, however, is assigned to this "singular epidemic": the estab-

instance of confusion, for the Select Society's *Edinburgh Review* was
at this period defunct, and the *Edinburgh Magazine and Review* of
1773–6 was actually established and conducted by Gilbert Stuart and
William Smellie (*Dictionary of National Biography*, LII, 401, LV,
83).

[83] Bailey Saunders, *Life and Letters of James Macpherson*, 1894,
72–8.

[84] Thomas Edward Ritchie, *Life and Writings of David Hume*,
1807, 93.

[85] *Ibid.*, 93–102.

lishment of the Regius Professorship of Rhetoric and Belles Lettres, the first incumbent of which was Dr. Hugh Blair.[86]

The Aberdeen Philosophical Society, which met first in 1758 and continued in existence as late as 1773, has been estimated to have had an unusually active influence upon Scottish philosophy in these years. One of the founders was Dr. Thomas Reid, who succeeded Adam Smith as Professor of Moral Philosophy at Glasgow.[87] The rules of this society provided that "the subjects of the discourses and questions shall be philosophical; all grammatical, historical, and philological discussions being conceived to be foreign to the design of this society."[88] But notwithstanding this embargo, a small number of the subjects discussed were in the nature of aesthetical controversies upon general, and usually very abstruse literary questions.[89] The society can therefore be granted an incidental, but only an incidental, importance for our purpose.

Some Scottish clubs whose chief object is admitted to have been conviviality may have possessed a casual relation to scholarly productivity because of the literary nature of their free deliberations. The most conspicuous of these were the Anderston Club, which was attended by most of the members of the Glasgow Literary Club, and which is said to have held discussions of some little literary dignity,[90] the Hodge Podge Club, of the same place and period,[91] and the Poker Club, of Edinburgh. The Poker Club was evi-

[86] *Ibid.*, 102.

[87] James McCosh, *The Scottish Philosophy from Hutcheson to Hamilton*, 1875; 227-9, 467-73. Dugald Stewart, *Life and Writings of Thomas Reid*, Edinburgh, 1803, 25-6.

[88] *Ibid.*, 228. Dr. McCosh comments, "It is evident that they had no idea of the importance of philology."

[89] A list of the subjects of discussion is given in an appendix to Dr. McCosh's work, 467-73.

[90] John Strang, *Glasgow and its Clubs*, Glasgow, 1856, 23-32.

[91] *Ibid.*, 45-7.

dently conducted as an adjunct to the Select Society, much as the Anderston Club seems to have been for its more distinguished contemporary.[92] It has been said that the Poker Club actually developed into a literary club; but this claim substitutes an accident for an essential feature. Hume's biographer tells us, "It met on Tuesdays and Fridays during four or five years, at a house, called the Diversorium, in the vicinity of the Netherbow of Edinburgh; and although it is here dignified with the character of a literary society, the reader will not, we hope, conceive an unfavourable opinion of it, when he learns, that the sole object of the members was conviviality."[93] After all, it must be said that social clubs of this type, whose membership was made up even in large part of men of literary distinction, possess no special importance in the history of intellectual movements, for when the social objects of the gathering become subservient to the intellectual objects, as they may be said to have become in Johnson's literary club, the club becomes by that fact an intellectual, and no longer a social organization. The historical identity of the two types seems to indicate that this distinction is not arbitrary or useless.

On the inevitable border-line, however, stands the well-known club whose central figure was the most impressive personality in eighteenth century literature. To assert that the Literary Club was in any sense a learned society would be, of course, to claim for it a kind of importance which it certainly did not possess, and the imputation of which its members, save a possible two or three, would have resented emphatically. But if any of the eighteenth century clubs whose purposes were primarily and assertively social can be said to have exerted a positive influence upon literary scholarship (not upon literary production),

[92] Tytler, *Memoirs of Kames*, I, 253–4.
[93] Ritchie, *op. cit.*, 83.

Johnson's club must unquestionably be placed first among them. It would be idle to assume that Johnson's own personality or literary tastes had very much to do with the revival of interest in literary antiquity, although, to be sure, he is known to have given Percy, as a fellow-member of the club, the advantage of some probably perfunctory advice previous to the publication of the *Reliques of Ancient English Poetry*.[94] On the contrary, Johnson's attitude toward medieval popular literature was wholly scornful. He parodied the simplicity of ballad poetry,[95] and ridiculed the collection of black letter books and literary rarities as a characteristic silliness of the antiquarian enthusiast.[96] The scholarly importance of the Literary

[94] Boswell's *Life of Johnson*, edited by George Birkbeck Hill, 1887, III, 276–7. *Reliques of Ancient English Poetry*, edited by Henry B. Wheatley, 1886, I, 14.

[95] Boswell's *Life of Johnson*, II, 136 n.

[96] In the *Rambler*, No. 177. Vivaculus, bored by his solitary lucubrations, entreats one of his "academical acquaintances" to introduce him to "some of the little societies of literature which are formed in taverns and coffee-houses." "The eldest and most venerable of this society was Hirsutus, who, after the first civilities of my reception, found means to introduce the mention of his favourite studies. He informed me that . . . he had very carefully amassed all the English books that were printed in the black character. . . . He had long since completed his Caxton, had three sheets of Treveris unknown to the antiquaries, and wanted to a perfect Pynson but two volumes, of which one was promised him as a legacy by its present possessor, and the other he was resolved to buy, at whatever price, when Quisquilius's library should be sold. Hirsutus had no other reason for the valuing or slighting a book, than that it was printed in the Roman or the Gothic letter, nor any ideas but such as his favourite volumes had supplied; when he was serious he expatiated on the narratives of 'Johan de Trevisa,' and when he was merry, regaled us with a quotation from the 'Shippe of Foles.' . . . Cantilenus turned all his thoughts upon old ballads, for he considered them as the genuine records of the national taste. He offered to show me a copy of 'The Children in the Wood,' which he firmly believed to be of the first edition, and, by the help of which the text might be

Club lies in its inclusion of a group of accomplished students whose interests in literary antiquity shamed Johnson's prejudice and belied Warburton's fatuous dictum that "antiquarianism is to true letters what specious funguses are to the oak."[97] Among these members of the Club were of course Garrick, who was an industrious ballad collector,[98] Percy, Thomas and Joseph Warton, the former the writer of the first distinguished history of English poetry, Steevens and Malone, giants in the history of Shaksperean criticism and biography, and later Dr. Farmer, acknowledged as one of the greatest scholarly figures of the day, although not a frequent combatant in the public lists of criticism of the time.[99] We know that in the cases of Malone, Percy, and the Wartons, the friend-

freed from several corruptions, if this age of barbarity had any claim to such favours from him.'' Johnson's judgment of the occupations and characters of antiquaries may be gathered from another paragraph: ''Every one of these virtuosos looked on all his associates as wretches of depraved taste and narrow notions. Their conversation was, therefore, fretful and waspish, their behaviour brutal, their merriment bluntly sarcastick, and their seriousness gloomy and suspicious. They were totally ignorant of all that passes, or has lately passed, in the world; unable to discuss any question of religious, political or military knowledge; equally strangers to science and politer learning, and without any wish to improve their minds, or any other pleasure than that of displaying rarities, of which they would not suffer others to make the proper use'' (*The Works of Samuel Johnson*, Oxford, 1825, III, 329–33). In a letter to Boswell relative to a previous disagreement with Percy, Johnson says: ''Percy's attention to poetry has given grace and splendour to his studies of antiquity. A mere antiquarian is a rugged being'' (Boswell's *Life of Johnson*, III, 278).

[97] *Bishop Percy's Folio Manuscript*, edited by John W. Hales and Frederick J. Furnivall, 1867; I, xxxviii–ix.

[98] Percy's *Reliques*, edited by Henry B. Wheatley, I, 14.

[99] The names of all but Farmer are given in Boswell's list of 1792 (Boswell's *Life of Johnson*, I, 477–9); Farmer was admitted to the Club in 1795 (Nichols, *Literary Anecdotes*, II, 639).

ships established in the Club were perpetuated in a valuable correspondence, largely upon literary questions;[100] and we may safely assume from the mere presence of so imposing a group of scholars in the Club that its meetings, particularly in the later years, provided frequent occasion for discussion of the topics of uppermost interest to them. With the close of the century, however, the Literary Club began to sink into an aristocratic decadence, an offence to the memory of its greatest member, and of course an absolute check upon essentially literary activities, from any point of view whatsoever.[101]

Apparently most of these pioneers were also members of Issac Reed's Unincreasable Club, a "dining club," as Nichols calls it, with some scholarly pretensions;[102] and Farmer, with Reynolds and Boswell, was a member of the Eumélian Club, founded by Dr. John Ash;[103] but there can be little doubt that in both of these clubs, as with most contemporary organizations, serious questions were not permitted to intrude upon conviviality.

Much more important is the fact that Percy, Thomas Warton, Malone, Farmer, Steevens, Tyrwhitt, and Reed were all members of the Society of Antiquaries during the last quarter of this century;[104] and it is of incidental interest that Ritson and Samuel Ireland were both black-

[100] Sir James Prior, *Life of Edmond Malone*, 1850, 117–9, 122–3, 282, 284–5, 321–2.

[101] John Timbs, *Club Life of London*, 1866; I, 213–5.

[102] [John Nichols], *Biographical Memoirs of the late Isaac Reed, Esq.; Gentleman's Magazine*, LXXVII, 80–2, 1807.

[103] Nichols's *Literary Anecdotes*, II, 638; and William Munk, *Roll of the Royal College of Physicians of London*, 1878, II, 379.

[104] Richard Gough, *List of Members of the Society of Antiquaries*, 1798. Tyrwhitt's name is not given in Gough's *List;* but he is said by Nichols (*Literary Anecdotes*, III, 147), to have been a member of the society.

balled by the Society in 1789.[105]   The Antiquaries had at
this time awakened to a more active existence than before
the middle of the century; and between 1770 and 1800
their principal communications were collected in the first
thirteen volumes of *Archaeologia*.   None of the papers
delivered during this period were from members of our
group, however, if we except a single indirect communication by letter from Bishop Percy upon an archaeological
topic.[106]   So evidently the membership of these students of
literature was due to their interest in antiquities in the
more general sense; indeed, Percy, Warton, Tyrwhitt and
Malone were antiquarians of the traditional stamp, as well
as literary scholars.   But the publications of the Society of
Antiquaries for this period are not without interest to the
student of literature.   During these thirty years there
were published in *Archaeologia* a number of articles of
interest upon English, French, Gaelic and Cornish philology, and a few records of Anglo-Saxon inscriptions.   Most
of these papers, however, exhibit a curious rather than a
scholarly interest in such studies.   The most important of
these articles was a series of lengthy dissertations by
William Drake, partly controversial in their nature, upon
the history of the English language; these demonstrate
with some effectiveness the relation of the Teutonic linguistic stock to the modern tongue.[107]   Other items of some
importance were Samuel Pegge's amicable *Observations on
Dr. Percy's account of minstrels among the Saxons*,[108] and
translations of four really learned papers communicated
between 1794 and 1797 by the Abbé de la Rue upon Wace,

[105] Edward William Brabrook, *On the Fellows of the Society of
Antiquaries of London who have held the Office of Director; Archaeologia*, LXII, 70 (1910).

[106] *Archaeologia*, VII, 158–9, 1785.

[107] *Archaeologia*, V, 306–17, 379–89, IX, 332–61.

[108] *Ibid.*, II, 100–6, 1773.

Marie de France, and the Anglo-Norman poets of the twelfth and thirteenth centuries.[109] It must be admitted, therefore, that the Society of Antiquaries accomplished during this period something of genuine importance in this province, even though the rarity of communications on literary subjects, and the apparent apathy among the noted literary scholars in the society to the exhibition of their special interests here, forbids our assuming that the society as a whole possessed more than a casual and half-indulgent approval of literary investigation as part of their learned business.

Two other permanent societies dating from the late eighteenth century, one in Manchester, and one in Dublin, displayed in the first years of their existence a disposition to foster literary scholarship. Their activity was neither more nor less effective than that of their older and more important contemporaries. The first of these, the Literary and Philosophical Society of Manchester, had its beginnings, as did almost all of the learned societies established before the nineteenth century, in a club of "inhabitants of the town, who were inspired with a taste for Literature and Philosophy."[110] This society, founded in 1781, was the first so-called provincial publishing society in England; for the powerful learned societies in London and Edinburgh were then, and have always continued to be, really national in their influence. The Manchester society was by its membership and environment destined to develop naturally into a scientific society; indeed its early leaning to scientific study may be seen in its first catalogue of honorary members, which included Erasmus Darwin and Priestley, residents of Manchester, and Delaval,

109 *Ibid.*, XII, 50–79, 297–326, XIII, 36–67, 230–50.

110 *Memoirs of the Literary and Philosophical Society of Manchester*, I, vii, 1785. R. Angus Smith, *A Centenary of Science in Manchester*, 1883, 22–4.

Franklin, Lavoisier, Volta, and Wedgewood.[111] Despite this rather unpromising outlook for literary study, a few papers of this nature appear in the first series of the Society's *Memoirs;* the only two published before 1800, however, were papers by a local physician, Dr. John Ferrier, on Massinger and Sterne.[112] With the opening of the next century this society became more strictly scientific, probably in part because of the expanding importance of the city as an industrial centre. In time, therefore, literary communications were dropped entirely from the society's meetings.

The Royal Irish Academy, which possesses a scope and importance comparable to that of the metropolitan societies in England and Scotland, was organized in 1782, and chartered in 1785, the names of Percy and Malone appearing on the list of constituent members.[113] The Academy seems to trace its descent more or less directly from a Physico-Historical Society, founded in 1740, and an antiquarian group known as the Dublin Society which flourished from 1772 to 1774. The immediate origin of the society, however, was apparently in the kind of essay club which was the first form of early societies generally.[114] The Royal Irish Academy was chartered for inquiry in science, polite literature, and antiquities; and the publications of the Academy, therefore, were divided under these heads.[115] The literary section of the *Transactions,* how-

[111] *Memoirs of the Literary and Philosophical Society of Manchester,* I, xviii–xix.

[112] *Ibid.,* III, 123–58, and IV, 45–85. Notes on the quality of these two articles are found in Smith's *Centenary of Science in Manchester,* 177–9.

[113] *Charter and Statutes of the Royal Irish Academy,* Dublin, 1786, 4.

[114] Robert Burrowes, *Preface* to *Transactions of the Royal Irish Academy,* I, xiii–xv, 1787.

[115] *Charter and Statutes,* 5.

ever, included at first papers on a variety of subjects. Those of the more strictly literary type published before 1800 comprise a number of essays in aesthetic criticism of the drama, and academic disquisitions upon classical literature. It is simply classing the Academy's publications with the bulk of similar productions of the time to say that the critical contributions to the literary section in these years possess very little value to the scholar of the present. In the nineteenth century the Academy abandoned English literature and fittingly turned its attention to the remains of Irish literature; and in this field it has accomplished much of the very highest scholarly importance.

Probably the most extensive and the most solid contribution on the part of any society of this period to a scholarship that had now beyond doubt become assured of its strength was the investigation conducted by the Highland Society of Scotland—an organization for wholly miscellaneous purposes—into the authenticity of the Ossian Poems. After Dr. Johnson's fulmination against Macpherson, interest in the question had subsided, although the adherents to the belief that the poems were wholly or largely genuine had by no means abandoned their convictions. The investigations of the committee of the Highland Society were begun in 1797. Eight years elapsed before the publication of their report,[116] which represented an extended inquiry into the remains of Gaelic poetry generally, and considerable research in the special questions connected with Macpherson's publication. The conclusions of the committee[117] recited that Macpherson's so-called translations are probably not to be taken as literal

[116] Henry Mackenzie, *Report of the Committee of the Highland Society of Scotland, appointed to inquire into the Nature and Authenticity of the poems of Ossian*, Edinburgh, 1805.

[117] *Ibid.*, 151–5.

renderings of actual ancient remains, although they may have been derived in part from the *disjecta membra* of old Gaelic poetry. With regard to Macpherson's use of his materials the committee was ''inclined to believe that he was in use to supply chasms, and to give connection, by inserting passages which he did not find, and to add what he conceived to be dignity and delicacy to the original composition, by striking out passages, by softening incidents, by refining the language, in short by changing what he considered as too simple or too rude for a modern ear, and elevating what in his opinion was below the standard of good poetry.''[118] Beyond these conclusions a century of occasional research in the subject has scarcely carried us.

The action of the Highland Society in settling, as far as settlement was possible, a literary dispute so vexed, and at the same time so closely indicative of the state of literary scholarship at this time, brings us to a consideration of the special conditions and problems with which scholarship found itself dealing during the last forty years of the seventeenth century.

The gradual growth of a general appreciation of old literature had been in progress since the early years of the century.[119] The development of this appreciation, which may be taken as one of the most significant marks of the romantic reaction, had been very slow, however, except possibly in Scotland, where a literary consciousness arose which found itself possessed of no literary reminiscence approaching in richness that of England's yesterday, but which resolved to make much of what it did possess—an

[118] *Ibid.*, 152.

[119] See Sir Walter Scott's *Introductory remarks on popular poetry,* in his *Minstrelsy of the Scottish Border,* edited by T. F. Henderson, I, 1–54, 1902; also John W. Hales's *The revival of ballad poetry in the eighteenth century;* in *Bishop Percy's Folio Manuscript,* edited by John W. Hales and Frederick J. Furnivall, II, v–xxxi, 1867.

ancient literature of rugged vitality and naturalness, but largely wanting in delicacy and polish. The spread of this new literary taste in England was furthered remarkably during the decade following 1760, partly through the rapid weakening of the classical tradition, but more particularly through the publication of three collections of ostensibly ancient poetry, Macpherson's *Ossian* in 1760, Percy's *Reliques of Ancient English Poetry* in 1765, and Chatterton's *Rowley Poems* from 1764 to 1770. What seemed to create the extraordinary vogue of these collections, where the publication of actual poetical remains up to this time had passed without enthusiasm, was the adaptation of all three to a poetical taste which, however much it might be attracted by vigor and simplicity, was repelled by a lack of refinement and finish. Far from being actual monuments of antiquity, the Ossian poems were, if not really forged, at least highly modernized; Percy's *Reliques* were generously and systematically refined; and the *Rowley Poems* were soon recognized as fabrications.

The result was that no sooner had a body of assumedly ancient poetry captured the liking of the reading public than scholars began to demonstrate that it was really not ancient poetry at all; for if it were not actually modern in composition, its adaptation to popular taste had been at the expense of some of its most characteristic virtues. Macpherson met a very torrent of criticism in England generally; Percy suffered at the violent hands of Ritson and his fellows, and Chatterton was shortly exposed by Gray, Warton, and Tyrwhitt.[120] The very prevalence of

[120] Prof. Skeat (*The Poetical Works of Thomas Chatterton, with an Essay on the Rowley Poems by Walter W. Skeat*, II, ix) says: "It is not too much to say that Tyrwhitt is the only writer among those that have hitherto handled the subject who had a real critical knowledge of the language of the fourteenth and fifteenth centuries, and who, in fact, had on that account a real claim to be heard."

uncritical emendation or downright dishonesty on the part
of editors and publishers, magnified later by the inventions
of Pinkerton and the spectacular Shakspere forgeries of
Ireland, established at once the supreme importance of a
well grounded critical scholarship in dealing with old
literary materials. The generation of students who built
up the new critical tradition found it no longer necessary,
therefore, to adopt an apologetic manner before the reading
public, but found instead a public which had gradually
but certainly formed its taste in a school of new literary
doctrines. The literary scholars of the age had something
that their predecessors had never possessed—not merely a
field to work in, but a general public interest to appeal to.
The way was prepared, therefore, for a degree of productive activity which could have met with no response
fifty years earlier. The eighteenth century closed when
the claims of literary scholarship no longer needed assertion, and the new century opened upon an entirely new
prospect.

Meanwhile the usefulness of the learned society had
become entirely established in diverse fields of intellectual
occupation; and although there was not yet in existence a
society devoted exclusively or even largely to the study of
English literature, a number of thriving organizations had
exhibited a more or less stable interest in the subject.

CHAPTER V

NINETEENTH CENTURY BOOK CLUBS AND GENERAL PUBLISHING SOCIETIES

Hitherto the occasional activity of societies in the field of literary study had been confined to ineffectual appreciative criticism and more or less valuable attempts at literary history. To be sure, the reprinting of old literature was going on with increasing rapidity, and was calling forth from time to time a kind of critical response even on the part of the learned societies themselves. But with the bulk of the important literature of the Anglo-Saxon and the middle English periods still unavailable, and with the societies engaged in no effort to continue or to systematize the reproduction of the actual materials for literary study, it is very much to be questioned whether their importance in this field would have expanded commensurately with the expansion of literary scholarship unless an outside force had placed the club function in a new light. This force was the wave of book-collecting enthusiasm which was one of the indirect results of the revival of interest in things medieval.

This wave of bibliomania was at its height during the first few years of the nineteenth century. Buyers of books had come to see that there were fewer Caxtons than there were collectors desirous of possessing them, and that Shakspere quartos were becoming so rare that a mere scholar could no longer afford to stack his shelves with them, as Malone had done in the previous century. The famous collection of the Duke of Roxburghe, which was sold at auction in 1812, brought in £23,000, although Dibdin estimated its cost to have been not over a fourth of that amount.[1] On the other hand, the collection of Richard Heber, which was gathered during these early years, and which Dibdin estimated to have cost between £100,000 and £150,000,[2] was sold between 1834 and 1836 for a total of only £67,000.

While the growth of preposterously artificial values for rare books could not be regarded as encouraging directly an interest in the contents of these books, such an enthusiasm could scarcely fail to awaken the interest of the public, already captivated by the charms of romantic literature, to a knowledge of the existence of the manuscript and printed materials of an older literature of unimagined extent and value.

Bibliomania had, then, as all collecting hobbies must have, an appreciable effect upon popular sentiment; but having prepared the field for the great projects of publishing societies throughout the entire nineteenth century, it possesses for us a more direct importance. Indeed, it is not too much to say that to the bibliophiles alone must be given credit for having established the first generally successful scheme for the systematic publication of original documents; and the example which they set in the domain of literary study was followed in the publication first of historical and biographical materials and local records, and later of the materials for the history of the useful sciences, typography, architecture, music, ecclesiology, and a score of special studies. The effect of their work, in fact, was not limited to the societies which sprang up about them, but it is also to be clearly seen in the great government undertakings, such as the Rolls Series, and in a host of private projects organized upon the same plan, illustrated, for example, in the publications of Carew Hazlitt and Dr. Grosart.

[1] Thomas Frognall Dibdin, *Reminiscences of a literary life,* 1836, I, 366-7.

[2] *Ibid.*

The general importance of all of these early book clubs, however, was greatly restricted by the conditions of their organization. They were without exception exclusive in their membership, and they limited the issues of their publications in many cases to the exact numbers upon their rolls. In no instance were club publications very far in excess of the actual number of members to be accommodated, for it was understood that the book clubs were not attempting to supply books for the public. This policy met with much unfavorable comment generally, some of it voiced in the periodicals of the day.[3] The Roxburghe Club, pioneer of these organizations, was the greatest source of offence in this respect; of the publications presented to the club during the first fifteen years of its existence, almost all were limited to between thirty and forty copies, while the membership during this period was seldom much over thirty. Even the Roxburghe Club, however, displayed a slightly more considerate spirit when it later resolved to issue copies of its publications to the most important British libraries, and increased considerably the number of copies—which have never in any event exceeded one ,hundred—issued at the direction of the club itself, and not presented to it by incoming members.

The story of the founding and early existence of the Roxburghe Club is told by Dibdin, with what he himself might have called "truly bibliomaniacal enthusiasm," in his

[3] See the *Gentleman's Magazine* for 1813, 211–12, 338–41, 544. The writer of the first protest says: "Selfishness must be the most appropriate term whereby to designate the proceedings of a body of men, who have determined annually to print or reprint some valuable or scarce work, but to confine the number of copies to be printed to the number of their club, . . . That they have a right, or, in other words, that it is lawful for them to do so, cannot be disputed; but it is doubtless selfish, and by no means becoming men who have any pretensions to literature; and is so far from tending to diffuse knowledge, that it can serve only to confine and repress it" (211–12).

Bibliographical Decameron and his *Reminiscences*.[4]   A less
temperate account, but one which does superb justice to
the gustatory side of the club's gatherings, is found in the
annals which Joseph Haslewood set down for his personal
delectation, but which were purchased at the sale of his
library after his death and published with ungenerous
comment upon the personality of the writer in the London
Athenaeum during January, 1834.[5] Haslewood's reminiscences are too slight and too personal to supply us with
anything more than suggestions of the society's history;
but from Dibdin's narrative, we may by scanning many
solid pages of meaningless literary gossip and irrelevant
foot-notes, interspersed generously with shrill *Italic* and
thundering ROMAN, gather the following definite facts.
On the night of the seventeenth of June, 1812, following
the afternoon on which at the sale of the Duke of Roxburghe's books the ephemerally famous Valdarfer Boccaccio
was knocked down to the Marquis of Blandford for upwards of two thousand pounds,[6] eighteen properly self-
styled bibliomaniacs met at the St. Albans Tavern to discuss
what was to that time the most celebrated event recorded in
the history of bookhunting.[7]   Dibdin himself claimed the
honor of having fathered the plan, although his fellow-
clubman, George Isted, was apparently inclined to dispute
with him this title to fame.[8] Earl Spencer, the unsuccessful competitor in the bidding for the Boccaccio, presided
at this festive meeting, and continued as president of the
club which grew from it until his death in 1834. The first

[4] Thomas Frognall Dibdin, *The Bibliographical Decameron*, 1817,
III, 69–75. *Reminiscences of a Literary Life*, 1836, I, 367–470.

[5] These articles were collected and republished, with some apology
for Haslewood, and some miscellaneous Roxburghiana, in *Roxburghe
Revels and other relative Papers*, 1837.

[6] See Dibdin's *Bibliographical Decameron*, III, 48–69.

[7] *Ibid.*, 69.

[8] *Ibid.*, 71.

meeting was attended by eighteen bibliophiles; within its first two years, however, the number of members of the Roxburghe Club was increased to thirty-one. The club prided itself upon exclusiveness, but an exclusiveness which belonged to the nature of its hobby, rather than to aristocratic preferences. In fact the organization consisted of two pretty distinct classes of members, between whom there was without question a very real social gulf; and it was, in fact, this social mixture in the early membership which later laid the club open to the rather unprincipled attack of the *Athenaeum.* The club, then, was composed of social lions and gentlemen of wealth on the one hand, such as Spencer and Gower, and on the other hand, of humbler bibliophiles, some of whom actually lived largely by the commissions of their wealthier associates. The most conspicuous of the latter class were Haslewood, the protegé of Sir Egerton Brydges, and Dibdin himself, who had executed at the Roxburghe sale extensive purchases for Sir Mark Masterman Sykes.[9] At the first anniversary meeting of the club the Duke of Devonshire and the Marquis of Blandford were among the six new members admitted;[10] and at the third anniversary meeting James Boswell the younger became a member.

The publishing plans of the Roxburghe Club were comprised at first in a resolution for "each member, in turn, according to the order of his name in the alphabet, to furnish the Society with a reprint of some rare old tract, or composition—chiefly of poetry."[11] The letter of this rule,

[9] *Reminiscences,* I, 373.

[10] There is a point of casual interest in the fact that the social discrimination of the Marquis of Blandford, who, as the purchaser of the Valdarfer Boccaccio, might have been regarded as the most "out and out" bibliophile in the club, was so far from being carried away by bibliomania that at least during the fourteen years following his admission into the sacred circle he was present at none of the anniversary dinners of the Roxburghers. (*Roxburghe Revels,* 45.)

[11] *Bibliographical Decameron,* III, 72.

and the tastes of the members, brought it about that the publications of the club came to include particularly ancient literature, rather than history or antiquities. The first book presented was Surrey's *Certaine Bokes of Virgiles Aenaeis, turned into English Meter,* which was distributed at the second anniversary, in 1814, by William Bolland. The gifts to the club were very numerous in the first few years of its existence, presumably because most of the members hastened to fulfill an obligation which was met at continually greater intervals when the membership was renewed merely by the filling of occasional vacancies. In any event, during the sixteen years from the foundation of the club to the issue of the first book at the joint expense of the members, in 1828, the clubmen had been the recipients of forty-five volumes, three of which had been presented by non-members. These first publications were confined practically to distribution among the members.

The issue of between thirty and fifty copies of such works was certainly not sufficient to be said to effect any very tangible service to English scholarship, especially when the majority of the club were probably collectors rather than readers, and when the reprints were as a rule brought out because of the rarity or singularity of the original, and not because of its intrinsic literary qualities. Indeed, it must probably be admitted that John Hill Burton was substantially correct when he declared that the Roxburghe Club scheme was, from the standpoint of the members, one of purely personal advantage.[12] It was inevitable that under these conditions much of the output of the club should be relatively worthless, for most of the members were wanting in the ability, the wherewithal, or the inclination to produce really important literary works for gratuitous distribution. The publications of this

12 John Hill Burton, *The Book-Hunter,* New York, 1883, 230–1.

period were, therefore, frequently far from valuable, and often lacking in scholarly significance.

The club, however, recognized by 1826 the deficiencies of its original plan; for it was resolved at the anniversary dinner in that year that a work of real literary magnitude should be printed at the joint expense of the members of the club.[13]   It was decided in the following year that the manuscript of *Havelock the Dane,* which had been recently unearthed in the Bodleian by Frederic Madden, should be edited by him for the club.   This was the first occasion on which the club resorted to outside aid in the preparation of its publications.   Madden's remuneration for the work was to be one hundred pounds, and the copies were to be two for each member, instead of being confined, as the gift books had been, to the actual number of members.[14] The *Havelock* was by far the most noteworthy Roxburghe book that had yet been produced; and the success of this trial was followed up by the club in the subsequent employment of some of the most gifted scholars of their day to oversee important publications.   Among these later editors were Madden again, Joseph Stephenson, Sir Henry Ellis, Collier, Thomas Wright, Furnivall, Aldis Wright, Gollancz, and Bond.

The selection of Madden, an outsider, to edit a Roxburghe book, seemed to be a thorn in the side of Haslewood, who had hitherto done a substantial amount of editorial work upon the publications of the club members; it may be that he even thought that he detected an injury in the failure of the club to choose him for the important position.   His chronicle of the Roxburghe doings records his opinion of the event: "A MS. not discovered by a Member of the Club, was selected and an excerpt obtained,

13 *Roxburghe Revels,* 47–8.
14 *Ibid.,* 51.

not furnished by the industry, or under the inspection of any one Member; nor edited by a Member—but in fact after much pro and con, it was made a complete hireling concern.''[15] Whether Haslewood was moved to these observations by pique at his position, or by real disappointment at what he regarded as a reflection upon the literary taste and scholarship of the members as a body, may be left to conjecture. The writer of the *Athenaeum* attack,[16] however, attributes Haslewood's feeling to pure jealousy: ''From his non-appointment, proceeded his disappointment. He gave vent to his vexation in the paragraphs we have cited, and he, moreover, stirred up a man, a little abler than himself (where could he find an inferior?), to put together some hasty 'remarks' upon Sir F. Madden's Glossary to *Havelock the Dane,* which remarks, in some respects, seemed a happy imitation of Haslewood.''[17] The attack referred to was S. W. Singer's *Remarks on the Glossary to the ancient metrical Romance of Havelock the Dane, in a Letter to Francis Douce,* to which Madden himself replied in the following year with a vigorous and thoroughly convincing defence.[18]

The election, in 1823, of Sir Walter Scott, who represented the ''author of Waverley,'' may be regarded as anything but a condescension on the part of the club.

[15] *Roxburghe Revels,* 50.

[16] *Ante,* 101.

[17] *Roxburghe Revels,* 52.

[18] *Examination of the ''Remarks on the Glossary to the ancient Metrical Romance of Havelock the Dane, in a Letter to Francis Douce, by S. W. Singer,''* London, 1829. Accompanying the copy of Singer's *Remarks* which was presented to Thomas Grenville, and which is bound in with the Grenville copy of Madden's *Havelock* in the British Museum, is a letter from Singer to Grenville stating that he had prepared a rejoinder for Madden's *Examination of the Remarks,* but had withheld its publication to avoid a literary controversy, and also because of '' Mr. Madden's then afflicted state.''

The "Wizard of the North" could scarcely gain by association with a body which vaunted what was generally regarded as an unnecessary and undesirable exclusiveness. But what the club had to gain by the possession of so popular a writer, so keen an antiquary, and so gifted a scholar, was a very measurable something. Sir Walter graciously accepted the election, although he attended only one of the club dinners, in 1828, when he presented his book, *Proceedings in the Court-Martial held upon John, Master of Sinclair, for the Murder of Ensign Schaw and Captain Schaw, 17th October, 1708*. Dibdin, the nature of whose literary and historical taste could scarcely enable him to discern interest in this kind of document, classes Sir Walter's gift as "among the least interesting and valuable in our garland."[19] The book was, in fact, a rather striking departure from the traditional substance of the club's publications, although it anticipated the character of many of the works issued by the Bannatyne, the Maitland, and the other early Scotch publishing societies.

After the brief storms of external criticism and internal jealousy which the Roxburghe Club seemed to weather serenely, the club became much less conspicuous than during its first twenty years, both because it had obviously demonstrated the general utility of its policies, and because four or five other bibliophile clubs had come to share its glory. Despite all that can be said in criticism of the privacy which makes its literary work decidedly less useful than it might be, it is really pleasant that to-day the first of the book clubs should without relinquishing its traditions continue a benign existence into a period when publishing societies represent possibly a more serious and efficient scholarship, but generally a less purely amateur spirit. The Roxburghe has never descended from its orig-

[19] *Reminiscences of a Literary Life*, I, 401–2.

inal exclusiveness—indeed, from the social standpoint, its membership list is probably more imposing to-day than it was a century ago. Social fastidiousness, however, it must be said, is not the sum of its existence; eminent names both in scholarship and public life appear upon its roster—so the election of a commoner is probably more than ever an enviable honor. The publishing policy of the club has been anything but static during its later years; passing over the trifling early issues, most of which have been printed elsewhere in more recent and emphatically improved editions, the genuine merits of the modern publications have made them not only the desiderata of book collectors, but indispensable material for scholars. Such are Stürzinger's three volumes of Guillaume de Deguileville, Gollancz's edition of *The Parlement of the Thre Ages,* Bercher's *The Nobility of Women,* edited by Warwick Bond, and Randle Holme's *Academy of Armory.* The Roxburghe Club has in its later period taken example from the early Scotch printing clubs by publishing historical material of decided value, but of such a character as to preclude the possibility of successful publication for the open market. In this class of thoroughly useful publications are the Copley and Gawdy letters, Herd's *Historia Quatuor Regum Angliae,* the *Ailesbury Memoirs,* chartularies, local records, and college accounts. Considering its importance, the fecundity of the club is to-day not remarkable; but there can be no question as to the satisfactory quality of its recent publications. In all, the books of the Roxburghe Club now comprise over one hundred and fifty volumes.

When Scott wrote to Dibdin in 1823 his acceptance of the election to the Roxburghe Club, he concluded with a bit of news which it must have rejoiced the heart of the gossipy cleric to repeat to his cronies: "It will be not uninteresting to you to know, that a fraternity is about to be established here something on

the plan of the Roxburghe Club; but having Scottish
antiquities chiefly in view, it is to be called the Bannatyne Club, from the celebrated antiquary, George Bannatyne, who compiled by far the greatest record of old
Scottish poetry. The first meeting is to be held on Thurs-
day, when the health of the Roxburghe Club will be
drunk.''[20]   A Scottish printing club had been first talked
over by Sir Walter Scott, Robert Pitcairn, and David
Laing.[21]   In their respect for Scott's attainments, his
friends wished to name the club in honor of him, Maidment
and Constable favoring the name of ''Abbotsford Club,''
which Scott ''pointedly declined'' to allow. It was firmly
in the minds of all the original projectors that the club
should be modeled upon the Roxburghe, but that its object
should be, as Sir Walter put it, ''different, and I humbly
think more useful.''[22]   Scott intended that the club should
accomplish something of real importance; he wrote in his
journal in 1827, ''I am in great hopes that the Bannatyne
Club, by the assistance of Thomson's wisdom, industry, and
accuracy, will be something far superior to the Dilettanti
model on which it started'';[23] and in his review of Pitcairn's *Criminal Trials*,[24] he enlarges upon the striking
differences between the purposes of the Roxburghe Club
and the Bannatyne. The Bannatyne, in the first place, led
a quasi-public existence; it had little of the family secrecy
about its concerns which had always characterized its pred-

20 John Gibson Lockhart, *Memoirs of the Life of Sir Walter Scott*,
5 v., 1902, IV, 97–8.

21 For a detailed account of the events and correspondence preceding the foundation of the Bannatyne Club, see [James Maidment's]
Notices relative to the Bannatyne Club, Edinburgh, 1836; v–xiv.

22 *Ibid.*, ix.

23 *The Journal of Sir Walter Scott* [edited by David Douglas], 2 v.,
1890; I, 350.

24 *Quarterly Review*, XLIV, 438–75, 1831. The introductory portion of this article is a very winning defence of the book club idea.

ecessor. It began with a membership of thirty-one—the
number of the Roxburghe—but applications for membership were so numerous that it was resolved to sacrifice the
dilettante character of the club in the interests of the
portion of the public which was disposed to support productive scholarship to the extent of five guineas a year,
and the number was accordingly increased to one hundred.[25]
Not being satisfied with having extended its membership
to such a point that it was practically freed from the re-
proach of unuseful exclusiveness, the club decided that its
publications which possessed an interest so general as to
make a strictly limited issue an object merely of public
envy should be printed in excess of the number actually
required for the members, and put out for public sale. It
is worth noting upon this point that the widespread
clamor that publications of this description should not be
withheld from a public anxious and ready to buy them,
failed absolutely to justify itself, since the fact is recorded
by the permanent secretary of the Bannatyne Club, that
the books which were offered by the club for public sale—
books of large value particularly to the Scottish antiquaries—"always proved a complete failure."[26] Another
fact which dignified the methods of the Bannatyne Club
was that lists of desiderata were constantly before the
members of the club, and it was from such lists, which gave
free opportunity for discussion as to the relative value of
publications in prospect, that its works were in the majority
of cases actually taken.[27] Further evidence of the wise
and unhindered seriousness of the club's purposes is found

[25] *Bannatyne Club; Testimonial to the secretary, presented 27th
February 1861* (appendix to *Adversaria, Notices illustrative of some
of the earlier Works printed for the Bannatyne Club*, 1867), 6.

[26] *Ibid.*, 6.

[27] See the three *Albums* of the Bannatyne Club, 1825, [1831], and
1854.

in its exchanges of valuable historical, antiquarian, and literary publications, and their occasional collaboration in such publications, with the Maitland Club, the Irish Archaeological and Celtic Society, the Wodrow Society, and the Spottiswoode Society.[28]

The first president of the Bannatyne Club was, of course, Sir Walter Scott. He was succeeded at his death by Thomas Thomson, who had formerly served as vice-president, and who was one of the club's most capable and energetic members. Of the one hundred and thirty odd publications of the club (excluding the garlands, catalogues, and albums) which are recorded by Bohn, thirteen were edited as a whole or in part by Thomson.[29] Indeed, the influence of his activity and personality upon the fortunes of the club seems to have been so great that after his death, in 1852, there was apparently some suggestion of permanently suspending its activities.[30] The club, however, was destined to survive but little longer. Interest in the Scottish book-clubs at least was by this time on the wane, and the Bannatyne was forced in 1851 to the rather humiliating expedient of inviting ten public libraries to subscribe to its publications as members, in order to sustain its former number. But even this plan proved inadequate as the older generation died away; and from 1856, when subscriptions to the club ceased, the body was very evidently moribund.[31]

The final general meeting of the club was held in 1861, when the members gave directions for the closing of its affairs. On this occasion a handsome testimonial was

28 See Henry G. Bohn's list of the publications of the Bannatyne and Maitland Clubs in his *Appendix* to Lowndes's *Bibliographer's Manual*, VI, 8–26, 1864.

29 Cosmo Innes, *Memoir of Thomas Thomson*, 1854, 251.

30 *Ibid.*, 207, 242.

31 Bannatyne Club, *Adversaria*, [app.], 7.

presented to David Laing, who had held the office of secretary to the club since its organization. It was at Scott's personal instance that Laing had accepted this unremunerative responsibility,[32] which, it was soon foreseen, could be competently administered only if it were made permanent. Laing's protracted activity in the club exceeded even Thomson's in its tangible results: for twenty-six of the club's imprints exclusive of the "albums" and "garlands," he was responsible wholly or in part,[33] and his secretarial duties undoubtedly gave him responsibilities in the preparation of much of the club's work which were not specifically acknowledged. His editorial work included what from the standpoint of the club must have been regarded as its most important productions, the works of and relating to George Bannatyne. His association with the Bannatyne Club was only a single instance of his influential connection with Scottish literary scholarship throughout the greater part of the nineteenth century. He occupied in the publishing traditions of his day, in fact, a position equalled later only by Halliwell and Furnivall. Laing was also a member of the Maitland Club—but resigned after two years[34]—and later of the Abbotsford Club. The printing societies for which he labored included the Wodrow, of which he was a founder, the Society of Antiquaries of Scotland, of which he was for some years president, the Shakespeare Society, and the Spalding Club; he also edited three volumes for the Hunterian Club, although he was not one of its members. The literary services which Laing rendered to his country are still regarded by Scotsmen with real sentiment. His editions of Dunbar, Henryson, and Lyndesay, for example, beautifully made, as well

[32] *Ibid.*, 5.

[33] See the valuable bibliography of Laing in Thomas George Stevenson's *Notices of David Laing*, 1878, 43–7.

[34] *Catalogue of the Works printed for the Maitland Club*, 1836, 35.

as effectively edited, are fondly sought for by Scotch collectors, even though their textual value has been considerably diminished by the appearance of the later editions of the Early English Text and the Scottish Text Societies.

The other prominent scholars who worked upon the publications of the Bannatyne Club included Cosmo Innes, John Hill Burton, Patrick Chalmers, and David Irving, who edited a great amount of local historical and record material, and also Sir Frederick Madden and Joseph Stevenson, more widely known outside of their connection with the Bannatyne. To specify the most notable titles among the club publications would be quite superfluous, but it may not be without profit to recall some of the most valuable in the literary field. These were, in addition to the Bannatyne memorials and works, Alexander Hume's poems, the *Buik of Alexander,* Buchanan's *De Scriptoribus Scotis,* the collection of Gawaine romances edited by Madden, Gavin Douglas's *Aeneid* and *Palice of Honour,* poems by Henryson, and a quantity of miscellaneous material of lesser literary value.

The Bannatyne Club may be said to have been, all in all, the soundest, the most useful, and the most democratic of all the book clubs. The genuine value of what it produced, contrasted, for example, with the merely curious interest of many of the early Roxburghe publications, is marked by Dibdin with what must have been a touch of humiliation: "Both the Bannatyne and Maitland Clubs must be allowed to have outstripped our own, not less in the rapid succession, than in the instructive complexion, of their publications."[35]

The Maitland Club, the object of which was "to print works illustrative of the antiquities, history, and litera-

---

[35] *Reminiscences of a literary Life,* I, 476.

ture of Scotland,''[36] was founded in 1828. Its personnel included many of the members of the Bannatyne—Scott, Laing, Pitcairn, Thomson, and Tytler among them—and its aims corresponded closely with those of the earlier club, although as a Glasgow organization, the Maitland Club inclined a little more towards localism than did its predecessor. The members of the Maitland were at first seventy in number, and later one hundred; but in spite of the limitation of its membership, the body was, like the Bannatyne, sufficiently alive to its public position to place its issues in general sale when they were ''of such importance as to render it expedient to extend their circulation beyond the members.''[37]   The most useful textual publications of this club were the poems of Richard Maitland of Lethington, the patron saint of the club, Henryson's fables, Drummond of Hawthornden's poems, the romances of *Beves of Hamtoun, Lancelot du Lak,* and *Clariodorus,* and the works of Sir Thomas Urquhart of Cromarty. Many of the publications of the Maitland were issued jointly with the Bannatyne Club, and the organization had less frequent associations of the same kind with the Abbotsford and the Spalding Clubs. The Maitland Club closed its publications in 1859, with the issue of its seventy-fifth volume.[38]

The Abbotsford Club, founded in 1834 by W. B. D. D. Turnbull in memory of Sir Walter Scott,[39] included likewise many of the most active members of both the Bannatyne and Maitland Clubs. The purposes of this club were substantially those of the two other Scottish book clubs,

---

[36] *Catalogue of the Works printed for the Maitland Club,* 3.

[37] *Ibid.,* 6.

[38] Henry G. Bohn, *Appendix relating to the Books of literary and scientific Societies;* in Lowndes's *Bibliographer's Manual,* VI, 1864, 20–26. Henry B. Wheatley, *How to form a Library,* 2nd ed., 1886, 187.

[39] Henry B. Wheatley, *op. cit.,* 187.

9

although the club was formed ostensibly for the purpose of publishing "all materials which can throw light on the ancient history or literature of any country, anywhere described or discussed by the Author of Waverley."[40]   The publications of the Abbotsford Club did, in fact, possess much of the tone and color of the literary preferences of the Author of Waverley.   Fourteen of its thirty-one volumes were reprints of literary material, including three volumes of mystery and morality plays, and eight medieval romances.[41]   This is a higher proportion of literary publications than is found in any of the contemporary book clubs save the Roxburghe.   The last volume issued by the Maitland Club was likewise the last one issued by the Abbotsford, although the organization apparently continued an inactive existence until 1866.[42]

The form of organization and the aims of the Roxburghe, Bannatyne, Maitland, and Abbotsford Clubs were closely similar.   The last three took example from the Roxburghe even to the detail of the external form of their publications—a luxurious quarto in the traditional "Roxburghe" binding; and although the Scottish clubs were considerably larger, and for that reason, considerably less exclusive, than the Roxburghe, the fact remains that the aims of all of these clubs were in no respect popular.   The Spalding Club,[43] the Spenser Society,[44] and the Hunterian Club[45] had all of them some of the distinguishing marks of the book clubs, as well as of the typical printing societies of a popular stamp—as for example, publications

[40] John Gibson Lockhart, *Memoirs of the Life of Sir Walter Scott*, IV, 100.
[41] Henry G. Bohn, *op. cit.*, 36–9.
[42] Henry B. Wheatley, *op. cit.*, 188.
[43] *Post.*, 126.
[44] *Post.*, 164–6.
[45] *Post.*, 169–71.

of a more expensive kind than the plain octavo of the publishing societies, and a limitation upon the number of members, in no case, however, less than two hundred. But the traditional form of the Roxburghe Club and its imitators was not followed by the few later bibliophile clubs; and with the demise of the three Scotch book clubs shortly after the middle of the century, the Roxburghe was left alone in the field which it had opened.

The social incentives of the bibliophile were satisfied at intervals, however, by the formation of publishing clubs of similarly defined, but generally more diffuse purposes than those of the Roxburghe. Probably the most important of these was the Philobiblon Society, which was apparently founded chiefly through the efforts of Richard Monckton Milnes, and under the patronage of the Prince Consort, in 1853.[46] The number of members of the Philobiblon Society was limited, as in the Roxburghe Club, to forty.[47] The purpose of the society was to publish annually a volume of historical, biographical, bibliographical, and literary miscellanies; and as the roll of the society included a number of distinguished foreigners, it was not considered necessary that the papers should be published in English. It was the boast of the society that "not a single copy" of its publications was placed upon sale.[48] The *Miscellanies* were exquisite octavos upon hand-made paper. The articles in these ten volumes of *mélanges* were separately paged throughout, by reason of the fact that the arrangement of the annual volumes was designed to be only temporary, and was ultimately to be replaced by a subject classification.[49] Needless to say, this method of classification was never carried out.

[46] Octave Delepierre, *Analyse des Travaux de Société des Philo-biblon de Londres,* 1862, 1; Henry G. Bohn, *op. cit.,* 82.

[47] Octave Delepierre, *op. cit.,* 2.

[48] *Ibid.,* 2.

[49] *Ibid.,* 4.

The contents of the volumes were largely inedited fragments, letters, notices, and bibliographical comments.   The
contributions of literary value were in rather a marked
minority, but included some useful items, such as unpublished letters by Sterne and Dr. Johnson, inedited poems
by John Donne and Samuel Daniel (and these latter, by the
way, were not by Daniel, but by Ben Jonson), a variant
version of Keats's *Hyperion,* eight letters between James
Thomson and David Mallet, Burke's Table Talk, and miscellaneous notes relative to Johnson, Walpole, and Chester-
field.   Under the name of this society there were also issued
by contributors nine extra volumes, including Lord Herbert
of Cherbury's *Expedition to the Isle of Rhe,* Henry G.
Bohn's *Biography and Bibliography of Shakespeare* (only
the biographical section of which was new), and two
volumes contributed by Henry Huth : *Ancient Ballads and
Broadsides,* and *Inedited Poetical Miscellanies.*[50]

The book club as an institution is now much less important from every standpoint than it was a half century ago.
The history of the Scottish clubs has apparently shown that
when the animating club spirit of exclusiveness is strongly
affected by considerations of public utility, the club as a
club ceases to exist.   In addition, it is probably true that
the higher practical value of the output of the larger publishing societies has demonstrated the relative inferiority of
the book club for any other than social purposes.   For these
reasons at least, the book clubs—always except the Roxburghe—have gradually disappeared, until all that passes
under the name to-day are a few private bibliophile clubs
which do not pretend to any public functions—for example,

[50] Delepierre's bibliography of the Philobiblon Society, which was
issued in 1862, is of course incomplete.   A complete bibliography of
the society may be found in Bernard Quaritch's *Account of the great
Learned Societies and Associations and of the chief Printing Clubs of
Great Britain and Ireland,* 1886; 43–8.

the Sette of Odde Volumes—and a number of clubs of restricted membership, such as the Malone Society[51] and the Edinburgh Bibliographical Society;[52] these are nevertheless .sufficiently large, and their publications of sufficiently wide circulation, to make it advisable for us to class them as publishing societies rather than book clubs.

Latterly the book club idea has acquired many commercial features, and has in some cases, probably more particularly in America, served purely commercial ends. It would be a difficult matter to say just where a book club ceases to be a book club, and becomes a promoter's venture, but there can be little question that the imprint of many of our modern clubs is nothing more nor less than a publisher's trade-mark; and it is obvious that in many cases of this kind it is generally unnecessary to take very seriously the scholarly quality of the work so produced.

Of much more importance in the aggregate than the publications of the book clubs were the publications of the printing societies, which began to spring up rapidly between 1830 and 1850, while the clubs were at the pinnacle of their vogue. There was in general no social aspect to these societies, since their existence was something in the nature of an actual protest against the undemocratic attitude of the printing clubs. Their meetings were ordinarily of a purely fiscal nature, for the greater number did not include in their programs any provision even for scholarly communications between members, one of the most familiar functions of earlier learned societies; hence most of these early publishing societies had no "transactions" to measure and record the reaction of their publications upon the scholarly temper. In fact, in most of these bodies the proceedings of the society were understood to be taken up so exclusively with the balancing of the accounts of income

51 *Post.*, 197–8.
52 *Post.*, 134–5.

and expenditure for publishing, that all the actual business of the society was conducted by a council or by the executive officers. It is of course quite apparent that such institutions have been called learned societies largely by virtue of what the word society does not imply, for in effect they were nothing more than simple publishing projects, in which the members—who might as well have been called subscribers—secured for a small sum annually a volume or two which came within the scope of the society's declared objects, but in the selection or preparation of which they had very little responsibility or choice.

This fact does not, of course, diminish the value of what was effected by these agencies. It might be said, indeed, that the conduct of these societies upon such lines was almost inevitable, since without question the majority of their members, scattered as they were in most cases not merely throughout England but throughout continents, could not have interested themselves in the routine business of their organizations. The concentration of the fiscal control and scholarly policies of the societies in the hands of a small minority of the membership, therefore, while it provided opportunities for exploitation and downright abuse of personal privileges, nevertheless placed the working machinery of such organizations in hands that were in nearly all cases capable of efficient and honorable administration. So the remark so often passed in criticism of these bodies, both then and now, that they are frequently "one man" organizations, means, in the last analysis, that the vigor and industry of a very few well-endowed scholars may produce direction and results out of an ill-defined purpose. It may be said, in fact, that throughout the history of all these bodies, the public have been with scarce an exception substantial gainers, and the managers and editors have been satisfied with a modicum of distinction and a minimum of remuneration in return for much hard labor and self-sacrifice.

The purposes of these printing societies, then, were frankly utilitarian. They endeavored to issue intrinsically important works in sufficient numbers to make the expense of publication relatively small; and the name and plan of a society organization assured an immediate sale for the bulk of their issues. Their primary consideration—the cutting down of the expense of publication to a minimum— necessitated a departure from the publishing policy of the old book clubs. For this reason the *recherché* volumes of the Roxburghe and the Bannatyne were replaced by the substantial and sometimes rather homely books that are familiar in the bindings of the Surtees, the Camden, and the Early English Text Societies. The gain in utility was naturally at the cost of sentiment, except in such instances as the English Historical Society and the Hunterian Club, which endeavored to restore some of the fastidious bookishness of the earlier clubs.

Before taking up in detail the question of the work of these general publishing societies in furthering literary culture, we must return to an organization with which we are already more or less familiar, and the chief claim of which upon our attention so far has lain in its complete failure to explore a field in which its publishing activities in the nineteenth century were to have a very substantial influence.

As early as 1811 John Josias Conybeare communicated to the Society of Antiquaries a series of papers relating to early English literature.[53] The papers included notices of the *Exeter Book* and observations upon Anglo-Saxon metrics; and they were followed by valuable communications of a kindred nature by Conybeare and others,[54] until apparently the society as a body was awakened to the

[53] These papers were published in *Archaeologia*, XVII, 173–5, 180–8, 189–92, 193–7, 257–66, 267–74, 1814.

[54] *Archaeologia*, XVIII, 21–8, XIX, 314–34, XXI, 43–78, 88–91, XXII, 350–398, 1815–29.

importance of the study of old English literature as something more than a mere adjunct to archaeological research. Conybeare's contributions to *Archaeologia*, with a large and valuable addition of illustrative material, were edited and published by his brother, William Daniel Conybeare, in 1826, but apparently not under the auspices of the Society of Antiquaries.

Conybeare's communications to the society had constituted one of the most powerful stimuli to a revival of interest among his countrymen in old English letters, which was contemporary with, and largely influenced by, the rehabilitation of Norse studies by Thorkelin and Grundtvig, and the investigations of the two Grimms in Germanic philology.[55] The most efficient leaders in the Anglo-Saxon revival in England were Bosworth, Kemble, and Thorpe; and it was at Thorpe's instance that the Society of Antiquaries in 1831 determined to take up the burden of publishing the remains of old English literature. It is probable that the arguments of Thorpe were powerfully seconded by Grundtvig's circulation of a proposal to begin a series of publications to include the valuable remains of Anglo-Saxon literature, a project which seems to have struck the English literary students of the day as something in the nature of a scholarly challenge.[56] Thorpe and his friends accordingly planned to redeem English scholarship from its neglect of opportunity, which was made all the more conspicuous by contrast with the industry of foreign scholars in old English studies, by endeavoring in 1831 to found a society for the publication of unprinted Anglo-Saxon works;[57] but since many of the supporters of the

[55] See Wülcker's *Grundriss zur Geschichte der angelsächsischen Literatur*, 1885, 45–8.

[56] John Petheram, *An historical Sketch of the Progress and present State of Anglo-Saxon Literature in England*, 1840, 141–2.

[57] John M. Kemble, *Letter to Francisque Michel;* in Michel's *Bibliotheque Anglo-Saxonne*, 1837, pp. 1–63 (21).

proposed society were fellows of the Society of Antiquaries, their proposals were submitted to the Council of the Antiquaries. It was decided soon afterward that the Antiquaries should undertake the projected publications, placing the issues on public sale, but permitting members of the society to receive them at half price. A committee of the society consisting of twenty-two members was therefore appointed to supervise the issue of these publications. On this committee were a number of scholars thoroughly equipped for the work, including Henry Ellis, Francis Palgrave, and Frederic Madden, all as yet undistinguished by knightly dignities. A concession to the undeveloped state of old English scholarship is seen in the decision of the society to print the works in the original tongue and character, but with an accompanying translation into modern English.[58] The result of these plans of the society was the publication of the Caedmonic poems by Thorpe in 1832, of the *Codex Exoniensis* in 1842, and of Sir Frederic Madden's edition of Layamon's *Brut* in three volumes in 1847. With the completion of this series, an emphatically necessary and very timely contribution to the national literary resources, the Society of Antiquaries once more withdrew from its active patronage of letters, but with the distinction of having been the first learned society to lend its support to early English textual scholarship.

To return, then, to the history of the general publishing societies: the Surtees Society, which was the pioneer among them, was established by the Rev. James Raine in 1834. The Society was founded in memory of the recently deceased Robert Surtees of Mainsforth, the distinguished, if possibly over-canny antiquary, and its specific purposes were announced to be "the publishing such inedited manu-

---

[58] *Prospectus of a Series of Publications of Anglo-Saxon and early English literary Remains, under the Superintendence of a Committee of the Society of Antiquaries of London* [1831 or –2], iii–iv.

scripts as illustrate the intellectual, the moral, the religious, and the social condition of those parts of England and Scotland, included, on the east, between the Humber and the Frith of Forth, and on the west between the Mersey and the Clyde, from the earliest period to the time of the Restoration."[59]   The society numbered in the first year of its existence about one hundred and thirty members, and increased in numbers rapidly.   A limit of three hundred and fifty was placed upon the membership; but the publications of the society, which were printed considerably in excess of this number, were also for sale to outsiders.[60] The earlier publications were edited for the greater part by Raine, who became secretary of the society upon its actual foundation, and whose services in this capacity were quite as indispensable as were Laing's to the Bannatyne Club.   Considering the limitations placed upon the scope of the society's work by the definition of its purposes, it has produced a series of publications really remarkable for their general importance.   Many societies of similarly local interests have produced works of much more restricted value; but the Surtees Society, while choosing its material from its elected neighborhood,—and over half of its publications are connected with the town and cathedral of Durham—has published materials of the broadest historical and literary value.   What it has contributed to the study of English literature generally is typical of the importance of its publications in other fields; the principal items in this class are the *Towneley Mysteries,* the Durham Anglo-Saxon ritual, Jordan Fantosme's chronicle, two volumes of *Anglo-Saxon and early English Psalters, Latin Hymns of the Anglo-Saxon Church, the Lindisfarne and Rushworth Gospels,* in four volumes, and a metrical *Life of St. Cuthbert.*

[59] Taylor, George, *A memoir of Robert Surtees,* New edition, with additions, by James Raine, n. d. [1852]; 195–6.

[60] Henry G. Bohn, *op. cit.,* 33.

The Camden Society was a still further concession to the popular demands upon English scholarship. This society, named in honor of William Camden, was founded in 1838,[61] four years after the formation of the Surtees Society, to the example of which the later society admittedly owed its existence. The Camden Society was, however, by reason of the fact that its interests were not restricted to a locality, and that its annual fee of only a guinea and its practically unrestricted membership made it emphatically a popular society, by all means the most widely important of the general publishing societies of this period. It was, in fact, the wholly practical basis of organization in the Camden Society which gave to Collier, Crofton Croker, Dyce, and Thomas Wright, all of them members of the Camden, their cue for the establishment of similar bodies for the furtherance of scholarship specifically in the literary field.[62] The objects of this society were "to perpetuate, and render accessible, whatever is valuable, but at present little known, amongst the materials for the civil, ecclesiastical, or literary history of the United Kingdom."[63] The society began publication on a large scale, but the five hundred copies of its first book were quickly taken up, and a reimpression was made in the same year. At the first anniversary meeting, when the members already numbered over a thousand, it was decided to limit the number of members for the future to twelve hundred. The publications of the society were fixed therefore at twelve hundred and fifty impressions until 1848, when the number was again reduced to a thousand, and subsequently to six hundred.[64] The decrease of popular interest in the society was

[61] For a sketch of the early history of the Camden Society see John Gough Nichols's *Descriptive Catalogue of the Works of the Camden Society,* 1862, iii–viii.

[62] *Ibid.,* iv.

[63] *Ibid.,* iii.

[64] *Ibid.,* iv.

apparently brought about partly at least by the formation of the Parker, Percy, and Shakespeare Societies within two years of its establishment, with the consequent attraction to their ranks of members of the Camden to whom the special interests represented in the newer societies appealed more strongly than the miscellaneous interests of the Camden.[65] But the membership in the Camden Society showed no marked decrease until the close of the following decade. A second effect of these later societies upon their predecessor was that the announcements of their provinces of interest served to limit considerably the field of the Camden Society's publications, as did also the opening of the Rolls Series in 1848.

The accomplishments of the society in the realm of historical scholarship, which has been altogether its most useful field, especially in later years, included the publication of some valuable chronicles, before the Master of the Rolls preempted this domain, and monastic, political, and social evidences of very great importance. Its literary publications opened with Bishop Bale's *Kynge Johan* and Thomas Wright's collection of *Political Songs;* and even though the literary societies soon appropriated this province, the Camden Society's contributions to literary study have since been, at least for the time being, invaluable. The 1842 volume of Arthurian romances, the *Promptorium Parvulorum*, the *Thornton Romances*, the *Peterborough Chronicle*, the works of or attributed to Walter Map, the *Ancren Riwle*, the *Milton Papers*, and a quantity of correspondence, diaries, miscellaneous poems, and other material of the greatest importance to students of literature, appeared first in the publications of this society. It is needless to say, however, that in most cases these early publications have been superseded. What the Camden Society, there-

---

[65] *Ibid.*, iv–v.

fore, has accomplished directly in the interests of literary scholarship gives it an undisputed place not merely as a powerful example and influence for the later literary publishing societies, but as a literary agency of emphatically great importance in itself.

The First Series of the Camden publications extended from 1838 to 1872, and comprised one hundred and five volumes. In this First Series appeared almost all the works of literary significance that the society produced. The Second Series of the publications, in sixty-two volumes, which was closed in 1898, included the commonplace book of John Milton, and the letter book of Gabriel Harvey. In 1897 the Camden Society was absorbed by the Royal Historical Society,[66] and the publications of the Camden Society were continued from that date as the Camden Series of the Royal Historical Society. The result of the amalgamation was of course to limit still further the scope of the Camden publications, and the new Camden Series has therefore been restricted almost exclusively to historical material. A single reprint of some literary connection has appeared in the re-clothed Camden Series—*The Travels and Life of Sir Thomas Hoby*.

The English Historical Society, founded in the same year as the Camden, was something of a book club, and something of a general publishing society. Its membership was limited to one hundred, and its list of members, being limited, was properly embellished with many aristocratic and bookish names. Many of the members were, however, scholars of note, including Joseph Stevenson, Thomas Duffus Hardy, Panizzi, and Kemble. To the members the society issued handsome tall octavo volumes on hand made paper; but issues of their publications on smaller paper

[66] *Transactions of the Royal Historical Society*, New Series, XII, 232, 1898.

were sold to the public—though at a price.[67] The object of the society was stated to be "to print an accurate, uniform, and elegant edition of the most valuable English chronicles, from the earliest period to the accession of Henry the Eighth."[68] It was intended, however, to include in the publications material of collateral historical value, including lives of saints and historical poems.[69] The society has, therefore, for the student of old literature, an obvious importance, both in its direct and indirect aims. The literary value, if not the historical value, of its publications, however, is diminished somewhat by a system of editing which deliberately eliminated from the text irrelevant and borrowed material.[70] In the eighteen years of the society's existence it issued a valuable series of Latin-English historical works, including Bede's *Historia Ecclesiastica* and minor works, Gildas and Nennius, and the chronicles of William of Malmesbury, Nicholas Trivet, and Florence of Worcester. The most important of the society's publications was Kemble's *Codex Diplomaticus Aevi Saxonici*, in six volumes, 1845–8.

The Spalding Club, established in Aberdeen in 1839, was in reality not a book club, but a publishing society, if we accept the established distinction between the social aims and exclusive nature of the one, and the business-like organization and missionary principles of the other. This society was brought into existence by Joseph Robertson and John Stuart,[71] and its field was intended to comprise "the literary, historical, genealogical, and topographical remains

[67] Henry G. Bohn, *op. cit.*, 131.

[68] *General introduction* [*to the publications of the society*]; in *Venerabilis Bedae Historia Ecclesiastica*, recensuit Josephus Stevenson, 1838; i.

[69] *Ibid.*, xiii–xiv.

[70] *Ibid.*, iii–xi.

[71] [John Stuart], *Notices of the Spalding Club*, 1871; 1.

of the north-eastern counties of Scotland.[72] The numbers of the club were at first limited to three hundred, but the extent of the public participation in the project soon made it advisable to extend the membership to five hundred. The prominent members of the Spalding Club included, in addition to Robertson and Stuart, Cosmo Innes, David Laing, William Knight, Thomas Thomson, and Robert Pitcairn. Conditions made the secretary's office in this society —as was true, too, in the Bannatyne Club and the Maitland Club—one of supreme importance, and acknowledgment of Stuart's services to the society in this position took the form of an elaborate memorial when the club was dissolved in 1871.[73] Exceptional as was the quality of the Spalding Club's publications relating to the history and antiquities of the northern shires, its sole contribution to Anglo-Scottish literary study was Cosmo Innes's edition of Barbour's *Brus,* issued in 1857. The *Book of Deir,* however, edited by Stuart, and published in 1869, was an important, and for the society, an expensive, reprint of Celtic material.

The Spalding Club was "re-constituted" as the New Spalding Club in 1886. The only publication of the revived club which may possess interest for the student of literature are the two volumes of *Musa Latina Aberdonensis,* 1892–5.

The first of the ecclesiastical publishing societies was the Parker Society, named in memory of Archbishop Parker. It was established at Cambridge in 1840, and continued in existence until 1853, publishing in this short period fifty-five volumes of ecclesiastical and devotional literature. In this amount of work there is, needless to say, much of the highest value to the student of English prose. The society's publications included complete or partial works, or remains, of Ridley, Grindal, Cranmer, Coverdale, Latimer,

[72] *Ibid.,* 2.
[73] *Ibid.,* 94–110.

Jewel, Tyndale, Bale, and Whitgift; and in addition a large quantity of liturgical relics and a volume of Elizabethan devotional poetry. The Parker Society had in its day a membership phenomenally large, extending at one time to more than seven thousand.[74] As evidence of the relative lack of interest in literary studies at this time, it is useful to compare this number with the mere thousand of the Shakespeare Society and the twelve hundred of the Camden.

The Wodrow Society was instituted in 1841, largely through Laing's endeavors, for the publication of the early writers of the Reformed Church of Scotland.[75] Its province is comparable, therefore, with that of the Parker Society in England. It would be impossible to place the bulk of its publications, however, upon the same plane of intrinsic importance as those of the Parker Society, for the simple reason that most of the Scottish "church fathers" count for relatively little in literary history. The society did publish, though, in 1846–7, two volumes of Knox's *History of the Reformation in Scotland*, edited by Laing, which were to form the opening volumes for a complete edition of Knox's works. The society collapsed, however, in 1848; but Laing, sticking to his prospectus, carried on the work of completing the promised edition, and issued the sixth and last volume in 1864. This publication, unsuccessful at first under the society's auspices, and later in the hands of the publishers who took over the third, fourth, and fifth volumes, is a real monument to Laing's scholarly devotion.

The Spottiswoode Society issued between 1843 and 1851 six volumes of the writings of the Episcopal clergy in

[74] A. Hume, *The Learned Societies and Printing Clubs of the United Kingdom*, 1853; 268.

[75] Thomas George Stevenson, *Notices of David Laing*, 1878, 23–5.

Scotland; none of these publications, however, requires special comment.

The Chetham Society, like the Surtees Society, limited its labors to a special district of England, "the Palatine Counties of Lancaster and Chester"; but, as with the Surtees Society, its interests were by no means restricted to unprofitable localism. The society was founded at Manchester in 1843, and included among its members from the beginning scholars and antiquaries of national reputation. Among the most active members of the early council were James Crossley and the Rev. Thomas Corser. The membership was limited to three hundred and fifty (at present there are almost one hundred institutions upon the subscription list), and the annual subscription was fixed at one pound; no significant change has been made in the rules of the society since its foundation. In sixty-eight years of existence the Chetham Society has issued one hundred and fourteen volumes in its original series (1843–92), and sixty-nine volumes in a new series. About thirty of the society's volumes supply more or less valuable material for the literary student, consisting largely of local poetry. The most noteworthy of these special works are Henry Bradshaw's *Holy Life and History of Saynt Werburghe*, John Byrom's poems, in four parts, edited by A. W. Ward, and Byrom's *Private Journal and Literary Remains*, edited in the earlier series by Richard Parkinson. A very substantial and interesting descriptive bibliography of early poetry was the *Collectanea Anglo-Poetica*, a catalogue of Corser's library in this field, begun by Corser in 1860 and completed by Crossley in 1883, in all eleven numbers.

The Caxton Society was established in 1845 "for the publication in a cheap and commodious form, of chronicles and other documents hitherto unpublished, illustrative of the history and miscellaneous literature of the British Isles

10

during the middle ages.''[76]   The society had no stated subscription, but the members placed themselves under obligation to take one copy each of all the books printed by the
society; and all the income from the sales of the separate
volumes remaining after the payment of the expenses of
publication were to be regarded as the remuneration of
the editors.   The original members were thirty-three in
number, and included Bosworth, the Rev. J. A. Giles, Palgrave, and Thomas Wright.   The Caxton Society published
between 1844 and 1854 sixteen volumes, the first three of
which were issued not with the imprint of the society, but
under the serial title *Scriptores Monastici.*   The first
volume to bear the society's name was Silgrave's *Chronicle,*
published in 1849.   The lack of system in publication seems
in many other respects to imply that the editors of the
separate volumes carried the arrangements very much in
their own hands and that there was no really effective administrative oversight for the work of the various editors;
the volumes were not numbered in the actual order of their
issue, and they were printed by different publishers without any approach to uniformity in their make-up.   The
great bulk of the society's publications are in Latin, largely
letters, brief biographies, and, most importantly for our
purposes, chronicles.   These last include Geoffrey of Mon-
mouth's *Historia Britonum,* the *Chronicon Angliae Petri-
burgense,* and others of less importance.   The society also
published two documents of more immediate literary interest: Peter Heylin's versified *Memorial of Bishop Waynflete,*
and Grosseteste's *Chasteau d'Amour,* with an English
version.

The only remaining society of the first half of the nineteenth century whose publications have had a wide impor-

[76] Information relative to the organization of the Caxton Society
is given in the announcements of the society in various volumes of
its publications.

tance in the study of English literature is the Hakluyt Society, which was founded in 1846 with the object of printing ''rare and valuable voyages, travels, naval expeditions, and other geographical records.''[77] The society opened with an annual subscription of one guinea, but increased this later to a guinea and a half. For this modest amount the subscribers received down to the year 1898 a First Series of one hundred volumes; and twenty-nine volumes of the Second Series have been issued to the year 1912. The Hakluyt Society has published a series of travel books which possess the greatest literary value, including not only early works by Hawkins, Ralegh, Strachey, Hakluyt, Dr. Giles Fletcher, Baffin, and others, but important sixteenth and seventeenth century translations of foreign books of travel. In addition to the regular series of publications, the society has supported as an extra series the Messrs. MacLehose's reprints of the most important early English travel books, including a complete Hakluyt in twelve volumes, and a Purchas in twenty.

It is of course important to mention that many monographs on literary topics appeared throughout the second quarter of the century in the publications of such bodies as the Society of Antiquaries and the British Archaeological Association. The most prominent of literary scholars found these agencies of publication indispensable when there were no special journals for literary scholarship. Less distinguished scholars found in the periodical or occasional publications of local societies opportunity for more or less meritorious articles on literary topics. The importance of these bodies for such purposes is not to be underestimated; and it is even now growing. The skeptic on this point would do well to look over a file of the publications of the Birmingham and Midland Institute, the Powysland

[77] [Announcement] The Hakluyt Society, 1912, ii.

Club, or the county archaeological and antiquarian societies
—for example, those of Cumberland, Devonshire, Norfolk,
Shropshire, and Somersetshire.

Since the middle of the nineteenth century there have
been comparatively few new societies formed, barring the
literary learned societies themselves, whose interests have
touched very closely those of literary students.   In the
collapse of society activities between 1850 and 1870, only
the most useful and influential survived; and to these very
few have been added since, save in special fields.   In addition, with the increase in the number of special societies in
later years there has been a distinct tendency to more
clearly defined specialization, so that if a text or an article
of literary import is included in the publications of an
historical or an archaeological society nowadays, it is
merely a coincidence.   Such organizations, therefore, as
the Oxford Historical Society, the Royal Historical Society,
and the modern ecclesiastical societies, have by no means
the points of contact with literary study that the Surtees
Society, the British Archaeological Association, and the
Parker Society, for example, had in their earlier days.   In
fact, those even of the general publishing societies which
have lived through their period of trial are, as we have
seen, to-day of very much less significance to the student of
literature than they were at an earlier date.   Sufficient
illustration of this is found in the fact that the Surtees
Society has published no literary text since 1891; the
Camden series has since its adoption by the Royal Historical Society been turned over entirely to historical material; and A. W. Ward's edition of Byrom's poems has been
the only literary work published by the Chetham Society
since 1873.   These facts explain at once the great increase
in the number of efficient and long-lived literary societies
that sprang up during the latter half of the nineteenth cen-

tury, and the extreme paucity of literary material among the publications of special societies in other fields, and even of the once receptive general publishing societies. What has been accomplished, then, since 1850 or thereabouts, for literary study by societies outside the field of literary publication may be dismissed very briefly, and without special consideration whether the nature of their activities should rank these bodies as book clubs or printing societies.

Of these later societies, the first both in point of priority of establishment and of the value of its output for students of English literature is the Folk-Lore Society, founded in 1878 chiefly through the efforts of W. J. Thoms, a worker in the earlier Shakespeare Society, the projector of *Notes and Queries,* and the inventor of the term "folk-lore." The society was organized for the "preservation and publication of popular traditions, legendary ballads, local proverbial sayings, superstitions, and old customs."[78] The program of the body was large, but its achievement has been quite equal to its declared purposes. The success of its work was, in fact, assured from the beginning by the quality of the scholarship which it represented: among the first members of the council were Andrew Lang, E. B. Tylor, W. J. Thoms, Max Müller, and Frederic Ouvry; and the English scholars who have contributed to the publications of the organization have included, in addition to these, Fleay, Havelock Ellis, York Powell, Alfred Nutt, Joseph Jacobs, Laurence Gomme, Napier, and Skeat. The *Folk-Lore Record* was the society's first organ, five volumes of which were issued from 1878 to 1882. This was followed by the *Folk-Lore Journal,* of which seven volumes appeared to 1889. In turn this was incorporated with the *Archaeological Review* under the title *Folk-Lore,* the present mouth-piece of the society. In these three

[78] *Folk-Lore Record,* I, *Preface,* 1878.

periodicals is to be found much literary material, including illumination of many crucial passages in the light of the society's special researches, and much matter which, if not strictly literary in itself, constitutes one of the most useful adjuncts to literary study, such as charms, mumming, proverbs, local rimes, place names, folk-tales, and a hundred related subjects. Besides its periodical, the Folk-Lore Society has published a number of separate treatises, including Aubrey's *Remaines of Gentilisme and Judaisme*, from the manuscript, Alfred Nutt's *Studies on the Legend of the Holy Grail*, and many volumes of local folk-lore, including a series of *County Folk-Lore* which has comprised so far five volumes. From this brief record it is apparent that the Folk-Lore Society has been, both in the magnitude and the intrinsic worth of its work, of the greatest importance in the literary field; indeed, it might not be too much to say that it has been the most continuously valuable of all the non-literary societies.

Two bibliographical societies have issued works of marked utility in our province, the Edinburgh Bibliographical Society, founded in 1880 as a private club devoted chiefly to local interests,[79] and the Bibliographical Society, founded in London in 1892. For the Edinburgh Bibliographical Society William Macmath issued a *Bibliography of Scottish popular Ballads in Manuscript*, James Cameron a *Bibliography of Scottish theatrical Literature*, R. A. S. Macfie a *Bibliography of Fletcher of Saltoun*, and J. P. Edmonds *Elegies and other Tracts issued on the Death of Henry, Prince of Wales, 1612*. Under the auspices of the later Bibliographical Society have appeared W. W. Greg's *List of English Plays written before 1643 and printed before 1700*, and his *List of Masques, Pageants, &c*, a supplement

[79] Charles Sandford Terry, *Catalogue of the Publications of Scottish historical and kindred Clubs and Societies, 1780–1908*, 1909; 66.

to the previous volume. The *Transactions* of this body contain also many items of interest. Both of these societies have issued a number of longer and shorter works on the history of printing, the book trade, and kindred subjects of much potential value to students of English literature.

A number of amateur and learned bodies of less general importance have printed from time to time within recent years texts and monographs of literary interest. Among these may be mentioned the Royal Historical Society, organized in 1868, the moving spirit of which was the Rev. Charles Rogers. In accordance with its announced purpose of pursuing some of the "less explored paths" of history, it published in its first two volumes of *Transactions* the *Poems of Sir Robert Aytoun*, and the *Poetical Remains of King James the First of Scotland*. To the ninth and tenth volumes of the *Transactions* the Rev. F. G. Fleay contributed two valuable papers, *On the Actor Lists* and *On the History of the Theatres in London*, both covering the period preceding the Commonwealth. In the third and fifth volumes of the third series of *Transactions* C. H. Firth published his *Ballad History of the Reigns of the later Tudors*, and *Ballad History of the Reign of James I*. Rogers established in London in the same year as the Royal Historical Society the Grampian Club "for the editing and printing of works illustrative of Scottish literary history and antiquities." The publications of this club included *Boswelliana*, the commonplace book of James Boswell, and three genealogical works by Rogers, *Genealogical Memoirs of the Family of Sir Walter Scott, Genealogical Memoirs of John Knox and of the Family of Knox*, and *the Book of Robert Burns*, three volumes of biography, family history, and memoirs. The club has published nothing further since 1891.

In 1877 two book clubs were established in Scotland, the

first the Scottish Literary Club, founded by Thomas G. Stevenson,[81] and the other The New Club, formed in Paisley, which republished Jamieson's *Etymological Dictionary of the Scottish Language* in four volumes from 1879 to 1882, with a supplement in 1887. It published also the *Buke of the Howlat* and *the Black Book of Paisley and other Manuscripts of the Scotichronicon.*

As types of societies of casual significance for our purposes, cursory mention of a few of the most generally known may close a chapter which has already descended dangerously near to mere enumeration. The Aungervyle Club, established in Edinburgh in 1881, was probably something in the nature of a proprietary name. In its four series of reprints, which appeared from 1881 to 1888, are included a number of short and curious poetical fragments and miscellaneous pieces of small intrinsic value. The Oxford Historical Society should be mentioned for the fact that although it has done little for essentially literary scholarship, its editions of *The Life and Times of Anthony Wood* and of Hearne's *Remarks and Collections,* together with its contributions to correlated subjects, such as printing, book collections, and the early history of the University, have provided very useful materials for the literary investigator. The Scottish History Society has published in its miscellanies a few monographs upon figures of at most secondary literary importance, including James VI, Maitland of Lethington, and Gilbert Burnet. The Viking Club, founded in 1892 as the Orkney, Shetland, and Northern Society, has printed thoroughly useful saga and folk-lore material, and in 1912 published a translation of Stjerna's essays upon *Beowulf.* The Royal Philosophical Society of Glasgow in 1902, one hundred years after the date of its foundation, instituted a Historical and Philo-

[81] *Post.,* 169.

logical Section; since then there have appeared in the *Transactions* of the society a number of papers by F. J. Amours, George Neilson, and other Scottish specialists, on topics in Middle English and Middle Scots literature.

These records, then, mechanical and formal as by their nature they must be, serve to show what our modern scholarship owes to a day when literary societies had no separate existence, and to a tradition which regarded literature as the handmaid of many related studies. When the literary societies themselves entered the field, the tendency was for the societies of general aims, or of special aims in other provinces of learning, to eschew literary studies, so that the history of the influence of such societies upon English scholarship is, as it has already been pointed out, one of progressive decline in importance and interest.

CHAPTER VI

PHILOLOGICAL AND TEXT SOCIETIES

The history of English societies for literary scholarship divides itself into two definitely marked periods. The first of these was contemporary with the effervescence of publishing society activities in the second quarter of the nineteenth century, apparently influenced by the success of the small and exclusive book clubs. The second period opened with Frederic J. Furnivall's establishment of the Early English Text Society in 1864, when a wholly new scholarly tradition, derived in large part from Germany, not only gave societies once more an excuse for existing, but made them indispensable as an agency for the effective realization of the rapidly expanding aims of contemporary scholarship.

The Royal Society of Literature of the United Kingdom was the only society of the nineteenth century whose position as a chartered society under royal patronage admitted it to the dignity shared by the Royal Society, the Society of Antiquaries, and other learned establishments of their rank. It was also the first important society organized definitely for the purpose of literary study; although, as we shall see, its aims as defined by its charter were rather miscellaneous, and so broad in their scope that it might have been foreseen that the society could not realize a number of its stated objects. In addition, the circumstances of its establishment made its activities, at least during its early period, more pretentious than serious; and it was at first burdened, as all such royal establishments must be to some extent, by a number of aristocratic figureheads. The first officers and council of the society were, in fact, men of title and ecclesiastical dignitaries, with not a single scholar of first rate literary attainments among them. Indeed, the entire constituent membership of the society at that time was distinguished by the almost total absence of names of scholarly prominence. Finally, the extension of the society's activities to the whole domain of literature, both English and foreign, resulted in the distraction of its attention from the revival of interest in Anglo-Saxon, which was at the moment of the society's foundation advancing rapidly in England, and in the concentration of much of its effort upon classical and oriental studies, especially Egyptology. As a significant influence upon English literary scholarship, therefore, the society which, from its name, should have been one of its most active organized forces, was in reality surpassed in activity and importance by a score of unsubsidized and unpatronized volunteer societies. The society remains to-day, in fact, less a really literary society than a dilettante organization for every kind of polite purpose.

This society was planned as early as 1820; the first general meeting was held in 1823, and its charter was granted in 1825.[1] Its declared objects, which promised much to English scholarship, were to promote the publication of valuable manuscripts, and to encourage the search for such materials, "to promote the publication of works of great intrinsic value, but not of so popular a character as to induce the risk of private expense,"[2] "to read at its public

[1] *Transactions of the Royal Society of Literature of the United Kingdom*, v. I, pt. I, London, 1827; *Advertisement*.

[2] One of the most interesting proposals to endow literary labor, and possibly the first fully developed scheme of the sort, is to be found in the plans of the Society for the Establishment of a Literary Fund, which outlined its work in its *Claims of Literature*, London, 1802; 93–163. The society actually distributed upwards of sixteen hundred pounds from the time of its establishment in 1790 to 1802. The present income of the fund is about four thousand pounds.

meetings papers upon subjects of general literature," "to adjudge honorary rewards to persons who shall have rendered any eminent service to literature, or produced any work highly distinguished for learning or genius; provided always, that such work contain nothing hostile to religion or morality," and "to elect, as honorary associates, persons eminent for the pursuit of literature; and from these to select Associates upon the Royal Foundation, or upon the Foundation of the Society, as circumstances may admit."[3]

The last of the society's stated objects was provided for by an appropriation from the Privy Purse of one thousand guineas annually, to be divided between the ten "Royal Associates" named by the society; and in emulation of the monarch's patronage of letters, the society itself elected ten "Honorary Associates," who were to receive the same emolument.[4] The Royal Associates were to be "persons of eminent learning, and authors of some distinguished work of literature." In addition, the society was empowered to award annually two Royal Medals to the writers of remarkable works. The appropriations for the Royal Associates and the Royal Medals, however, were discontinued after the death of George IV. In the period during which both were granted, the Royal Associates had included Coleridge and Malthus, and the Honorary Associates Crabbe and Southey. Among the recipients of the medals were Mitford, Dugald Stewart, Scott, Southey, Crabbe, Washington Irving, and Hallam.[5]

The further activities of the Royal Society of Literature have not placed English scholarship under a very great debt. Its province has at one time or another included the whole of classical and oriental antiquity, British archaeology, political economy, numismatics, history, comparative reli-

---

[3] *Transactions*, v. I, pt. I, vii–viii, 1–2.

[4] *Ibid.*, xiv.

[5] *Biographia Britannica Literaria*, II, [*Advertisement*] iii–iv.

gion, biblical criticism, comparative philology, and geography. Its chief promise of special aid to English letters was its effort to publish a complete *Biographia Britannica Literaria,* which was undertaken under the editorship of Thomas Wright in 1842, and the expenses of which were defrayed from a bequest of five thousand pounds by the Rev. George Richards.[6] This work, however, was never carried beyond the second volume, published in 1846, which brought the undertaking only through the Anglo-Norman period. In addition to this publication the society issued in 1876 a valuable autotype reproduction of the manuscript *Common-Place Book of John Milton,* and in 1897 a facsimile of the Princess Elizabeth's prose translation of Margaret of Navarre's *Mirror of the Sinful Soul.* Latterly the society has given two series of popular lectures, to commemorate the five hundredth anniversary of Chaucer's death, in 1900, and the tercentenary of Milton's birth in 1908. Our final judgment of the society's work, however, must be that in both bulk and quality it suffers by comparison with that of private societies of more serious and concentrated aims.

The first society to limit its field to publications illustrative of the history of English literature was the Percy Society. This society was founded in 1840, as were the Shakespeare and the Parker Societies, and curiously enough, it was dissolved in the very year in which these two societies ceased publication. The question of priority might be disputed between the Percy Society and the Shakespeare Society, but it seems to be generally accepted that to the Percy belongs the distinction of having been the first society to devote itself exclusively to the printing of English texts. In point of value, however, the publications of the Percy Society are much less noteworthy than those of the Shakespeare Society, for the former are by

[6] *Ibid.,* II, iv.

comparison slight, fragmentary, and generally unimposing. The leading workers in both societies were in the main the same, including Thomas Wright, Halliwell, Dyce, and Collier, and less importantly, Rimbault, Cunningham, and Fairholt. The two societies were, however, conducted on quite different principles. The Percy Society was by the nature of its publications more prolific, averaging during its early period one issue a month; the Shakespeare Society, on the other hand, printed works not merely of high value in the aggregate, but almost without exception of the greatest importance each in itself. A point of further difference lies in the fact that the Percy Society, like the earlier general publishing societies, was organized merely for the purposes of publication; the Shakespeare Society, on the other hand, held meetings at which scholarly questions were discussed and critical and historical papers read, and the most valuable of these were published from time to time as the *Shakespeare Society's Papers*. These scholarly meetings, which gave the Shakespeare Society a greater distinction as a veritable learned society, were thought to constitute one of its most important functions.

The Percy Society issued during the thirteen years of its life ninety-four numbers of its publications, with two others that were withdrawn from general circulation. These issues were in the form of thin unbound volumes; for the frequency of their appearance and the relatively small income derived from the modest subscription of only a pound yearly from five hundred members prevented the publications from showing much bookish pretentiousness. The fact that the society was named after the erstwhile Bishop of Dromore implies something as to the nature of the works which it published. Twenty-three of the numbers were made up of popular ballads, songs, carols, and nursery rimes; another twenty-three included tracts, pamphlets, and curious pieces illustrative of manners, tra-

ditions, and customs; fourteen of the numbers were reprints of miscellaneous verse, and nine of Middle English
and Scots poetry, including Hawes's *Pastime of Pleasure,*
selections from Lydgate's minor poems, and Thomas
Wright's new text of the *Canterbury Tales;* five numbers
were interludes and dramatic dialogues, and five medieval
tales and romances. In addition to these there first appeared in the Percy publications Massinger's *Believe as
you List,*[7] Henry Porter's *Two Angry Women of Abing-
don,* Wotton's poems, and Barnfield's *Affectionate Shepherd.* The remaining volumes comprised collections of
proverbs and conceits, scriptural paraphrases, devotional
poetry, Lord Mayors' pageants, and other material.

The Percy Society's product is not to be scorned because
its bulk seems on the surface to be more imposing than its
quality. Since in these productions the objects of the body
were very effectively realized, it would be vain to wish that
the society's aims had been larger or better directed. That
the reading public seemed to feel, however, that the Percy
Society had distinguished itself for industry rather than
solid accomplishment is apparently to be inferred from a
note in the *Athenaeum* in 1855, in reference to the prospective organization of the Warton Club, which was formed
to succeed the Percy Society: "Certainly it will be a relief
to book-buyers to be spared the infliction of another series
so long as that of the Percy Society. Several smaller series

---

[7] In the main, the history of the early societies is one of amicable
relations one with another. Over Croker's edition of this play, however, developed a personal quarrel between Croker and Collier in
which the council of the Percy Society took a part. The dispute
originated in a paper, *On Massinger's Believe as you List* (*The
Shakespeare Society's Papers,* IV, 133–9, 1849), which found a
reply in Croker's anonymous *Remarks on an Article in the Papers
of the Shakespeare Society* [1849].

would be better than one which is altogether indefinite and interminable."[8]

The Shakespeare Society dated its existence from 1840.[9] The prospectus of the society stated its chief object to be "the publication or republication of works connected with and illustrative of the plays of Shakespeare and his contemporaries; and of the rise and progress of the English

[8] *Athenaeum*, May 26, 1855; 609.

[9] The Shakespeare Society of general fame was not the first of its name, or the first, in all probability, to attempt some tangible memorial to Shakspere. As early as 1770, a society of the name existed in Edinburgh, the objects of which were apparently in the main—and like those of the majority of the Scotch clubs of the time—convivial (*Notes and Queries, 2nd Series*, IV, 185–6). The first Shakespeare Society to leave traces of any serious interest in the works of its nominal patron and to issue a publication was probably the Sheffield Shakespeare Club, founded in 1819 as a protest against the fulminations of a local cleric upon the immorality of theatregoing (Sheffield Shakespeare Club, *Proceedings from its commencement in 1819, to January 1829.* Sheffield, 1829; v). This club "bespoke" a play annually, and held dinners in honor of its bard. Its meetings, judging from the reports of them, were of no more impressive dignity than those of the Roxburghe Club immortalized by Haslewood, or the gathering of the Bannatyne Club recorded by Scott, as a wind-up to which Lord Eldin "had a bad fall on the staircase," and Scott himself "did not get to his carriage without a stumble neither." (*Familiar letters of Sir Walter Scott*, 1894; II, 178). The reports of the dinners of the Sheffield Club are, in short, a record of endless toasts, rather undiscriminating praise of the object of their admiration, and small talk upon everything from music to politics. In a word, none of the reminiscences of the Sheffield Shakespeare Club could convince us that it had any project for systematic or serious study of Shakspere. There was also founded an Edinburgh Shakespeare Club in 1820; it must, however, be taken even less seriously than the Sheffield body, for its objects are stated to have been "the cultivation of literary pursuits, and the promotion of sociality and friendship among the members (*Rules and Regulations of the Edinburgh Shakespeare Club and Library*, Edinburgh, 1826). Its title was certainly not intended to suggest a particularly serious attention to any aspect of literary study.

stage and English dramatic poetry, prior to the suppression of theatrical performances in 1647.'' The publications of the society were also to include old plays and tracts, and of the latter especially those which shed light upon Elizabethan stage history. The organization was admittedly modeled after the Camden and Percy Societies: its administration was vested in an elective council of twenty-one members; its dues were only one pound annually; and its publications were to be inexpensive, and for that reason more numerous than would have been the case if the form and character of the book club publications had been followed. A significant provision of the prospectus was that members of the society should be "invited to contribute works for publication.''[10]

The first council of the Shakespeare Society included Thomas Amyot, Campbell, Collier, C. W. Dilke, Dyce, Halliwell, Knight, Macready, Sir Frederic Madden, Milman, and Thomas Wright. Much of the heaviest executive work was carried on by Collier, the first director, and throughout its history altogether the most industrious member of the society. Halliwell and Collier found an outlet in this body for great energies and intense, though possibly unnecessarily spectacular, scholarly application. It must be admitted, indeed, that whatever the shortcomings of these two students were, it was through their efforts particularly that the earlier Shakesperean study of the age secured its impetus and influence.

The Shakespeare Society led an active existence until the year 1851, publishing in this time forty-six volumes; after the society was practically defunct, it issued its final two volumes, which had been previously in preparation, in 1852 and 1853. One volume which the society had in hand at the time of its dissolution was never published; this was

[10] ''*It is acknowledged on all hands*'' . . . [*Prospectus*, 1840].

11

Peter Cunningham's selections from Oldys's notes to Langbaine's *English Dramatick Poets.*

The publications of the Shakespeare Society, it must be remembered, contained material which was then generally unfamiliar. For example, the treatises on the stage by Gosson, Heywood, and Northbrooke, well known as they are to us, were first made popular property through their publication by this society. Their reprints of source plays, pre-Shaksperean plays, Heywood's dramatic works, mystery cycles, and kindred material, though more or less faulty in the eyes of modern scholarship, must be looked upon as opening up to the reading public a field which had been heretofore practically closed. In addition to its reprints, the society published four volumes of its *Papers,* selected from those presented at its meetings. In these volumes is to be found a great deal of historical, interpretative, and illustrative criticism which is less valuable now than it once was merely because it has been absorbed into the traditions of scholarship.

It is unfortunate that much of what might have been the most noteworthy of Collier's labors for the society forms to-day part of the ground upon which his veracity has been impugned. There can scarcely be a doubt that the suspicion which had already begun to attach itself to Collier's work in the fifties was largely responsible for the decline of the Shakespeare Society's activity and the failure of popular support for it.[11] It must also be apparent that

---

[11] It is difficult to find printed evidence of the suspicions of Collier's dishonesty at so early a date, for the public outcry against him did not begin until after the publication of his *Notes and Emendations to the Text of Shakespeare's Plays* in 1852, and the law of libel was then as now probably sufficiently deterrent to prevent the publication of suspicions unbacked by evidence; but in T. Crofton Croker's *Remarks on an Article inserted in the Papers of the Shakespeare Society* [1849] there are undoubted intimations that by this time Collier's discoveries were beginning to be seriously called into question (*op. cit.,* 8, 9, 12).

Halliwell, Knight, and Dyce, who were among the first scholars of the time to express their skepticism as to the authenticity, if not the honesty, of Collier's emendations to Shakspere, must have been impressed by the tone and the evidential value of the criticism which greeted Collier's letters to the *Athenaeum* in 1852;[12] and with faith in the society's most strenuous leader so sadly shattered, and the genuineness of a handful of the society's publications called into open question, it was of course impossible that the remaining workers in the society should continue to appeal to public confidence as they had done for eleven years. It is true that the society's generous scale of publication in its earlier years had impoverished its resources to some extent, for it was necessary for the council to explain upon this ground the appearance of only two volumes for the year 1851;[13] but this does not diminish the importance of the fact that the publications of the society ceased to appear in the year in which the Collier controversy arose, only two volumes, already in preparation, remaining to be issued in the following two years.

The works edited by Collier for the Shakespeare Society which had been suspected are those which contain documents from Dulwich College now proved to have been doctored by Collier; these were the *Memoirs of Edward Alleyn*, *The Alleyn Papers*, and the *Diary of Philip Henslowe*.[14] The results of Collier's misconduct are of course more far-reaching than their effect upon the value of

[12] For an account of the history of Collier's critical forgeries and the ensuing controversies see *Notes on the Life of John Payne Collier* by Henry B. Wheatley, 1884; 30–38, 47–8, 51–67.

[13] *Athenaeum*, May 1, 1852; 490.

[14] The extent of Collier's forgeries is discussed in George F. Warner's *Catalogue of the Dulwich Manuscripts*, and further investigation of the treatment of Henslowe's diary is to be found in Mr. W. W. Greg's new edition of the document.

works which are now known to be unreliable, for all that he produced—including almost half of the Shakespeare Society's publications—must clearly be affected by some degree of uncertainty as to its complete authenticity and accuracy.

The oldest of the societies whose record has been one of unbroken and unterminated service to English scholarship is the Philological Society, organized in 1842.[15] The society's revised rules state that it was formed "for the investigation of the structure, the affinities, and the history of languages; and the philological illustration of the classical writers of Greece and Rome;" the special reference to the domain of classical philology, however, was by resolution omitted in 1878. The constituent members of the society numbered upwards of two hundred, among whom the most conspicuous in English studies were Bosworth, Garnett, Hallam, Kemble, Thorpe, and Trench. In the beginning, however, none of these distinguished scholars was as active as two others probably less accomplished, Edwin Guest and Hensleigh Wedgwood, both of whom contributed numerous papers on syntax and special etymologies to the *Proceedings* and the later *Transactions*. These records of the meetings of the society contained from its early years useful articles on English dialects, Anglo-Saxon and Middle English grammar, place, animal, and plant names, and etymologies; interest in the English field, which was at first overshadowed by that in classical philology and anomalous tongues, increasing until it became the first concern of the organization.

[15] There were without question other philological societies of similar aims in active organization before this date; but although some of them were known to the members of the Philological Society, their records have apparently disappeared. A sketch of the history of a single one, the Etymological Society at Cambridge, which published some of its papers—in part on English subjects—in the short lived *Philological Museum*, may be found in the *Proceedings of the Philological Society*, V, 133–42 (1854).

The last and the present generation of English scholars began to enter the society soon after its foundation, Furnivall, Wheatley, Morris, Ellis, and Sweet beginning their contributions in the sixties, and Murray and Skeat in the following decade. The infusion of new blood, which brought with it enthusiasms and not unrealizable dreams, turned the society eventually into the channels of activity which have brought it its greatest usefulness and distinction: textual publication, spelling reform, and most importantly, the stupendous project for an historical English dictionary.

The publication of the dictionary was first proposed by Richard Chenevix Trench, an English scholar of considerable note, in 1857, and was urged in two papers read before the society in 1858, *On some Deficiencies in our English Dictionaries.* The principal points in these two papers were those which determined the attitude of the society upon the subject of a dictionary from this time on: that a dictionary should be complete, and should exercise no principle of exclusion for the purpose of establishing a puristic standard, or upon grounds of obsoleteness, foreignism, or localism; and that it should treat extensively etymological history and relationships. Trench's original proposal, however, contemplated only a supplement to the dictionaries of Johnson and Richardson, and when work was undertaken by the society, it was for that purpose. But after an extended analysis, by over one hundred collectors, of the most typical materials for further etymological studies, it was thought that the magnitude of the work upon which the society found itself actually embarked called for a completely new lexicon upon scientific principles. To this end, two committees were appointed, one Literary and Historical, composed of Trench, Furnivall, and Herbert Coleridge, and the other Etymological, including Hensleigh

Wedgwood and Prof. Henry Malden, a classical scholar.[16]

The system of work upon the dictionary was to be volunteer coöperation, especially for the work of collecting illustrative quotations. There were to be readers of examples of English from all periods subsequent to the decline of Anglo-Saxon, and sub-editors for the arrangement of the materials alphabetically and historically. For this purpose lengthy and specific rules for the guidance of collectors were drawn up, and the arrangement of the dictionary was outlined in the *Canones Lexicographici* in 1860. As the dictionary was at first planned, it was to consist of three parts: a main non-technical section, a section of technical and scientific terms and proper names, and an etymological appendix. This plan was, however, ultimately abandoned. After 1861, when Coleridge died, Furnivall carried much of the work of collection and arrangement upon his own shoulders. But in 1876, when he had a few publishing societies upon his hands (and the first impulse to his revival of the publishing society plan came from his wish to make available in print the materials for the Middle English portion of the dictionary), he proposed placing the work under the supervision of a special editor.[17] Dr. J. A. H. Murray was appointed to this position in 1878.

In 1879 Murray announced[18] that contracts with the Delegates of the Clarendon Press had been signed early in that year, and gave at the same time a highly interesting picture of the extended and careful preparations for the reception, classification, and digestion of the raw material, and of the varied and complicated problems which presented themselves when the undertaking was actually under

[16] *Proposal for the Publication of a new English Dictionary by the Philological Society*, 1859; 1–2.

[17] *Frederick James Furnivall, a Volume of personal Record*, 1911; xliv.

[18] *Transactions of the Philological Society*, 1877–8–9; 567–86.

way. The society in the meantime had been incorporated for the purposes of the contract. The contract itself excited some little comment among the members of the society, Furnivall and Sweet objecting strenuously to the small percentage of the profits of the enterprise which was to fall to the society; but it was accepted by the society in consideration of the large advance which the Press was required to make for initial expenses, and of the difficulty which the society had already had in getting any publisher to undertake a work of the magnitude they wished.[19] As it was, the Clarendon Press contracted for a dictionary of between six and seven thousand pages, limiting considerably the scope of the etymological portion as it had been originally planned; and the society, therefore, reserved the right to publish after the completion of this first dictionary an expanded dictionary of about ten volumes of sixteen hundred pages each. The contract stipulated that three years should be spent upon the accumulation and arrangement of material, and that the dictionary should be completed within ten years after the actual beginning of publication.

In 1879, then, the real work of the editor was begun; but it was found immediately that there were large hiatuses in the material already collected, and for this reason renewed appeals were made for readers. When it was considered that the preliminary work for the first parts was completed, the apparatus consisted of over three million quotations from five thousand authors, which had been collected by thirteen hundred readers. The sub-editors who had given gratuitous service to the project then numbered thirty.[20] The delays in the progress of the work,

[19] *Ibid., App.*, xv–xviii. A copy of the contract itself is to be found in *App.*, xlix–lix.

[20] *A New English Dictionary on Historical Principles founded mainly on the Materials collected by the Philological Society*, I, v–vii, 1888.

however, were much greater than any of the workers concerned had anticipated; for the general magnitude of the labor, and the care necessary in completing information and settling points in word history, had occasioned serious stoppages in the machinery.[21] The first copy was finally sent to the press in 1882, the first part was issued in 1884, and the first volume was completed in 1888. The work has to-day progressed almost through the ninth volume, with a single volume necessary to complete it. In spite of the fact that it has not been constructed upon the scale which the society at first intended, it represents in extent and convenience of arrangement an achievement quite unparalleled. Indeed, it is as far in advance of the other two great national dictionaries, Littré's and Grimm's, as these are superior to their predecessors.

It was through the recognition of the need of more Middle English texts in the compilation of the dictionary that Furnivall first secured the Philological Society's approval of a plan for the publication of desirable English texts. In this way were issued in 1862 Furnivall's *Early English Poems and Lives of Saints,* and Morris's edition of the *Liber Cure Cocorum,* in 1863 Morris's edition of Richard Rolle of Hampole's *Pricke of Conscience,* and in 1864 a fourteenth century *Castel of Loue,* translated from Grosseteste, edited by R. F. Weymouth. The society's lack of funds, however, prevented its continuing such work,[22] and the Early English Text Society was accordingly organized by Furnivall in 1864 to carry on the undertaking.

In 1869 Danby P. Fry, one of the members of the Philological Society, endeavored to induce the society to institute some methods of reform in English orthography. A com-

21 *Transactions of the Philological Society,* 1882–4, 508 sq.
22 *Transactions of the Philological Society,* 1873–4, 236.

mittee was appointed, consisting of Ellis, Morris, Joseph Payne, Russell Martineau, Fry, and later Wheatley and Murray, to report upon the question, but the members were unable to agree upon a course of action.[23] After the committee was dissolved, Fry and Ellis submitted two proposals, embodying their individual ideas of the direction and extent of revision,[24] but the matter soon ceased to engage the serious attention of the members. After attempts at spelling reform in America had brought the matter once more before the Philological Society's notice, Dr. Murray made the question one of the points of his presidential address in 1880.[25] He did not favor a wholesale amendment, for, as he put the matter in his own words, "My own opinion is that at present and for a long time to come, until indeed the general principles of phonology are understood by men of education, no complete or systematic scheme of spelling reform has the least chance of being adopted in this country, and I do not think that the promulgation or advocacy of such bears any practical fruit." He did, however, favor action on the part of the society, "representing the English scholarship of the country," to the end of issuing a list of amended spellings, the alterations in which should be confined to "the omission of such letters as are both unphonetic and unhistoric, and for which no so-called etymological plea can be submitted." Following these recommendations, Henry Sweet issued as a basis for discussion some notes upon suggested changes,[26] and after two meetings of debate on the subject, the society printed its *Partial Corections of English Spellings aproovd by the Philological Society.*[27] Although from this time on, many

[23] *Transactions of the Philological Society, 1870–72,* 19.
[24] *Ibid.,* 17–88, 89–118.
[25] *Transactions of the Philological Society, 1880–1;* 139–155.
[26] *Ibid., App.,* *65–*89.
[27] *Ibid., Supplement,* 1–38.

individual members used the corrected spellings, the position which the society was courageous and confident enough to take seemed to have very little influence upon English usage generally. The matter slept, therefore, until Henry Bradley, in his presidential address in 1892,[28] gave it as his opinion that the whole project is really not as simple as most of his colleagues assumed, that after all the older spellings do convey somewhat adequately useful suggestions of etymological history, and that this fact, especially in a tongue so rich in technical and other special word constructions, is of more practical significance than most of the reformers seem willing to admit. Since this time the society has given no important formal expression of its attitude on the still seriously debated question.

The Philological Society continues to-day as one of the most vital forces in English scholarship; and its *Transactions* continue to publish much of the highest value in literary, but more especially linguistic, study, by the most capable English scholars of our day. When we consider that from the Philological Society actually sprang Furnivall's project for the Early English Text Society, and indirectly his other publishing society schemes, and Ellis and Skeat's plan for the English Dialect Society, it must be admitted that in the actual extent of its influence, if not in the bulk of its published results, this society has been the most powerful and fruitful organized aid to English scholarship that the last century produced.

The Aelfric Society, which was founded in 1843, outlined in its prospectus a much more modest program than had been attempted as yet by any publishing society.[29] Its plan was to publish "those Anglo-Saxon literary remains which have either not yet been given to the world, or of

[28] *Transactions of the Philological Society*, 1891–4, 263–6.
[29] "*It is proposed to establish* . . . " [*Prospectus*, 1842 ?].

which a more correct and convenient edition may be deemed desirable.'' The first class of its proposed publications was to include the Anglo-Saxon homilies and lives of saints, and the second class the *Anglo-Saxon Chronicle* and Alfred's Bede and Orosius. It was considered that the undertaking could be carried to completion in four years, and at a cost of about five pounds a member if a hundred members were secured. The society actually opened its existence, however, with less than half that number.[30] On the first membership list appeared the names of Bosworth, Kemble, Madden, Thorpe, and R. M. White; the remaining members included a generous proportion of clergymen, schoolmasters, and amateur antiquaries. It can be seen, therefore, that the society quite failed to excite anything like a general interest in its plans.

The publications of the Aelfric Society were issued in parts, with translations of the texts. All of its program that was completed was Thorpe's *Homilies of the Anglo-Saxon Church,* in ten parts, 1843–6, Kemble's *Poetry of the Codex Vercellensis,* in two parts, 1844–56, and *The Anglo-Saxon Dialogues of Solomon and Saturnus and Adrian and Ritheus,* in three parts, 1845–6. Upon the issuance of the second part of the Vercelli Book in 1856, the society was dissolved.[31]

No new literary club was organized in England for another eleven years, when the Warton Club appeared in 1854. Its first volume was issued in the following year. This club was designed to succeed the Percy Society, discontinued in the preceding year, although it was to have only two hundred members, as against the Percy's five hundred. A curious fact in relation to this body is that its existence was planned to terminate at the end of six

---

[30] *Aelfric Society for the Illustration of English History and Philology* [*Announcement*, 1843].

[31] H. G. Bohn, Appendix to Lowndes' *Bibliographer's Manual*, 67.

years, an assurance that was evidently intended to antici-
pate objections to a series of publications of undetermined
length and inclusiveness. Thomas Wright and Halliwell
appear again as the promotors of the new society, which
was to be administered in a novel and in some respects ob-
jectionable manner. It was, as the *Athenaeum* reviewed
the scheme, "to be entirely under the management of a
committee of 'six gentlemen,' who announce in their prospectus that they are 'known for their attainments in this
branch of literature.' There are to be no general meetings,
no president, no treasurer, no secretary, no auditors of
accounts, none of 'the forms of a society.' The 'six gentlemen' are to be a Permanent Committee, and nobody else is
to say a word."[32]　The proposed object of the club seems to
have been "the reprinting of such rare but well chosen
tracts by Greene, Nash, Breton, Taylor the Water Poet, &c.,
as afford valuable illustration of manners, or are interesting in any other point of view."[33]　The club, however, did
not realize any of these specific purposes; in fact, it did
not live out its predetermined existence, for with the publication of the Anglo-Norman text of *Fulke Fitz-Warine*, the
Latin Exercises of Mary Queen of Scots, and two fifteenth
century miscellany manuscripts, the Warton Club came to
an end in 1856.

The foundation of the Early English Text Society in
1864 marks the beginning of a remarkable revival in literary society activity.[34]　No large or influential English
society had been founded since the Percy and Shakespeare

[32] *Athenaeum*, May 26, 1855, 609.

[33] *Notes and Queries, 1st Series*, V, 238.

[34] A large part of my information as to the Early English Text
Society has been taken from the annual announcements, especially
from that for November, 1911. For further facts, particularly with
reference to the society's fiscal organization, I am under obligation
to W. A. Dalziel, Esquire, the Honorary Secretary.

Societies in 1840, but a number of efficient organizations, many of them the creations of the founder of the Early English Text Society, took example from the success of this project and lived long and energetic lives. Of the private societies for the furtherance of literary scholarship which had preceded it, none were still in existence save the Philological Society, and the field of this society was divided with the study of other tongues. The decline of the early societies which published English texts is without doubt to be assigned primarily to the wane of the first vogue of the society idea; but it was probably accelerated also by the personal scandal which became associated with the most prominent of all, the Shakespeare Society. It is probably true, in addition, that since the earlier text societies had exploited the Elizabethan field fairly thoroughly, there was little reason or incentive as yet for the exploration of the provinces of Old and Middle English—which had without question failed to appeal to more than a narrowly confined interest—until the actual necessity of publishing the earlier materials loomed large in the minds of scholars.

As Scott had received the dilettante club idea and converted it into something more generous and practical, and as Halliwell, Collier, and Thomas Wright had dominated, with good purpose, and to good ends, the later democratic societies, Furnivall revived the scheme, so common in the eighteenth century days of publication by subscription, of providing a market for a needed series of reprints which could not have been supported by the conditions of everyday publication, and organized a society upon the plainest and simplest business proposition: "I'll furnish the books if you'll pay for them." It may be said of the Early English Text Society, as of most of the other societies which Furnivall founded, that it was *his* society from the day of its organization to the day of his death.

This society, however, even though it was primarily a business proposition pure and simple, was not without a basis of sentiment, and this Furnivall did all he could to foster. Its origin, as has been seen, lay in Furnivall's desire to make accessible the bulk of the unprinted and scarce linguistic material which should properly form the foundation of the Philological Society's projected etymological dictionary.[35] It could scarcely be hoped that the class of literary material promised by such a plan could by the remotest possibility appeal to anything like a general literary taste. The society began in fact with one hundred and thirty-seven members, and now after very nearly a half-century it numbers scarcely over three hundred. There is real cause for remark in the fact that the membership of a society of such illustrious aims and attainments should compare so unfavorably with that of some of the earlier publishing societies, which in a few cases exceeded a thousand. But the reasons for the marked difference seem simple and obvious. In the first place, the objects of the Shakespeare and Percy Societies, and in their own fields, of the Camden and Parker Societies, after all were intended to appeal to a taste that had been under popular cultivation for a comparatively long time; but the publications of the new society could appeal continuously only to scholars of special training. On this point there was really little to justify the querulous complaint that Furnivall published in his announcements from year to year, that "the society's experience has shown the very small number of those inheritors of the speech of Cynewulf, Chaucer, and Shakspere, who care two guineas a year for the records of that speech." The society's publications were to have, and have had, little to do with Shakspere; most Englishmen "have a feeling for" Chaucer, but not for the

[35] *Ante*, 150, 152.

majority of his contemporaries; Cynewulf is a name without meaning for the great number. If this were all there were to be said for or against the project from the standpoint of its failure in popular appeal, the plea might not be unjustified; but to ask an Englishman, even with a well developed respect for his national traditions, to take with his Chaucer and Cynewulf reams upon reams of homilies, dull metrical romances, interminable didactic poems, saints' lives, cook books, and surgical treatises, was and is unreasonable. The society has received fair support from the classes of subscribers whose wants it might be expected to fill—trained philologists and institutions; but it has never succeeded in its general appeals to readers at large, chiefly because these appeals are not grounded in reason. There may have been more substance in Furnivall's characteristically direct comparison: ''it is nothing less than a scandal that the Hellenic Society should have over a thousand members, while the Early English Text Society has not three hundred.'' The complaint itself is the best evidence in the world that for most educated people a dead language which has no important traditional culture associated with it is indeed a very dead thing. And whatever enters most significantly into the general cultural traditions of our day, it is not derived from any intellectual force of medieval England or Anglo-Saxon England.[36]

[36] That Furnivall started his project in the face of a really profound lack of interest in and preparation for ancient English literature seems to be attested by the tone of some of the early reviews of the society's publications. For example, the *Saturday Review's* judgments (November 5, 1864) upon the first two books issued by the society: With reference to Furnivall's *Arthur*, ''As matters of philological study, we are ready to receive texts about King Arthur or about any other subject under heaven; but in any other point of view, we must confess that we are tired of King Arthur. . . . We must confess that we do not enter into the apparently prevalent love of everything Arthurian for its own sake.'' And with regard to

Another thing which without question affected the success of the Early English Text Society was Furnivall's personality. As strongly endeared as he was to his near friends by exceptional personal qualities, he possessed other qualities—summed up in the word "bumptiousness" by one of the distinguished English scholars of the time who could not work in harmony with him—which cost him the affection, and even the tolerance, of many men of attainments who otherwise would probably have been glad to aid his projects. His constant bullying, for instance, of some of the old Shakespeare Society group, must have prejudiced his undertakings in the public mind and made him appear as a rather irritating apostle of scholarly integrity. His complete autocracy, also, in practically all of his society schemes, while it may have been in part necessary to their continued existence, was probably a source of occasional pain even to his collaborators.[37]

But even though Furnivall's reiterated protests against the general lack of popular interest in English literary antiquities may not have been wholly justified by the conditions of the society's organization and administration, and the nature of the texts which it was its business to pro-

Morris's *Early English Alliterative Poems:* "The first poem, called by Mr. Morris 'The Pearl,' is one of those visions of Paradise of which we have already seen so many. . . . What strikes the ordinary reader at first sight is the extreme difficulty, and what we would call the uncouthness, of language in these poems."

[37] I am not speaking wholly at random here. A collection of correspondence to and from the Rev. Joseph Woodfall Ebsworth, which is now in my possession, contains comments from Furnivall's acquaintances upon the value of the personal equation in the Furnivall projects which are not strictly in harmony with the opinions expressed by his friends in the memorial volume. I intimate this not from any desire to quarrel with the common judgment of a great character, but to suggest what seems one clear reason why his societies were in comparison with other societies of similar objects, both before and since, relatively weakly supported.

duce, it must be said that the setting afoot and successful conduct not merely of the Early English Text Society, but, in time, of the Ballad and Chaucer Societies, the New Shakspere Society, the Browning Society and the Wiclif Society, was a task which required Atlantean strength and energy, not to say unquestioned scholarly attainments and high executive capacity. It is to be doubted whether anyone other than Furnivall could at this time, in the face of slow interest and a variety of discouragements, have carried through such a series of editorial and administrative labors over so long a period of years. The Early English Text Society was from the date of its foundation until Furnivall's death in 1910 under his directorship; which is to say that practically the entire history of the society is a history of his personal labors for it.

In the Original Series of the society's publications, which opened at a guinea a year at the time of the society's foundation, there have appeared in forty-eight years one hundred and forty-three numbers. In the Extra Series, which was opened in 1867, there have appeared one hundred and nine numbers. This series was issued for the reprinting of black letter books and already published manuscripts which were either scarce or inadequately edited. To indicate even in the most general fashion the variety and extent of the society's work would be to give a bibliography of its publications; and this, fortunately, is issued annually in satisfactory form by the society itself. The society has, in a word, already printed the bulk of important Old and Middle English literature, exclusive of Chaucer and ballad material; so its work of the present and future is less within the purely literary field than formerly, and within that field is being given over inevitably to what must be regarded as of secondary value or interest. Its most monumental publications are *Merlin*, Lyndesay's works, Skeat's edition of *Piers Plowman* (since revised for the Clarendon

12

Press), the *Cursor Mundi* in four texts, the *Blickling Homilies*, Aelfric's *Metrical Lives of Saints*, the Old English version of Bede's *Ecclesiastical History*, and the autotype edition of the Beowulf manuscript. The most important publications in the Extra Series are probably Ellis's *Early English Pronunciation*, Barbour's *Bruce*, Lovelich's *Holy Grail*, the *Charlemagne Romances*, many of the extant mystery cycles and fragments, Hoccleve's works, and Lydgate's works. These suggestions of what may be merely of the greatest intrinsic value and scholarly magnitude among the society's publications serve at least to emphasize by omission the importance of the vast body of poetry, philosophy, romances, saints' lives, books of manners, homilies, scriptural paraphrases, moral and devotional works, and miscellaneous treatises which have not been named.

The workers engaged upon the Early English Text Society's publications have included most of the distinguished English scholars of recent years. To enumerate them would be to run through a list of scholarly names of late or present prominence. A substantial measure of what the society has actually accomplished for English literature and linguistics is to be found in its statement of the year 1911 that the publications had to that date covered a cost of over thirty thousand pounds. For the future the society announces that at the present rate of production it has in preparation or prospect material sufficient for fifty years to come; and the amount of work which the society feels it ought to undertake would require a century or two of publication after the appearance of what is at present upon its lists. A point of generosity—and probably well rewarded generosity—in the Early English Text Society's plans is that its back volumes are for sale to non-members at an advance of fifty percent over their cost to members.

This provision gives the society a greater range of public usefulness than any of the older societies or most of those of the present day possess.

The form of organization of the Early English Text Society furnishes in general the model for most of Furnivall's later societies, that is, for all the remaining text societies founded before the close of the nineteenth century save the Spenser Society, the Hunterian Club, and the Scottish Text Society. These societies of Furnivall's have been very close corporations; it would be scarcely accurate to call their form of organization even oligarchic, though the control of the Early English Text Society, as the type, is nominally vested in a Committee of Management of about twenty members. The exigencies of wholesale publication such as Furnivall planned have always, of course, required extensive collaboration and administrative responsibility on the part of a large number of gifted co-workers; but it has been generally understood that the founder and director of the Early English Text Society was not merely a nominal head. As for the administrative arrangements of the society, the Committee of Management possesses all the governing powers of the body—fiscal, editorial, and executive; the members possess no voting powers. The executive body is self-continuing; it selects the society's publications, appoints its editors, makes no provision for recommendation by subscribers of works which they may think it advisable to undertake, and allows the members no judgment upon the works proposed. All this contrasts rather strongly with the custom of the Bannatyne Club, which published at intervals lists of desiderata, and made the vote of the members the final word upon what the society should undertake; it is in just as strong contrast to the administrative policies of the Camden Society, the Shakespeare Society, and the Scottish Text Society, for instance, all of which constantly solicited from their members suggestions and advice. There is, however, it must be admitted, a patent difference between the aims of the Early English Text Society and of most of the other text societies; and this difference may justify a special and undemocratic kind of organization. In the societies whose activities have been compared with those of the Early English Text Society the principle underlying the selection of the works to be printed has been established upon the clear consideration that whatever was to be published could be no more than representative or illustrative of a very large field of choice. The Early English Text Society, however, set out from the beginning to print an entire *corpus* of early and middle English literature and linguistic material; and for this reason the questions of selection and order of publication were clearly secondary to the necessity of accepting special opportunities—editorial proposals, offers of manuscripts or copies, and so on. Indeed, it may be that the founder of the Early English Text Society foresaw that if his subscribers were left to choose their publications, the "plums" might have been quickly harvested, and an impoverished body might have been forced to struggle unsupported through the task of publishing a quantity of material pronouncedly lacking in popular appeal, or even have been obliged to abandon its scheme in the end. Its plan, then, which was to offer everything as it came, with the understanding that in the end everything was to be produced, contains no elements of real unfairness; in fact, the society's willingness to sell copies of its works to outsiders upon reasonable terms is a concession to purely popular demands which it was not required, in the chosen nature of its work, to make, but which has justified more than anything else its appeal for extended popular support.

The Spenser Society, which, curiously enough, issued

none of Spenser's works,[38] was formed in Manchester in 1866[39] with James Crossley, a local scholar and antiquary of recognized gifts, as its first president. He was succeeded upon his death by A. W. Ward. The announced purpose of the society was "the reprinting of the rarer poetical literature of the sixteenth and seventeenth centuries."[40] A notable departure from the aims of any scholarly organization hitherto existing, however, was its resolution "to reprint the works of each author in as complete a form as possible." The society was to be limited to two hundred members, and its issues were to be of an expensive character. The dress finally chosen for the publications was a small quarto on a curious ribbed paper, with reprints in folio of the works which had been originally issued in that form. In the first year of publication, 1867, the membership lists were closed with the number provided for.[41] The publications of the society consist of two series, the Original Series containing forty-seven volumes, and the New Series six volumes, with two extra ones. The issues comprised the complete works of John Taylor the Water Poet, Michael Drayton, and George Wither, the non-dramatic works of John Heywood, and separate pieces by Alexander Barclay, Bodenham, and Churchyard. The society was closed in 1894,[42] its last volume, Oliver Elton's *Introduction to Michael Drayton*, the only purely critical volume published by the society, appearing in the following year. The reprints of the Spenser Society were produced upon a high plane of

[38] The society received an apportionment of Grosart's edition of Spenser, but with the editing of this work the society had of course nothing to do.

[39] *Dic. Nat. Biog.*, XIII, 229.

[40] *Notes and Queries, 3rd Series*, XI, 308.

[41] *Athenaeum*, June 15, 1867, 792.

[42] *Athenaeum*, October 13, 1894, 496.

textual accuracy and general excellence; in fact, with the Hunterian Club, this society is the best example of the purely amateur type of organization, which, combining the aims and methods of both the dilettante clubs and the scholarly societies, achieve work which is at once of the highest practical value and the greatest aesthetic attraction.

The work of Hales and Furnivall upon the *Percy Folio Manuscript* in 1867 brought to Furnivall the plan of founding a society for the publication of all the extant English ballad material.[43] The Ballad Society was therefore advertised to commence publication in 1868. The Pepys collection at Magdalene College, Cambridge, the largest in existence, was the one which Furnivall wished to attack first; he accordingly proposed to the Fellows of Magdalene that they should act in union with the Ballad Society for the publication of their collection; but his proposal was rejected.[44] William Chappell then undertook to edit the Roxburghe collection, but he insisted that the entire body of these ballads should be copied before publication was begun; so in the meantime Furnivall himself began the publications of the society with his series of classified *Ballads from Manuscripts,* the first part of which appeared in 1868. The first number of Chappell's *Roxburghe Ballads* came out in the following year, and publication went on apace, Furnivall's issue of *Captain Cox's Ballads* appearing in 1871, his *Love Poems and Humorous Ones* in 1874, and J. W. Ebsworth's *Bagford Ballads* in 1877 and 1878. Chappell's declining health had meanwhile compelled him to stop work upon the completion of the third volume of the *Roxburghe Ballads* and Ebsworth took up the work from this point. From this time on, Ebsworth was the sole editor of all that came from the

[43] *Bishop Percy's Folio Manuscript,* edited by John W. Hales and Frederick J. Furnivall, 1867–8; I, xxv–xxvi.

[44] [*Announcement of the Ballad Society,* 1878.]

society, the remaining five (really six) volumes of the *Roxburghe Ballads* taking up exclusively all the time and money of the society after the *Bagford Ballads* were completed. The twenty-fifth and final part of the *Roxburghe Ballads*, which was the last of the society's issues, was published in 1899, thirty years after the opening of publication. A general index to this collection which Ebsworth had in preparation did not receive enough subscriptions to permit its publication,[45] and an edition of Civil War Ballads which he was to have undertaken was carried no further than the announcement.

The Ballad Society is a rather striking example of the eventual failure of a society not founded upon a genuinely collaborative basis. From the beginning Furnivall was the nominal head of the society, but from 1875 on Ebsworth was the really responsible head, and carried all the editorial work quite unaided, as he said to his friends and to the public in his valedictory notes. The society when it commenced publication in 1868 had very nearly two hundred members; but, Ebsworth says, the first income "was frittered away in payments to incompetent copyists, of texts that would not be needed for a score of years," and considerable portions of which were not to be used at all; and "the most wasteful extravagance of space was persisted in" in the early publications.[46] In 1880, when only the *Roxburghe Ballads* remained to be completed, the membership had decreased to about one hundred and thirty, and for the concluding number of the *Roxburghe Ballads* there were considerably less than one hundred subscribers. All this seems to speak of weak administrative methods; we may take Ebsworth's word for it. But it reflected also poor editorial policies on Ebsworth's part. Not taking to

[45] *The Roxburghe Ballads*, VIII–IX, 878.
[46] *The Roxburghe Ballads*, Preface to Part XXV, viii**–ix**.

heart the admonition of the editor of *Notes and Queries,*
who found fault with the bulky critical apparatus of the
first of the society's volumes,[47] Ebsworth loaded down his
books with useless and facetious (and latterly mis-
ogynistical) comment, fragmentary quotations, editorial
confidences, doggerel of his own, and a thousand needless
editorial obstructions of all kinds. The quality of the
work, in comparison with that of the Early English Text
Society and the Chaucer Society, could have been only dis-
appointing to those who had supported the enterprise;
and it can not be questioned that these silly extravagances
cost him many subscribers. It was apparent for many
years, therefore, that the Ballad Society could not outlive
the completion of the monumental work then in hand, and
it passed away when the Roxburghe collection was printed
off.

The Chaucer Society, Furnivall's third society project,
was established in the same year as the Ballad Society, and
has led an industrious and thoroughly useful existence
ever since. Furnivall served as administrative head of this
society until his death, and was the responsible editor of
most of its publications. Upon his death he was succeeded
by Professor Skeat. Since the society had by this time
completed most of the important textual work which it had
undertaken, its textual publications, which constituted its
First Series, had been for some time appearing at wider
intervals; and its works upon sources, analogues, language,
chronology, contemporary illustration, social studies, por-
traits, and syntax, to which its Second Series was devoted,
had been taking up a larger proportion of its time and
effort. The great work of this society was its publication
of the six parallel text edition of the Ellesmere, Hengwrt,
Cambridge, Corpus, Petworth, and Lansdowne manuscripts

[47] *Notes and Queries, Fourth Series,* III, 255.

of the *Canterbury Tales*. These texts were also reprinted separately, with the addition of the Harleian and Cambridge Dd manuscripts. The ninety-seven volumes of the First Series contain also all the manuscripts of the minor poems, in parallel and separate texts, a parallel text edition of *Troylus and Criseyde, The Romaunt of the Rose, Boethius, The Treatise on the Astrolabe,* autotypes of manuscripts, rime indexes, and related material. Among the prominent contributors to the special publications of the Second Series were Skeat, Koch, Littlehales, Kittredge, Spielman, and Ellis. The dissolution of the Chaucer Society was announced in 1912.

The moving spirits of the Hunterian Club, of Glasgow, which began its publishing activities in 1871, were members of the faculty of the University; the name of the society, in fact, was taken from that of the University library and museum. The club limited its membership to two hundred, and printed only ten copies of its publications in excess of this number. The aims of the club were apparently not social. Its membership was gathered largely in and about Glasgow, but included a number of outside subscribers, among them Collier, Halliwell, Grosart, and Furnivall. None of these prominent scholars, however, were directly concerned with the issuance of the club's publications; these were produced almost entirely through the efforts of local students. David Laing, who edited three gift-books for the society, was, curiously enough, never a member, although there seems to have been the best of feeling between this patriarch of Northern scholarship and the club. One detail of the club's aim was unique as a society project, in that it contemplated issuing all of its texts in fac-simile, as far as the necessity of setting up the texts in type would permit. The first works undertaken by the club were those of Samuel Rowlands, which began to appear in 1871 and were completed in 1880. Of equal importance with the club's edition of Rowlands's tracts is its edition of Thomas Lodge. Its most important and extensive work, however, was the reproduction of the entire Bannatyne manuscript, with some of the old Bannatyne Club's critical apparatus, but without excisions or changes of any sort. The first number of this publication was put out in 1873, and the seventh, which completed the reprint itself, in 1881. The glossary to the work was not issued until 1894, six years after the club had practically ceased to exist.

When the Hunterian Club was nearing the end of its publication of the Bannatyne Manuscript, it decided to rest upon the achievements of the past. In the whole period of its activity it had shown an enviable industry and scholarly responsibility; but from the fact that its membership never reached the expectations of the founders, it is probably safe to assume that the financial affairs of the body were a source of pretty constant anxiety on the part of the administrative officers. That the society accomplished so much systematic and entirely finished work is, in view of its small numbers, really remarkable. There is probably no body of its kind throughout the century which, proportionately to the brief period of the Hunterian's existence, succeeded in producing in all of. its publication from first to last so much of intrinsic worth with scholarly accuracy and unimpeachable taste in book making. The club, in short, appropriated what was happiest and most useful in both the bibliophile clubs and the printing societies.

It is regrettable, in view of what the Hunterian Club accomplished, that the closing of its activities should be marked by an extraordinary instance of the essential narrowness of the bibliophile instinct. In giving notice of the discontinuance of the club after the completion of the Bannatyne volumes, the *Eighth Annual Report* in-

formed the members that "the Council has further decided
that all previous issues remaining in stock after the 1st of
July, 1888, shall be destroyed, so as effectually to prevent
any of the club's publications finding their way into the
book market as remainders."[48] It is difficult to excuse this
kind of action under any conditions; still there is a trace
of justice in the council's explanation that it would be un-
fair to the members who had borne the pains and expenses
of publication if a large quantity of their product should
be thrown for a trifling price into the hands of those who
had stood aloof from the enterprise when it had entailed
a degree of personal and financial sacrifice.

In the autumn of 1873 Furnivall published his prospectus for a New Shakspere Society. This document is a
rather interestingly thorough-going Furnivallian piece. It
begins with the characteristic appeal to the national
honor,[49] and defines a field of activities for the society's
entire existence; which was in short the establishment of
a Shakspere canon of authorship and chronology. The
society's principal publications were to comprise parallel
reprints of the quartos and folios, and possibly a critical
edition of Shakspere's works and a biography; although
Furnivall apparently intended to attempt little with the
Shakspere text, upon which, said he, "there will not be
much to do, thanks to the labours of the many distinguisht

[48] *Hunterian Club, Eighth Annual Report* [1887], 3.

[49] "It is a disgrace to England that while Germany can boast of a
Shakspere Society which has gathered into itself all its country's
choicest scholars, England is now without such a society. It is a
disgrace, again, to England that even now, 257 years after Shakspere's death, the study of him has been so narrow, and the criticism
so wooden, that no book by any Englishman exists which deals in any
worthy manner with Shakspere as a whole, which tracks the rise and
growth of his genius from the boyish romanticism or the sharp
young-mannishness of his early plays, to the magnificence, the
splendour, the divine intuition, which mark his ripest works."

scholars who have so long and so faithfully workt at it.''
Incidentally, the society was to take up conjectural readings, pronunciation, ''under Ellis's leadership,'' and
Shaksperean spelling. Tennyson was first offered the position of Honorary President, but declined; so the presidency
of the society remained unfilled until 1879, when Browning accepted it. A long list of honorary vice-presidents
included the best known English, German, and American
scholars of the time, with a sprinkling of distinguished
men from other professional walks. Furnivall insisted from
the first that German scholarship was to form the basis
and method of the society's entire work; so the *Saturday
Review* ventured to admonish him that ''caution would be
more necessary than any other quality in the prosecution
of this cardinal part of the society's labors,'' continuing
with a gentle *argumentum ad personam:* ''The caution is
perhaps more needed here than in Germany; for English
literary men are apt, like English men of science, to sit
down in companies and to overrate the necessity of supporting the views of 'authority.' It may be all very well
for Mr. Furnivall to inform us that Mr. Tennyson 'tells'
him that Fletcher's hand 'workt out Shakspere's original
conception' of *Henry VIII.* We are well aware that Mr.
Tennyson is 'the greatest living poet in England,' but still
we venture to ask, If Mr. Tennyson told Mr. Furnivall, who
told Mr. Tennyson?''[50]

The society was to maintain an active interest in its
work by regular meetings, with papers and discussions,
''the papers being shorter, and the discussions much fuller,
than in other bodies.'' The proceedings of the meetings
were to be chronicled in the *Transactions* of the society,
which were to form the First Series of the society's publications. The other series of the publications were to be

[50] XXXVII, 12; January 3, 1874.

divided into seven classes. The Second Series was to include the original quarto and folio texts of the plays; the Third Series originals and analogues of the plays, the Fourth Series Shakspere allusion books, the Fifth Series (in which no numbers were ever published) selections from the contemporary drama, the Sixth, works on Shakspere's England, the Seventh, English mysteries, miracles, masks, interludes, and comedies, and the Eighth, miscellanies, including specimens of Elizabethan and Jacobean handwriting, and reprints of Shaksperean criticism. Furnivall wished a thousand members for the new society, but at its maximum the membership never reached much more than a third of that number, this including libraries, institutions, and lastly "branch societies," a feature of Furnivall's scheme of organization.

The first meeting of the New Shakspere Society was held on a truly ominous day, Friday, the thirteenth of March, 1874. At this meeting Furnivall, who in his introductory address reviewed the progress of the lines of investigation upon which the society was to work, "handed the society over, in full working order, to the Committee of Workers."[51] The membership at the opening was about two hundred

[51] *The New Shakspere Society's Transactions, 1874*, I, viii. There is a characteristic note here: "With regard to the formation of the society I wish to say a word or two, because some people have complained that I have taken too much on myself in this matter. I can only say that I formd this society in the same way that I formd all the other societies I have founded; that is, having a special work to get done, I askt people to come forward and help to do it. I didn't ask people in general to come forward, and tell me what to do, because I knew (more or less) what special things I wanted done; and when this was the case, I have always found the best way was, to say so, and let anybody who thought your object a worthy one, come forward and offer to help in attaining it. But to let a number of people come together haphazard, sit down on your objects, and turn your means to other ends, is a way I don't see the good of; a way I never have taken, and never mean to take."

and fifty. The society immediately precipitated itself into
the machinery of German critical scholarship, and busied
itself with the "tests," metrical, pause, and speech-ending,
with great enthusiasm. From the beginning the society had
in view the attainment of definite conclusions, finality, the
absolute settlement of questions; and this confident attitude seemed to many outsiders to imply that the conclusions were likely to be reached before the proofs were
adduced; but in the main the members worked with care
and restraint; and there were really but few of them who
sacrificed themselves to hasty or one-sided judgments.

The society was very active during the first few years of
its existence. By the year 1886 it had issued thirty numbers of its publications, exclusive of its *Transactions*.
These numbers included in the Second Series a promising
beginning for the society's projected quarto and folio reprints, including separate and parallel reprints and revised
reprints of *Romeo and Juliet* and *Henry V*, and further
editions of *The Two Noble Kinsmen* and *Cymbeline*. The
Third Series contained only one volume, Arthur Brooke's
Tragicall Historye of Romeus and Iuliet. The first of the
series of allusion books contained entire reprints of well-
known Elizabethan material, such as Greene's *Groatsworth
of Wit* and Chettle's *Kind-Hart's Dream;* the other two
volumes in this series being composed of shorter critical
and allusive excerpts. In the Shakspere's England series
appeared Harrison's *Description of England*, Stubbes'
Anatomie of Abuses, and a number of shorter pieces. The
only volume in the proposed series of emergent dramatic
genres was Furnivall's edition of the *Digby Mysteries*.
Four numbers of the Miscellanies Series had also been published. In the *Transactions* of the society from the first
there had appeared papers exceeded in importance only
by the best analytical work of the Germans, and also, inevi-

tably, some papers more remarkable for daring than discretion. F. G. Fleay was the earliest constant contributor to the proceedings; and throughout the period of the society's activity papers were read by J. W. Hales, John K. Ingram, Delius, Spedding, P. A. Daniel, Ruskin, Brinsley Nicholson, Grace Latham, Robert Boyle, Sidney Lee, Stopford Brooke, and a multitude of others of greater or less prominence; in all, a singular array of scholars. The most conspicuous feature of the meetings was, as Furnivall had proposed, protracted discussion, in which Furnivall himself appropriated a large portion of the general time and opportunity.

An unfortunate distraction to the society, when it was at the supreme point of its accomplishment, however, arose in the form of a long-continued and very bitter controversy, which involved Swinburne, Furnivall, and Halliwell-Phillipps, and was pursued with a reckless rancor that would have done credit to Ritson or Gifford.[52] The quarrel began when in 1876 Swinburne, venturing upon an almost exclusively aesthetic study of Shakspere, possibly in deliberate opposition to what he regarded as the mechanical methods of German scholarship which were made so much of by the New Shakspere Society, attempted to decide for Shakspere's unaided authorship of *Henry VIII*,[53] and in particular against Spedding's critical judgment of the metrical questions involved.[54] Furnivall replied to Swinburne's arbitrary and hasty opinion in a letter, not very

[52] Furnivall's management of the society had already been made the object of an absurd attack issued anonymously by John Jeremiah: *Furnivallos Furioso and "the Newest Shakespeare Society,"* *a dram-attic squib of the period in three fizzes*, London, 1876.

[53] *Fortnightly Review*, XXV, 37–45, 1876.

[54] *Of the several Shares of Shakspere and Fletcher in the Play of Henry VIII, Gentleman's Magazine*, August, 1850, 115–23. Reprinted in *The New Shakspere Society's Transactions, 1874*, Appendix to Part I, 1*–18*.

provoking, to the *Academy*,[55] in which he submitted evidence of the error of Swinburne's pronouncements. In the succeeding number of the Academy,[56] Swinburne took issue with Furnivall's criticisms in ungracious fashion, but the substance of his argument was an evasion of the statements to which he had committed himself, and Furnivall answered this in the second number following.[57] There was really no reply possible to Furnivall's use of exact evidence; so Swinburne for the time being held his peace. He soon retaliated, however, with the publication of two scathing and thoroughly laughable parodies upon the learned investigations of the New Shakspere Society,[58] ridiculing the use of metrical and related tests, and the rash manipulation of internal evidence. In 1879, however, the quarrel became more bitter, when, in a *Note on the Historical Play of King Edward III*,[59] Swinburne again held up to ridicule the "New-Shakespearean synagogue" and their "New Shakespeare." Relying too much upon his "delicacy of ear," he ventured in this article to pronounce final judgment upon some questions of Shakesperean diction; and Furnivall descended upon him with naked dirk gleaming in his hand. In two letters addressed to the editor of the *Spectator*,[60] he took up specifically Swinburne's confident decisions upon

[55] IX, 34–5, January 8, 1876.

[56] IX, 53–5, January 15, 1876.

[57] IX, 98–9, January 29, 1876.

[58] *Report of the First Anniversary Meeting of the Newest Shakespeare Society (April 1, 1876)*, *Examiner*, April 1, 1876; *The Newest Shakespeare Society; Additions and Corrections*, *Examiner*, April 15, 1876. Both of the papers are reprinted in the appendix to *A Study of Shakespeare*, 1880.

[59] *Gentleman's Magazine*, August and September, 1879; 170–81, 330–49. This paper also is appended to *A Study of Shakespeare*, 1880.

[60] September 6 and 13, 1879. The two letters were reprinted, with comments, by Furnivall in the same year under the title *Mr. Swinburne's "Flat Burglary" on Shakspere*.

the questions, and with the incontrovertible evidence of quotation and reference he attacked Swinburne's pose as a critic whose intuitive faculties were superior to the systematic analysis of the ''Newest Shakespeare'' school, and practically annihilated his pretensions.

Early in 1880 appeared Swinburne's *A Study of Shakespeare*, which was elaborated from two articles, *The Three Stages of Shakespeare*, published in the Fortnightly[61] in 1875 and 1876; the two articles which, by the way, had provided Furnivall with his first ammunition. This volume was reviewed very harshly by Dowden in the first number of the *Academy* for that year,[62] and with special emphasis upon Swinburne's contumacy in sticking to his old assertion that Shakspere was the sole author of *Henry VIII*. The review was greeted with letters from both Swinburne and Furnivall,[63] and later in the year another couple of letters followed,[64] leaving Furnivall in the attitude of challenging Swinburne to ''dispute his facts and argument,'' and Swinburne satisfied that with ''such a person'' he would ''almost as soon think of entering into correspondence as of entering into controversy.'' Furnivall fired a parting shot in a letter, again crowded with damaging evidence of Swinburne's fatuity, in the next number of the *Academy*.[65] Swinburne was without question disastrously beaten.

At this point Halliwell-Phillipps joined the encounter. When Swinburne was preparing to publish his *Study of Shakespeare*, which was to include in an appendix the three articles in criticism of the New Shakspere Society, he decided to display his reverence for the old canons of

[61] XXIII, 613–32, XXV, 24–45, 1875–6.
[62] XVII, 1–2, January 3, 1880.
[63] *Academy*, XVII, 28, January 10, 1880.
[64] *Ibid.*, XVII, 476, June 26, 1880; XVIII, 9, July 3, 1880.
[65] XVIII, 27–8, July 10, 1880.

Shaksperean criticism by dedicating his volume to Halliwell; and Halliwell, whose vanity was apparently easily tickled, accepted what he probably regarded as a gracious compliment. Whether Halliwell, who up to this time had been a peaceful and inactive member of the New Shakspere Society, could read to the bottom of Swinburne's idea, and actually saw that Swinburne was hiding behind him to take a shot at Furnivall, is of course hard to say; the probability is that he relished the compliment and was a bit slyly pleased that Furnivall, whose new scholarship had so greatly overshadowed that of his own day, would have to swallow Swinburne's aspersion. In any event, there was no question in Furnivall's mind as to the state of things. "I at once wrote to Mr. Hell.-P.," he says,[66] "saying with what astonishment I had heard that he, affecting then to be my friend, had agreed to let these insolent Reprints, &c. be dedicated to him. I pointed out to him that, as the character of the Pigsbrook articles was known to him, and all of the Shakspere set, his acceptance of the dedication of them would be a deliberate adoption by him of the insults in the articles; and I told him that if his name appeared before the book, it would stop all relations between him and me; I would cut him dead; and that if he thus adopted and offered insults to my friends and me, he would find it a game which two could play at." Halliwell denied his responsibility for the contents of the book, but Furnivall reiterated his threat. The volume appeared in 1880, with the dedication to Halliwell.

Furnivall's revenge appeared in his Forewords to his reprint of the second quarto of *Hamlet*, the second of the *Shakspere Quarto Fac-Similes*. Here he referred to Swinburne and Halliwell under the corporate name of "Pigsbrook and Co.," and called "what they are pleased to call

66 *The "Co." of Pigsbrook & Co.*, [1881], 2.

their opinions," "porcine vagaries," descending to rather
meaningless vulgarity throughout his foot-notes to the preface. Halliwell then appealed to the Committee of the New
Shakspere Society, asking their censure for Furnivall's
attack,[67] but the Committee replied that they did "not
consider the matter as falling within their jurisdiction."[68]
Halliwell thereupon wrote to Browning, the Honorary
President of the society, asking him to use his office for the
purpose of securing a retraction from Furnivall,[69] whose
position as Director of the Society was proclaimed upon
the title-page of the *Quarto Fac-Similes,* and who had
advertised the volumes as appearing "with the approval
of the Committee of the New Shakspere Society, and the
co-operation of its leading editors." Browning wrote in
reply that his connection with the society was purely honor-

[67] Furnivall closed his pamphlet with a P. S.: "You will see that
I have said nothing of Mr. Hell.—P.'s action as regards the Committee; but as I see it, this it is. After two warnings not to do an
act which I, being Chairman of the Committee, tell him will be an
insult to our Society, and each of us, he deliberately does the act. I
retaliate, in a book for which I am solely responsible. He then
comes coolly to the men whom he has insulted, and using fresh
insulting expressions to me, their Chairman, asks them to blame me.
Had I been free to act for them, I should of course have torn
Mr. Hell.—P.'s letter into four pieces, and sent 'em back to him
with the inscription "Mr. Phillipps's insolent epistle is returned to
him." But the Committee treated him with great forbearance, and
he, unfortunately, has not been able to appreciate it." *The "Co."
of Pigsbrook & Co.,* 6.

[68] [*Halliwell's published Correspondence with Browning*], 3.

[69] "The obvious course would have been to have appealed to a
general meeting of the Society, but here a difficulty arises, there being no provisions under which such a meeting can be summoned,—
no constitution, no laws, no regulations, and no power whatever
vested in any of the members,—there being, in fact, no Society at
all. . . . Under these circumstances, . . . you will, I feel sure, excuse
my asking if you will not insist upon the Director's withdrawal of
the above-quoted disreputable language." (*Ibid.,* 4.)

ary and that he had not as yet, in fact, attended any of its meetings; but the point of Halliwell's appeal he did not touch. Halliwell then wrote him another letter, assailing the management of the society, and chiefly its Director, and published the correspondence.

Furnivall again returned to the fray with a very arrogant open letter, *The "Co." of Pigsbrook & Co.*, in which, after accusing Halliwell of evasion in disclaiming responsibility for the contents of Swinburne's book, he sought refuge for himself by endeavoring simultaneously to dissociate his personal action from his official connection with the society, and to justify that action as retaliation for "an insult to our society."[70] After Halliwell's publication of his correspondence with Browning, the *Athenaeum* took up the cudgels for him.[71] It gave its opinion that "the Committee ought at least to express its disapprobation" of Furnivall's "flowers of rhetoric," and added that it was "hopeless for them to deny responsibility for the preface in which Mr. Halliwell-Phillipps was wantonly insulted." In the early part of the same year a memorial was addressed by some of the prominent members of the society to the Committee, asking for censure. The Committee again, however, refused to interfere.[72] As a result there was something of an exodus of members from the society,[73] and

[70] *The "Co." of Pigsbrook & Co.*, 6.

[71] February 5, 26, March 12, 19, 26, April 16, 1881.

[72] *Athenaeum*, March 12, 19, 26, April 2, 1881; 367, 397, 429, 461.

[73] Among those who expressed in this manner their disapproval of Furnivall's part in the controversy were R. C. Jebb, J. W. Hales, Buxton Forman, C. M. Ingleby, Henry Morley, and Leslie Stephen. Spedding, whose position as to the authorship of *Henry VIII* was the immediate ground of Furnivall's attack upon Swinburne, was among those who resolved to retire from the society. He wrote shortly before his death (which occurred before the final action of the Committee upon the memorial): "If the society has no organization

Skeat, Grosart, Aldis Wright, Ulrici, Delius, Elze, and Leo resigned their honorary vice-presidencies. The gaps were then filled up by Sweet, Murray, and Prof. Paul Meyer of the Collége de France. Furnivall addressed a note to the seceding members of the society: "On the point taken by you," this ran, "opinions differ. My opinion is that 'the duty' of the New Shakspere Society is to mind its own business,—that is, to study Shakspere. . . . I regard as an impertinence your intrusion of yourselves into a dispute declared by me to be private between Mr. Halliwell-Phillipps and myself, and I am now glad to be rid of you, whose return for the faithful work I have given you (and others) is this present censorious caballing against me."[74]

It has been said, though possibly with some degree of prejudice, that this episode was the immediate occasion of the decline of the Shakspere Society's effective work.[75] In any event, it is certain that with decimated numbers, and discord still grumbling within the society's ranks, it was in a much weaker state than before, and it is a fact that from 1882 on, the publications of the society, barring the *Transactions*, became noticeably fewer and less important, until they ceased altogether in 1886. The eight volumes of Furnivall's "Old Spelling Shakspere," which were advertised from 1883 to 1886 as "at press," never came out; and the dozen volumes, more or less, which the society had "in preparation" or under consideration at this date joined the "Old Spelling Shakspere" in the limbo of books all but published. From this time on, the only issues of the society were its *Transactions*, which chronicled its activities until 1892, the last paper recorded bearing date June tenth of

capable of putting a stop to the use of such language by its Director, it is not a society to which a gentleman can belong." (*Athenaeum*, March 26, 1881, 429.)

[74] *Athenaeum*, April 30, 1881, 593.

[75] *Shakespeareana*, 1892; 185–6.

that year. In the same year Furnivall announced what proved to be the society's last publication, a reprint of *Robert Laneham's Letter,* from the plates of his edition of *Captain Cox's Ballads* for the Ballad Society in 1871, for, as he explained, "the falling off in the subscriptions to the New Shakspere Society makes it needful that a cheap reprint shall be provided for the issue of 1887"[76] (then five years delayed). The society afterwards passed quietly out of existence, no notice being given of its dissolution, if it was ever formally dissolved, and none of the contemporary reviews commenting upon its disappearance.

The first suggestion for the formation of a society for the scientific study of English dialects was made by Aldis Wright in a letter to *Notes and Queries* in 1870.[77] This letter was followed by comments from a number of linguistic scholars,[78] and finally Alexander J. Ellis proposed the formation of the English Dialect Society in the introduction to the third part of his *Early English Pronunciation,* published in 1871. The society was soon afterward organized with about one hundred and twenty-five members; it planned the issuance of four series of publications, to include bibliographies of all works illustrative of provincial dialects, reprints of old glossaries, original glossography, and miscellanies. As a beginning for the society's collective work, there was issued in the first year a set of *Rules and Directions for Word Collectors,* and the Philological Society's plan was followed of gathering and filing slips containing illustrative examples contributed by a large number of workers. The result was that through this collaborative research and the trained scholarship of a few

[76] *Jahrbuch der deutschen Shakespeare Gesellschaft,* XXVII, 249, 1892.

[77] *Notes and Queries, 4th Series,* V, 271, March 12, 1870.

[78] The communications are quoted in the announcement of the English Dialect Society for 1873.

gifted leaders, the society published between 1873 and 1896, when the publications were closed, eighty volumes of county and other local glossaries, old lexicons, and other important linguistic material. The society was rather an exceptional example of distributed activity, for a large number of scholars, many not very well known, appeared as editors of its issues. The most prominently active of these were Skeat and Ellis, J. H. Nodal, F. T. Elworthy, James Britten, Thomas Hallam, Joseph Wright, and R. O. Heslop. The English Dialect Society was brought to a close at the moment that Joseph Wright began to carry out the society's original purpose of publishing a dialect dictionary; and Wright's *English Dialect Dictionary* itself is of course derived in large part from the great mass of linguistic material published in the society's eighty volumes.[79]

The first important society of a type more or less familiar and more or less generally ridiculed during the last decades of the nineteenth century was the Wordsworth Society. This society, like other societies of its kind, devoted itself exclusively to spreading the appreciation of the works of a single author, and an author, too, not very far removed either in point of time or of intellectual outlook from those who endeavored to study him. The limitation of the field of interest of a considerable body of men in such a manner tended almost inevitably to the cultivation of a scholarship that was not always measured by common sense, and an enthusiasm touched at times by very narrow prejudices. It is a matter of common remark that in a number of the greater and lesser societies and clubs formed for the exaltation of a single literary figure, careless and precipitate judgment interfered with sound study and often invited irritating ridicule. Before the close of the century there

[79] *The English Dialect Dictionary*, edited by Joseph Wright, I, vii.

was a Carlyle Society, a Brontë Society, a Ruskin Society, and Shelley Societies, Browning Societies, and Burns Societies not a few. The vogue of these organizations unquestionably did much to increase general interest in their favorite authors, and, more tangibly, to provide historical and biographical material of very real value; indeed, these projects enlisted the efforts of small bodies of original workers who, without the incentive and the direction of collective study, could have produced absolutely nothing of themselves. On the other hand, the laudation of a single literary personage no doubt warped the vision of many of the participants in these pleasant projects, and prepared the way for much futile appreciative criticism and much purely nonsensical speculation. There is something intrinsically absurd in the introduction of literary culture as a diversion at afternoon teas; and this was what the vogue of many of the later Browning Societies, for instance, apparently meant. On the other hand, taken seriously, by scholars of adequate training, and readers of literary judgment, such societies could, and did, accomplish much; and nothing is more significant of the difference between a real and an affected literary cultivation than the solid results of the activities of the more important of what we might call the "personage societies," as contrasted with the trivial or pretended interests of others. For there is something well worth while after all even in the collection of anecdotes, the tracing out of localities in literary allusions, the unearthing of remarks and fragments of correspondence, and a dozen other slight kinds of literary crusading. No one can deny that the Wordsworth Society was very largely instrumental in re-creating Wordsworth's reputation, and that the general recognition of the intellectual substance of Shelley's work owes a very great deal to the members of the Shelley Society. The Browning Society, with all its followers, great and small, cultivated a specious popularity for Browning's work which has left a very solid and healthy residue of understanding appreciation, even though the popularity of the poet among many of his following consisted at one time in the mere fun of endeavoring to rationalize his phrasal surds.

By the very nature of the case, however, less of the meaningless partiality inherent in such projects was to be found in the Wordsworth Society. This society was first planned in 1879,[80] and was established at Grasmere in the following year.[81] The organization contemplated at first no public function, but the number of applications for membership induced the organizers to enlarge their original scheme. From the first the society possessed a social purpose, as well as that defined as its special aim: textual and chronological work upon the poet, and the collection of letters, reminiscences, and related matter of biographical interest. William Knight was throughout the existence of the society, from 1880 to 1886, its secretary and its principal worker. In its closing year the society numbered nearly three hundred and fifty members. The council of the society included at various times Knight, Dowden, Stopford Brooke, Arnold, Lowell, Browning, and Lord Houghton, the last four of whom were presidents of the body. During its life the society issued no extensive work upon Wordsworth's text, its *Transactions* including principally critical, biographical, and exegetical essays and addresses. In addition to these, however, the volumes contain a good bibliography of Wordsworth[82] by Prof.

[80] The *Transactions of the Wordsworth Society*, issued in eight numbers from 1882 to 1887, furnish information on all important points in the history of the body. This information is effectually digested, however, in Prof. Knight's preface to *Wordsworthiana*, 1889.

[81] *Wordsworthiana*, v.

[82] *Transactions*, I, 5–15. Subsequently corrected and again published in vol. VII, 121–9.

Knight, W. F. Poole's *Bibliography of Periodical Reviews and Criticisms of Wordsworth*,[83] reprints of correspondence, and Knight's invaluable *List of Wordsworth's Poems arranged in chronological Order*.[84] The most important of the addresses before the society were published by Knight in 1889, after the dissolution of the society, as *Wordsworthiana*.

All in all, the Wordsworth Society must be said to have been one of the sanest and most discriminating of all the societies which cherished a personal cult. Among its members were many men of letters, scholars, and critics of irreproachable taste and discernment—Leslie Stephen, Canon Ainger, Aubrey De Vere, Professor Jebb, Richard Herne Shepherd, Professor Masson, Ruskin, and others of only less distinction. It would be difficult to accuse such men of having cultivated a meaningless enthusiasm; indeed, the attitude of the society in fleeing as from the death the term "Wordsworthian" is sufficiently indicative of the good sense that marked its purposes and proceedings. Its history is from beginning to end, in short, a demonstration of the usefulness of a definite, even though a possibly sentimental, bond of union for the furtherance of careful and not over-academic study of a single literary character.

The Browning Society was in many respects the most important of its type; and the most criticized and ridiculed, because its founders had the temerity to undertake the serious study of a living poet—a poet, too, who was looked upon by many readers and critics in England as a mere turner of cryptic phrases. The first meeting of this society was held on October 28, 1881, with three hundred in attendance, of whom seventy were members.[85] The society was

[83] *Ibid.*, V, 95–102.
[84] *Ibid.*, VII, 55–117.
[85] *Monthly abstract of Proceedings*, in *Browning Society's Papers*, Pt. III, 1*.

founded, apparently with Browning's tacit acquiescence, by Furnivall and Miss E. H. Hickey.[86] From the first, great interest was shown in the undertaking, and within a year of its foundation the original membership was doubled. One noteworthy feature of the Browning Society was the number of women comprised among its members, including such active and enthusiastic workers as Miss Hickey, Mrs. Orr, and Mrs. Ireland. The plan of the New Shakspere Society, and later of the Shelley Society, to encourage the organization of branch societies wherever possible was adopted by the Browning Society with remarkable success, to the point even of establishing an esoteric vogue which extended literally to the farthest corners of the English speaking world.

The first number of the *Browning Society's Papers* included Browning's introductory essay to the spurious *Letters of Percy Bysshe Shelley*, originally published in 1852, and the first instalment of Furnivall's *Bibliography of Robert Browning*.[87] Beginning with the second number, the *Papers* reflected the activities of the members in criticism, exposition, and illustration of the poet's works. Among the best known contributors were James Thomson, Walter Raleigh, Arthur Symons, C. H. Herford, Furnivall, and William M. Rossetti; writers less known outside the exclusive realm of Browning study were J. T. Nettleship, Edward Berdoe, Helen J. Ormerod, and Mrs. Alexander Ireland.

Plans for a number of special publications appeared at an early date. Thomas J. Wise was to undertake a lexicon or concordance to Browning's works, but this was aban-

[86] *Ibid.*

[87] Furnivall's ''Forewords'' contain a characteristic division of Browning's works into four ''periods,'' with an interesting anticipation of a fifth.

doned for lack of funds.[88]   An interesting proposal from Hiram Corson to reprint the Latin and Italian documents which formed the foundation for the story of *The Ring and the Book* was relinquished only upon Browning's withdrawal of his permission to print "the book."[89]   Mrs. Orr was also to undertake a cheap primer; but this project was taken over by the Bells,[90] who issued in 1885 her *Handbook to Browning's Works,* a much larger book than the society had looked for.   Mrs. Orr's *Handbook* was distributed to the members of the society, as were a number of trade publications on Browning, including Arthur Symons's *Introduction to the Works of Robert Browning,* and Sharp's *Life of Browning;* the writers of most of the volumes distributed in this way were themselves members of the society.   The only book outside the *Papers* which was issued for the Browning Society alone was the facsimile reprint of the excessively scarce *Pauline,* which was delivered to the members in 1887.   The reprint of the prose *Life of Strafford* was issued through arrangement with a Boston publisher.

The entertainments and plays offered by the society were interesting side-issues of its work.   The plays produced were *In a Balcony, A Blot in the 'Scutcheon, Colombe's Birthday,* and *Strafford.*   The last of these was given in 1888, after which it was decided that the expense of production was scarcely justified, in view of more pressing obligations.

Until this year the society's history was apparently one of continually growing success, the membership having risen in seven years to something over two hundred and fifty.   There was from the beginning, however, some differ-

[88] *First Report of the Browning Society's Committee,* 1882, 2; *Second Report,* 1883, xii.
[89] *First Report,* 3; *Third Report,* xxi.
[90] *First Report,* 3.

ence of opinion as to how long the body should continue in existence. Mrs. Orr suggested in 1883 that it should be closed in five years; this Furnivall stoutly opposed, and his views were supported by a vote on the question.[91] In 1888 E. C. Gonner moved the dissolution of the society forthwith, as he was dissatisfied with its want of critical aim, the missionary character of its work, and the growing tendency to theological discussion. Gonner's motion was seconded by Bernard Shaw, and was followed by very heated discussion, in which Furnivall gave it as his conviction that "the society should not be wound up, and that this meeting should say distinctly that the time had not even come for asking the members' opinion about it."[92] The conclusion from the debate was that the society should move out of the theological rut and should devote itself more seriously to critical and expository work. Upon the vote, only one member, J. Dykes Campbell, supported the sponsors for the motion; there seems to be some significance, however, in the fact that the three who stood together were all members of the society's Committee. In 1889 there was a sharp decline in the recorded membership of the society, which was given then as two hundred; this decrease in the membership had its effect upon all the interests of the society.[93] Browning's death, at the very close of this year, could not fail, under these circumstances, to mean for the society either of two things: resurrection, or calamity. It proved to mean the latter. In spite of the natural appearance of a reawakened interest in Browning's work, the society was evidently doomed. At three meetings following close upon the death of the poet there were no papers presented. It was resolved in the next year, 1891, that the

[91] *Browning Society's Papers*, Pt. IV, 83*.
[92] *Ibid.*, Pt. X, 274*–280*.
[93] *Eighth Annual Report*, xxxiii.

society should be discontinued after 1892.[94]   Four years later the last echo of its activity was heard when Thomas J. Wise issued in the name of the Committee a call for two years' subscriptions from former members for the purpose of publishing a bibliography, a collection of letters, and Part VI of the *Papers*, which had been due for several years. Evidently there was not sufficient response to this appeal to enable the Committee to conclude the society's publications and announce its existence as formally closed.

The effect of Scotch sentiment in reviving and sustaining a hearty interest in Scottish literary antiquity, which we have already seen reflected in the accomplishments of the Bannatyne, the Maitland, the Abbotsford, and the Hunterian Clubs, is seen in its most gratifyingly practical aspect in the Scottish Text Society, founded in 1882.[95]   The organizers of this society whose names have been identified most continuously with the scholarly traditions of the nineteenth century were Aeneas J. G. Mackay, Masson, Skeat, Thomas Graves Law, and Sir James Murray. In its very earliest years the society received a support that the Early English Text Society, whose publications, it must be assumed, should have appealed to a much larger number of readers, has scarcely surpassed even at the present day. That the Scottish Text Society should have begun its existence with three hundred members, while the Early English Text Society began with considerably less than half that number, and that the present membership of the Scottish society should exceed that of its sister organization by about one hundred and fifty, although the society is actually eighteen years younger, are both facts that excite questions. This marked difference in the amount of interest shown in the

[94] *Tenth Annual Report*, ix–x.

[95] For information relative to the history of the Scottish Text Society I am largely indebted to Mr. W. T. Dickson, Honorary Secretary of the Society.

schemes for the revival of the literary past of the two
nations is probably explained in part by the real affection
on the part of Scotsmen for all that the language and literature of the nation have meant to it, the like of which is
assuredly not to be found south of the Cheviot Hills. It is
probably to be explained to some degree, too, by the more
liberal and unautocratic administration of the Scottish
Text Society. On this point there are some marked differences in the government of the two societies which it is
worth while to point out.

The Early English Text Society is still, as we have seen,[96]
governed by a self-continuing council, in whose hands the
entire administration of the society is held; its members
have no voice in the selection of texts, and no voting
powers of any sort. In the Scottish Text Society, on the
other hand, the council is elective, going out by rotation;
this insures the expression of the will of the members in
the administration of the society without sacrificing the
advantage of a relatively permanent executive establishment. In addition, in the Scottish Text Society the opinions and criticisms of members on the proposed publications are invited, and its fiscal accounts are published.
There can be little question, it would seem, then, that an
administrative program of this kind is more effective and
more generally to be approved than one in which the name
of a society may be utilized, as it has been utilized at
times, to carry forward what is ostensibly a collective
scheme upon lines of personal preference. A further reason for the larger success of the Scottish body may lie in
the fact that its first and plainest function was the reprinting of a series of literary monuments acquaintance with
which has been part of the culture of every representative
Scotchman, while the English society was to undertake the

96 *Ante*, 163.

publication of a number of works of distinctly inferior importance, many of which were practically unreadable by anyone not specially trained in an unspoken tongue. Another consideration which may in part account for the better support for the Scottish Text Society is that, with a proper Scotch recognition of what is at least proverbially a proper Scotch characteristic, the Society gives its subscribers extremely good book value for their guinea a year of subscription.

Since its organization the Scottish Text Society has published sixty-three numbers, comprising the works of Dunbar, Henryson, Ninian Winzet, Mure of Rowallan, and Alexander Montgomerie, the poems of Alexander Scott and Alexander Hume, Blind Harry's *Wallace*, James I's *Kingis Quair*, *Sir Tristrem*, George Buchanan's vernacular writings, Barbour's *Bruce*, the *Gude and Godlie Ballatis*, Bellenden's *Livy*, Wyntoun's *Chronicle*, six volumes of saints' legends, four volumes of *Satirical Poems of the Reformation*, the histories of Lindesay of Pittscottie and Bishop Lesley, *Lancelot of the Laik*, and William Geddie's *Bibliography of Middle Scots Poets*.

The Shelley Society, founded at London in 1886,[97] had aims and working methods generally similar to those of the Browning Society. The bulk of its published work consisted of a valuable series of textual reprints, from early editions and manuscripts. The plan of the Shelley Society, it seems, was the outcome of a proposal made to Furnivall by Henry Sweet that he should found such a body. Furnivall jumped at the suggestion, and the exact words of his reply, as he repeated them to the members of the society at its first meeting, giving as they did a glimpse of Furnivall's self-confident enthusiasm, formed the theme of a very

[97] The first three years of the society's history are covered in the *Note-Book of the Shelley Society . . . Vol. I, Part I* [all published], London, 1888.

clever and amusing bit of quizzing by Andrew Lang in the *Saturday Review* for March 13, 1886.[98] It was considered when the society was inaugurated that ten years would suffice to accomplish all its purposes, and as part of its program, it was decided to follow the plan of the New Shakspere and Browning Societies of furthering the influence of its work by the establishment of as many branch societies as possible, which should maintain an occasional correspondence with the London body.

One of the earliest projects of the Shelley Society, and one which met with the bitterest opposition from many of the earnest defenders of the national morality, was a dramatic production of *The Cenci;* in fact, this was one of the declared objects of the society at the date of its foundation. The performance, in 1886, was of course, because of the prohibitions of the censor, a private one, Miss Alma Murray playing in the principal rôle.[99] In the same year the society produced *Hellas,* but naturally with much less comment, either favorable or adverse.

The publications of the Shelley Society were to follow the arrangement of those of the New Shakspere Society in a serial division, in this case into four parts, including

[98] " 'By Jove, I will; he was my father's friend!' Thus Dr. Furnivall, in choice blank verse, replied when he was asked by Mr. Sweet (Sweet of the pointed and envenomed pen, wherewith he pricks the men who not elect him a Professor, as he ought to be), 'twas thus, we say, that Furnivall replied to the bold question asked by bitter Sweet. 'And what that question?' Briefly, it was this— 'Why do not you, who start so many things, societies for poets live and dead, why do not you a new communion found—'Shelley Society' might be the name—where men might worry over Shelley's bones?' 'By Jove, I will; he was my father's friend,' said Furnivall; and lo, the thing was done!' "—and much more in the same strain.

[99] Comments covering the whole history of the staging of *The Cenci,* from the first notices of the proposal to the criticisms of the performance, may be found in the Shelley Society's *Note Book,* 39–93.

14

respectively the *Papers* of the Society, fac-similes of the manuscripts and early editions of the poet, memorials, and bibliographical works. The Second Series, as it actually appeared, included some volumes which were not fac-similes, however; no volumes were published in the Third Series; and eventually an Extra Series was undertaken in order to hasten the publication of volumes which could not be printed immediately from the available funds of the society. Furnivall did none of the editorial work of the Shelley Society; in the production of the texts of the Second Series Thomas J. Wise was by far the most active of the members; Buxton Forman contributed occasional volumes, and Bertram Dobell, Dowden, Stopford Brooke, and T. W. Rolleston lent a hand in others. It is doubtful whether the reprinting of the Shelley Society texts was of at all the same degree of usefulness as it usually is in societies which give their attention to more remote periods. It is probably not too much to say that there is not the same field for this sort of labor upon Shelley as there might be upon earlier authors, exposed to the uncertainties of manuscript publication and very careless printing. Outside of the texts, the publications of the society were not of specially great importance, since William M. Rossetti's *Memoir of Shelley* and Browning's *Essay on Percy Bysshe Shelley* were not originally issued for the society. The serial arrangement, which was designed to form an effective classification for the publications, as a matter of fact turned out to be cumbersome and misleading, as none of the series was completed, and hiatuses occur in all of those in which any volumes appeared.

The Shelley Society continued in active existence until 1892, gathering in this period of six years a large amount of material valuable to the Shelley student, but accomplishing less, probably, than it had intended in the direction of encouraging a more general interest in Shelley and his writings. It was, in fact, probably the case with the Shelley Society, as with most others of its class, that its benefits were confined in the main to its own members.

The remaining years of the nineteenth century produced no new literary societies of wide prominence. Since 1900, however, two or three important organizations have begun with promise, one of which has also closed its career.

An organization of unique interest among English learned societies is the British Academy. When in 1899 there was established the International Association of Academies, it was urged by the newly instituted body that steps should be taken toward corporate representation of the branches of study not dealt with by the Royal Society. The Royal Society itself, therefore, made overtures to a number of representative scholars; and at a conference which followed it was decided that the establishment of an entirely new academy would be more effective than a federation of societies whose interests lay within the unrepresented fields. The Royal Society, however, was unwilling to carry further its initial effort; so those who had received the Royal Society's first communication undertook the steps toward organization upon their own responsibility. In 1901 a meeting was held at which it was resolved: "It is desirable that a society representative of historical, philosophical, and philological studies be formed on conditions which will satisfy the requirements of the International Association of Academies,"[100] and invitations for membership in the British Academy for the Promotion of Historical, Philosophical, and Philological Studies were soon afterward sent to a number of prominent scholars in these branches. The Academy held its first meeting in 1901, and received a royal charter in the following year. The names upon the

[100] *Proceedings of the British Academy*, 1903–1904, ix.

original list of fellows which should particularly interest us were E. Maunde Thompson, A. W. Ward, Gollancz, Murray, Skeat, Leslie Stephen, and Whitley Stokes; there were subsequently added within the year A. H. Firth, Furnivall, W. P. Ker, W. R. Morfill, A. S. Napier, and Joseph Wright, and in later years A. C. Bradley, Henry Bradley, W. J. Courthope, Andrew Lang, Sidney Lee, and George F. Warner.

The work of the British Academy in its special fields was to be prosecuted through the activities of Sectional Committees;[101] and a point of interest in its intellectual outlook was the early announcement of the policy of avoiding the presumption of acting as in a position of scholarly authority.[102]   In relation to the special field of English scholarship, the Academy had at the time of its foundation no specific plan, beyond the encouragement of the programs of linguistic and literary research already on foot.[103] Since the establishment of the Academy, the fellows chosen to represent English philological scholarship have presented to the meetings of the body valuable monographs upon diverse subjects; but the Academy has so far undertaken no comprehensive work in this field.

The Early English Drama Society, apparently less an actual association than a proprietary name, was founded by John S. Farmer in 1905, "to provide a *corpus* of early English dramatic literature, commencing with the transition period between interlude, comedy, and tragedy,"[104] and also to re-issue book and manuscript rarities in facsimile reprints.   The society published between 1905 and 1908 a series of thirteen volumes of *Early English Dramatists* in modernized spelling, comprising the complete works

---

101 *Ibid.*, 3.
102 *Ibid.*, 9.
103 *Ibid.*, 11.
104 *The Early English Drama Society*, [Announcement, 1905], 1.

of John Heywood, and a practically complete body of pre-Elizabethan moralities, interludes, comedies, and tragedies, both well and little known, and containing also an extra volume of discoveries, *"Lost" Tudor Plays*. A second series of twelve volumes of early Elizabethan plays was planned and announced to succeed the published series, but the society closed before this was set on foot. The dissolution of the organization was probably hastened by a scathing review of its first publications in the *Academy* for March 24, 1906,[105] a review which questioned both the good faith of the organizers and the scholarly character of their texts. As a result of this criticism, four of the six honorary vice-presidents withdrew from the society. Setting aside the personal questions connected with the break-up of the organization, it must be said that the society had done little more than to print in a new form a number of plays already generally available, the three volumes of John Heywood, for example, having been issued originally by the Spenser Society, two even of the three *"Lost" Tudor Plays* having been already published by the Malone Society, and a large number of the remaining plays having appeared in previous collections, particularly in Carew Hazlitt's Dodsley.[106] The Early English Drama Society also published a *Facsimile Series* of early manuscripts and rare printed plays, and a series of *Museum Dramatists*, which was simply a selection of separate plays from the *Early English Dramatists* series, printed off in compact volumes as students' texts.

One of the most productive societies of the present day is the Malone Society, founded in London in 1906 through the

[105] March 24, 1906, 280–1. See also *The Academy*, for March 31, April 7 and 28 (315, 323, and 338–9).

[106] From Hazlitt's Dodsley, by the way, the *Academy* reviewer intimates, *Hickscorner* was apparently reprinted; and not from the text of Wynkyn de Worde's edition.

recommendations of a committee consisting of F. S. Boas, E. K. Chambers, R. B. McKerrow, A. W. Pollard, and W. W. Greg.[107] Mr. Chambers has been the president of the society since its foundation, and Mr. Greg the general editor of its series of publications. The society has been publishing during its five years of existence, at the uniform rate of five a year, a series of type facsimile reprints of Tudor plays, in the format of the familiar Elizabethan quarto. It has also published every year one number of its *Collections*, consisting mainly of dramatic fragments and theatrical records, and paged continuously to form a volume of four or five numbers. In its productivity, its care in the preparation of texts, and in the charm of its books as books, the Malone Society has set a standard of efficient and tasteful publication which has already placed it in a position of unusual and well deserved distinction.

The English Association was founded in January, 1907, "to enforce the truth . . . that the accurate and pliant writing of English, the correct speaking of English, and the just appreciation of English literature are not less important acquirements than any other that can come of educational training."[108] The incidental purposes of the society are "to afford opportunities of intercourse and coöperation among all who are interested in English language and literature; to discuss methods of teaching English and the correlation of school and university work; and to encourage and facilitate advanced study in English language and literature." The project was suggested by a group of secondary school masters; and from the beginning the program of the society has been mainly educational. Its publications so far have been its *Essays and Studies*, which have ap-

[107] *Athenaeum*, October 20, 1906, 488. Mr. Greg has been kind enough to send me information relative to the organization of the society.

[108] *Academy*, January 19, 1907, 71–2.

peared annually for the last three years, and which have included papers and addresses by Henry Bradley, W. P. Ker, George Saintsbury, F. S. Boas, A. C. Bradley, and other prominent scholars and educators.

It would be impossible to cover in detail the work of a number of minor literary societies which have published material of great potential value to students. Among the great number of such societies, however, may be mentioned the Manchester Literary Club, founded in 1861, and issuing a series of annual *Transactions* in which contributions have been printed from a group of workers of some note outside of the society itself, among them George Milner, W. E. A. Axon, and J. H. Nodal. The Scottish Literary Club issued in 1877 and 1892 two publications of local literary interest;[109] and the Paisley Burns Club, likewise, between 1878 and 1881 published three volumes of local eighteenth century authors. The Wiclif Society, organized by Furnivall in 1882, is still engaged upon the publication of the body of Wiclif's Latin works. The Brontë Society, of Bradford, has led since 1894 an active existence, publishing in its annual *Transactions* a number of good Brontë items, including a well executed bibliography in two parts. The Rymour Club, founded at Edinburgh in 1903, has issued a few numbers of useful records of purely popular literary material. Local philological societies are of course rarer than local literary societies. Two, however, seem deserving of special notice. The Cambridge Philological Society, composed of trained scholars connected with the University, has printed in its *Transactions* since 1881 notes of a number of valuable contributions on phonology, etymology, and the like. The Yorkshire Dialect Society, organized in 1886, has done a commendable amount of serious work in local linguistic study.

[109] C. S. Terry, *op. cit.*, 160.

A few societies which have not issued regular publications have nevertheless exerted a perceptible influence upon literary scholarship; examples of these are the Carlyle and Ruskin Societies—both of which were formed for the study of the artistic, social, and literary theories of the writers of their choice, rather than for objective literary study. Other societies of importance are the Modern Language Association, the Elizabethan Society, and a host of local Shakspere and Browning societies and the like, including all classes of students, and ranging over a wide scale of effectiveness and accomplishment. The cultural aims of such institutions are as a rule, however, so general or so vaguely defined, that to include such societies among our learned societies would be to test severely the elasticity of the term.

It is difficult to draw definite conclusions from this historical review as to anything beyond the tangible value of the aid which these bodies have given to English scholarship. We have seen that the form of the society's organization has always been determined largely by the nature and the extent of its literary interests; that societies made up at first of mere dilettanti were replaced by associations of interested students whose capacities were to be measured by the earnest but undeveloped scholarship of the first half of the nineteenth century; and that these societies in turn died out after the middle of the century, and were succeeded by a number of organizations established and conducted by men ripened in careful and efficient modern scholarship, and determined to make the entire field of English literature available for general study—and their fight has been always up-hill. The quality of the results obtained by these various and varied organizations has been affected by a number of conditions, their period, their personnel, the extent of popular interest in their projects, and most of all, of course, their working efficiency. It can not be said that the number of any given society can be taken as a measure of the actual value of its work, even when there is no numerical limit placed upon its membership. Numbers generally means wealth, and wealth means opportunities for wide diffusion of the special aspect of culture for which the society stands as advocate and agent; but the Early English Text Society, which from the standpoint of the bulk and the scholarly value of its published product must be regarded as clearly the greatest of all, is in the actual number of its members still a small society.

Nor can much be said in a general way as to what is the most effective method of organization. We have reviewed all types of association, from the aristocratic club of a handful of members, which can make its business the subject of an evening's informal talk, to the large text society, international in its scope, with which the members have scarcely what might be called a speaking acquaintance. All these forms of organization are adapted to special purposes; each must be more or less effective in its own way. In general it may be said that unreasonable limitation upon the membership places an unnecessary restriction upon a society's usefulness; on the other hand, where the object of the society is not merely to sell books, and where there is in addition a social purpose to be served, such a limitation is practically unavoidable. As to administrative methods, probably the most successful society is the one whose corporate organization does not view the members merely as subscribers, but as constituents, and to a certain extent, even as collaborators. The advantage which the Scottish Text Society seems to enjoy in this respect over the Early English Text Society has already been referred to.[110]

[110] *Ante*, 191–2.

Most societies in this field, at least in England, are what insurance statisticians would call "bad risks." To be sure, a few of these organizations, such as the Warton Club and the Shelley Society, have at their foundation placed a more or less definite limit upon the period of their existence. Others, like the Wordsworth Society and the Browning Society, are confined by the nature of their interests to relatively brief life. Causes really unconnected with the essential work of a society have too often cut off prominent organizations before their utility has been effectively realized; this was apparently the case with the Shakespeare Society and the New Shakspere Society, in both of which the personal concerns of important members exercised a serious if not fatal influence upon the fortunes of the society. But taking all these special conditions into consideration, the fact remains that the average literary society may count itself fortunate if it has seen, say, its fifteenth anniversary. On the whole, the text societies may be said to have a more promising outlook for long service than what for want of a better term we might call the critical societies. In the latter, the general indefiniteness of the program, the reaction in interest in the chosen subject after a certain period of strenuous activity has been passed, the undue importance of personalities, big and little, all combine to produce friction and disarrangement when the machinery seems to be running most smoothly. In the text societies the definiteness of the program, the constant rate of progress, the tangible value of the product, may not capture the unthinking enthusiasm of a large number, but may be counted upon to retain the interest of a faithful and thoroughly appreciative few, still sufficient in number to make the project easily self-supporting from year to year. Of all the societies devoted exclusively to English literary studies, the Early English Text Society has been so far the most enduring. The Chaucer Society, the junior of its sister body by only four years, and the only society of the sort approaching the longevity of the Early English Text Society, was dissolved after forty-four years of service, having completed in this time a series of texts and treatises unequalled by any organization save the first and favorite of Furnivall's printing societies. The Early English Text Society, at the close of fifty years' activity, seems to have before it many years of profitable labor; and if the signs of its present vitality are not deceptive, it should live to accomplish fully one of the most monumental publishing projects of our age of monumental works—a project, in fact, paralleled only by a few series produced either with the aid of heavy subsidies or under the auspices of strong and wealthy institutions.

CHAPTER VII

AMERICAN SOCIETIES AND CLUBS [1]

It is not to be expected that the activities of learned societies in the United States should produce results to be compared in a large way with those secured by such societies in Great Britain. Although the work of American scholars upon English literature has for many years earned the respect of both British and Continental students, and although latterly American scholarship has frequently contributed to the publications of foreign text societies, isolation, special interests, the remoteness of manuscript material, have all provided an effective bar to extensive coöperative publication in this country. In addition, English literary antiquity is something in which America does not and can not directly share; an American society for the publication of English texts would be, therefore, for sentimental as well as geographical reasons, almost an impossibility. The history of publishing societies in the United States has shown that this fact is very generally appreciated; so we find the really scholarly societies working along lines subordinate to or collateral with the labors of

[1] Two facts have made it advisable to treat our American publishing societies less in detail than English organizations of a similar nature. In the first place, very few of them rank in importance, either historically or in the extent of their production, with the English societies; in the second place, the history and bibliography of American societies has been altogether very well done, in four works to which in most of this chapter, except the portion dealing with purely philosophical societies, I have been under continuous obligation. These are Growoll's *American Book Clubs*, 1897, Bowker's *Publications of Societies*, 1899, Griffin's *Bibliography of American Historical Societies*, 1907, and Thompson's *Handbook of Learned Societies and Institutions*, 1908.

European scholars, or devoting their efforts to the literature of their own nation. With the book clubs, which to-day occupy a much more important place in the United States than in England, the case is somewhat different, for manuscripts, memorabilia, curiosa of every sort, of the modern period, migrate much more readily than the literary treasures of medieval or Saxon England; and since at any rate this kind of literary material does not antedate the American civilization, it is actually more or less a part of American literary culture. Book Clubs in America, therefore,— and these are practically the only literary organizations which have produced reprints on an extensive scale—have drawn largely upon English literature and literary remains of the last three centuries, as well as upon the less promising field of American literature.

Societies devoted extensively or seriously to philological study have been in the United States very few in number. The oldest of them all is the American Philological Association, organized in New York in 1868 for investigation in the entire field of philology.[2] Its scholarly outlook at the time of its establishment was similar to that of the Philological Society of London; but for patent reasons the American Association at first showed a special interest in aboriginal American dialects. In the early meetings of the Association papers upon English linguistics were not infrequent; at present, however, none of the English scholars in the Association exhibits a specially active interest in its work, though the society still includes in its membership many of the best known modern language students. The American Philological Association was affiliated in 1900 with the Philological Association of the Pacific Coast.[3] This new section of the Association still shows an

[2] *Transactions*, 1869–70; App. 1–30, 1871.
[3] *Transactions*, XXXI (*Proceedings*), xxix, 1900.

active interest in modern language studies, and many papers in this province are read at its annual meetings. The discontinuance of the American Philological Association's work in modern philology must be ascribed largely to the appropriation of this field in 1884 by the Modern Language Association of America; and the reason that the Pacific Coast Association still continues its interest in modern languages is probably that the meetings of the two divisions of the Modern Language Association are practically inaccessible to Far Western scholars.

The American Philological Association first identified itself with the spelling reform movement in America in 1875,[4] six years after the Philological Society had introduced the question in England.[5] The provisional work of the Association in turn redirected attention to the subject in the English organization, after interest in it had for the time being apparently waned.[6] In 1883 the two societies entered into a working agreement for the furtherance of spelling reform. Following up the initial efforts of the American Philological Association, the propaganda was spread by the Spelling Reform Association, and in 1892 the Modern Language Association approved the adoption of the Philological Association's rules. The cause is being advanced in the United States to-day chiefly by the militant Simplified Spelling Board, which was organized in 1906 "to carry on the process of simplification and regulation,"[7] and in England by the Simplified Spelling Society, established in 1908. After the problem was brought up by the members of the Philological Society of London, altogether the most fruitful work in this direction was accomplished—and is still being accom-

[4] *Transactions*, XXIV (*Proceedings*), xxxv–xxxvi, 1893.
[5] *Ante*, 152–4.
[6] *Ibid.*
[7] *Simplified Spelling Board, Circular No. 16*, 1907.

plished—by American organizations. Whether this is because of the greater activity of these societies, or the less strongly intrenched tradition of conservatism in the United States, is of course an open question.

The Modern Language Association of America was organized at a conference of forty modern language teachers at Columbia College in December, 1883.[8] The first aims of this body were almost exclusively pedagogical. The weakening of the tradition of purely classical culture had been much more rapid in the United States than in England, and the demand for modern languages in both the cultural and the vocational branches of university instruction had resulted in a concentration of the attention of teachers of these languages upon scientific methods of teaching them. It was in response to the growing importance of questions connected with the changing order of things that these teachers formed their union; and for the first few years of the Association's existence, therefore, it was occupied primarily with educational questions, particularly with the problem of standardizing requirements and instruction in the modern languages. Although the special interest of the Modern Language Association placed it for this reason in a position of natural opposition to the classical languages, the organization was as a matter of fact in its early years opposed to radical action in favor of substituting the modern for the classical tongues in the university curriculum.[9]

This association has from its earliest period included in its membership the great majority of well known American scholars; for although the exclusively pedagogical outlook was abandoned shortly after its foundation, in actual fact the organization is made up to-day almost entirely of modern language teachers in the colleges and universities, in all

[8] *Proceedings at New York*, 1884; in *Transactions*, I, i–vii, 1886.
[9] *Ibid.*, xviii–xix.

well over a thousand. The nature of its work, however, is to-day quite changed: it is concerned principally with questions of pure scholarship; and its *Publications* have been for twenty years a distinguished medium of scholarly communication.

The *Publications*, which represent effectively the association's present interests, include in the main literary and linguistic monographs, frequently of more considerable length than is generally acceptable to reviews less generously supported. The confinement of the scholarly labor of the members to purely historical and commentative work is accounted for in large measure by the circumstances which naturally prevent American scholars from developing an original tradition in English scholarship. And it is worth noting in passing that the conditions which limit the possibilities of English textual scholarship in America have brought it about that in this subsidiary field of scholarship there is in general a much greater productivity in the United States than in England. American scholars, for example, are maintaining a larger number of modern language periodicals and reviews than are to be found in England. The condition may also be explained in part, it is true, by the fact that American students have borrowed the monograph habit from Germany, while the paraphernalia of German scholarship has not been taken over in England either as readily or as thankfully as in America.

The Modern Language Association of America is now separated for working purposes into two divisions. In 1896 a number of members in the Middle West, considering the inconvenience of attending meetings in the East, proposed a separate conference.[10] As a result of this action, the Central Division of the Association was established, with its own officers and its own place of meeting, but using the *Publications* as its organ.

10 *Publications,* XI (*Proceedings*), lviii–lix, 1896.

Out of the Modern Language Association have grown two independent organizations which, although they have no formal connection with the older society, usually for reasons of convenience hold their meetings at the place and time appointed for the annual meeting of the Association. These are the American Dialect Society and the Concordance Society, both of which have issued some valuable publications.

The first of these, the American Dialect Society, was organized in 1889 for the investigation of the English dialects of America. Professor Child, then one of the most important figures in American scholarship, was its first president[11] In its first year the society numbered over two hundred members, well distributed throughout the country, and for a time there was a gratifying and continuous increase in membership; but the numbers of the society are now apparently decreasing, as the last report of the society gives only about 150 names. The society has published since its organization *Dialect Notes,* a serial devoted to dialect records and history, word lists, and similar material. It has also aimed at the publication of an American Dialect Dictionary, but no definite steps have been taken toward the realization of this plan; and in the present state of the society, which is making ominous appeals for increased financial support, it is unlikely that the Dialect Dictionary will be, for some years to come, anything more than a glorious hope.

The Concordance Society, established at the annual meeting of the Modern Language Association in 1906, aims to provide subventions toward the publication of concordances and word indexes to English writers, "to formulate plans for the compilation of such works, and to assist intending compilers of such works with suggestions and

[11] *Dialect Notes,* I, 1, 1896.

15

advice.'"[12]   The Society has numbered from its organization about one hundred members.   Its first publication was a *Concordance to the English Poems of Thomas Gray,* published under the editorial supervision of Albert S. Cook in 1908; and this work was followed in 1911 by its *Concordance to the Poems of William Wordsworth,* edited by Lane Cooper. The society's method of support for such projects is to appropriate amounts from its income, derived from annual dues of five dollars, as payments to publishers, not to compilers, toward the expenses of publication of these works, which could not under ordinary conditions be looked upon as promising commercial ventures. Its work is one of the best examples of the effectiveness of coöperative labor and financial support for a large plan of publication which, however useful, it would be impossible to realize under private auspices.

Local societies for literary study, especially of the type most familiar toward the end of the nineteenth century, have been very numerous in the United States.   There have been, of course, many Shakspere societies in the most important cities; and in the eighties and nineties there was a rather remarkable growth, followed in most cases by a rapid decay, of Browning societies. Few of these local bodies achieved the dignity of publishing anything of permanent value to literary students; but two or three merit special, if only passing mention.

The Shakspere Society of Philadelphia, actually the oldest Shakspere Society in existence, was established in 1851.[13] Its importance is largely due to the fact that at an early date Horace Howard Furness became associated with it; it is even apparently true that the plan for Furness's *Variorum Shakspere* originated among the members

12 *The Concordance Society, Circular No. 7* [1911].

13 *New Shakespeareana,* III, 108–9, 1904.

of this society.[14]   The only publications of the society are
five brochures, two relating to its own history, and three
of them critical essays.

The most widely known society of this type is probably
the Shakespeare Society of New York, established and
incorporated in 1885.[15]   For the first twenty-two years of
the society's existence its destiny was directed by Appleton Morgan, a lawyer of local repute.   Within this period
it produced a series of publications in their bulk quite
imposing, including the *Bankside Shakespeare,* a series of
parallel reprints of quarto and First Folio texts, issued
in twenty-one volumes from 1885 to 1906.   The *Bankside
Sequel,* for the reprinting of texts of which no printed
copy exists prior to the First Folio, has supplied so far
only a single volume.   The *Bankside Restoration Series,*
designed for the reproduction of Restoration adaptations
of Shakspere, now numbers five volumes.   In addition the
society has published twelve numbers of its *Papers.*   Altogether the record of the society is readily seen to be one
of commendable industry; in particular, its series of reprints have without doubt a very definite potential value; yet
it must be said that the organization does not possess the
scholarly importance which the bulk of its publications
would lead one to assume.   From 1889 to 1893 it conducted a periodical called *Shakespeareana,* and from 1902
on, its successor, *New Shakespeareana.*   In these two publications, as well as in some of its *Papers,* are to be found
the society's contributions to Shakspere criticism; and
this criticism, it must be admitted, tends in the main to be
rather provincial.   Moreover, the attitude of some of the
most influential members of the society toward the criticism
and scholarship represented in the work of other institutions and other individuals, is generally a little over-

14 *New Shakespeareana,* II, 30, 1903.
15 *Shakespeareana,* II, 264, 1885.

confident, and in controversy almost always needlessly provocative. The real importance of the society, therefore, lies rather in its published reprints than in its larger but rather careless and whimsical body of critical work.

Among the numerous Browning clubs which sprang up in America after the establishment of Furnivall's Browning Society, only one, the Boston Browning Society, has published any work of serious value to students of the poet. *The Boston Browning Society Papers,* published in 1900, and covering the activities of the society from 1886 to 1897, included contributions from Thomas Wentworth Higginson, George Willis Cooke, and other local scholars of repute.

Book clubs came into vogue in America during the period when their popularity in Great Britain was beginning to wane, when, in fact, the famous Scottish clubs were struggling for continued existence. These American book clubs possess naturally less interest and significance for the student of the broader field of English literature than their English predecessors. This is true in part because the English field has usually been regarded in the United States as belonging for reasons of sentiment to English scholars; and in part because the strong nationalism, indeed localism, of most of our American organizations has without doubt directed their activities into lines mainly of national interest. Moreover, since the history of early American literature is in the main representative of an intellectual tradition which has been in the past, and is therefore likely to continue to be, of small interest save to the "good American," it is quite apparent that the dearth of important literary publications among American printing clubs is emphasized by the relatively slight value of much of their published product. There are, however, three notable exceptions to this rule: the Grolier Club, the Dunlap Society, and the Bibliophile Society.

The best known among American book clubs is the Grolier Club, organized in 1884 by a group of men "interested in the arts entering into the production of books." The distinguished press-maker and collector, Robert Hoe, was the first president of the club.[16] The organization was formed with the idea that a union of book lovers and book makers could accomplish much for bibliophile interests in America; with so clear and practical an aim, it was inevitable that it should take its place among the makers of tradition in this field.

Because of its consecration to the bibliophile cause, however, some of its numerous publications in the domain of English letters possess no special merit beyond their exquisite quality as books; such are the issues of Fitzgerald's *Rubáiyát*, Irving's *Knickerbocker History of New York*, Charles Reade's *Peg Woffington*, and Milton's *Areopagitica*. In a class of real scholarly distinction, however, are Richard de Bury's *Philobiblon*, *The Poems of John Donne*, with emendations by Lowell, *Two Note Books of Thomas Carlyle*, Copeland's translation of the *History of Helyas*, from Wynkin de Worde's edition of 1512, and two important bibliographical works: a *Catalogue of original and early Editions of some of the poetical and prose Works of English Writers from Langland to Wither*, published in 1893, and three volumes of similar nature covering the period from Wither to Prior, published in 1905. The catalogues of the club's occasional exhibitions also contain something of distinct value to either dilettante or student. So far these have included exhibitions in honor of Dryden in 1900, Franklin in 1906, Milton in 1908, Johnson in 1909, Pope in 1911, Thackeray in 1912, and Dickens in 1913.

The Dunlap Society was established in 1885 at the suggestion of Professor Brander Matthews for the purpose of

[16] Brander Matthews, *Bookbindings Old and New, with an Account of the Grolier Club*, 1895, 302.

preserving and publishing material pertaining to American dramatic writing and the American stage.[17]   The society was inactive from 1891 to 1896, and its printing has again been suspended since 1902.   Its publications consist entirely of American dramatic literature and theatrical records.   The First Series of fifteen volumes, running from 1887 to 1891, included four early American plays, an equal number of dramatic biographies, and a number of papers and addresses relating to the American stage.   The New Series of the society's publications began with its reorganization, in 1896, after five years of inactivity.   In this series appeared in 1900 two valuable bibliographies, Oscar Wegelin's *Early American Plays, 1714–1830*, and Robert F. Roden's *Later American Plays, 1831–1900*.   All the remaining volumes in this series of fifteen were concerned with American stage history and dramatic biography.   The Dunlap Society possesses, apparently, a unique interest as the only organization which has devoted itself exclusively to the entire domain of a nation's dramatic literature and history.

The Bibliophile Society, founded in 1901 in Boston, "for the purpose of the study and promotion of the arts pertaining to fine book making and illustrating,"[18] has in its twelve years' of life distributed to its members an imposing series of publications, many of them possessing great and at times unique importance to students of English and American literature.   The first president of the society was Nathan Haskell Dole.   Its first issue was four volumes of Horace's Odes and Epodes, with a selection of the best English versions; and in its second year it produced an elaborate edition of Dibdin's *Bibliomania*.   The earliest volume of significance to the English scholar was a facsimile reprint of Rossetti's *Henry the Leper,* a paraphrase

17 Growoll, *American Book Clubs*, 1897, 278–80.
18 *Tenth Year Book*, 1911, 171.

from Hartmann von Aue. In 1906 was published a memorable edition of *The Letters of Charles Lamb,* in five volumes, and in the following year three volumes of unpublished manuscripts by Thoreau. In 1907 appeared *The Romance of Mary Wollstonecroft Shelley, John Howard Payne, and Washington Irving,* from a series of letters, and later *The Private Correspondence of Charles Dickens and Maria Beadnell* and *The Dickens-Kolle Correspondence.* The society's latest publication is its *Note Books of Percy Bysshe Shelley,* edited in three volumes by Buxton Forman. In addition, the regular publications have included unpublished poems by Bryant, Thoreau, and Keats, letters from Thomas Love Peacock, and unpublished orations by John Fiske, the *"Geddes Burns",* and a reprint of Thoreau's *Walden,* from the manuscript, containing many points of difference from the trade edition. In the *Year Books* of the society are also preserved many valuable pieces, including unpublished fragments by Whittier, Longfellow, Thoreau, Bayard Taylor, Scott, Cooper, and Tom Moore. This survey of the issues of the Bibliophile Society shows it to be one of the most important clubs publishing English texts. Indeed, considering its brief existence, its industry and the scholarly character and the rarity of the originals of its productions place it second to no body of its kind.

In the United States there have been for more than a half century a number of clubs, some of them consisting of no more than four or five members, which have published occasionally works of literary interest. The majority of these strictly private clubs have put their attention principally upon local American history and literature; but the publications of a few of them possess a broader significance.[19] The earliest of these, the Bradford Club,

[19] For the history of most of these smaller institutions see Growoll's *American Book Clubs,* 1897, and Thompson's *Handbook of Learned Societies and Institutions,* 1908.

founded in New York in 1857, issued three years later *The Croakers* of Halleck and Drake, a series of satires contributed in 1811 to the *Evening Post* of New York. The Naragansett Club, of Providence, sent out between 1865 and 1874 six volumes by or relating to Roger Williams. The Club of Odd Volumes, organized in Boston in 1886, published from 1894 to 1898 five volumes of *Early American Poetry* and some useful histories of the Massachusetts press and book-trade.

The Rowfant Club, established in Cleveland in 1892, has published a number of works in English literature, most of them more noteworthy for bibliophile excellence than for original or critical value. Among its issues are a volume of Drake's poems, Landor's *Letter to Emerson,* Frederick Locker's *Rowfant Rhymes,* and Franklin's *Autobiography.* In a class of superior merit, however, are Samuel Arthur Jones's *Bibliography of Henry David Thoreau,* 1894, Lowell's *Lectures on English Poets,* delivered in 1855 before the Lowell Institute, and published by the club in 1897, and W. H. Cathcart's *Bibliography of the Works of Nathaniel Hawthorne,* 1905.

The Society of the Duodecimos, a club of twelve members organized in 1893, issued in 1897 an important edition by Charles Eliot Norton of *The Poems of Mrs. Anne Bradstreet.* The Caxton Club of Chicago, formed two years later, published in 1898, *Some Letters of Edgar Allan Poe to E. H. N. Patterson.* The Club for Colonial Reprints, founded at Providence in 1903, has issued two small Freneau and Roger Williams items. Besides these minor book clubs, other kinds of organizations have rendered service of more or less magnitude to English studies in America; for example the Acorn Club, with a series in Colonial history and bibliography, the Princeton Historical Association, with its three volumes of *The Poems of*

Philip Freneau (1902–1907), and the Bibliographical Society of America, with many papers in literary bibliography. In addition to these must be mentioned the American Historical Association and a number of local historical societies in the East, most notably the Prince Society and the Massachusetts Historical Society, which have included in their publications from time to time occasional examples of early American literature or historical documents which possess a value for literary students.

It will be seen from the present brief review of American literary organizations that the place of learned societies in the traditions of American literary scholarship is relatively unimportant. The Modern Language Association only has produced work comparable in volume and significance to the productions of English learned societies. The book clubs, however, have played, and are likely to continue to play, an important part in the furtherance of literary culture; in fact they compare favorably with their great predecessors in England and Scotland. Altogether, America's part in this special movement is very creditable.

BIBLIOGRAPHY

(Prospectuses, announcements, advertisements, and annual reports of societies have been omitted from this bibliography. Where such leaflets have furnished information of substantial value, foot-note references to them have been given in full. See *infra*, Aelfric Society, Ballad Society, Browning Society, Concordance Society, Early English Dialect Society, Early English Drama Society, Early English Text Society, English Historical Society, Hakluyt Society, Hunterian Club, Philological Society, Royal Society of Literature, Scottish Text Society, Shakespeare Society, Simplified Spelling Board, and Society of Antiquaries.)

American Book Prices Current . . . . 18 v., New York, 1895–1912.

(AMERICAN DIALECT SOCIETY.) *Dialect Notes. Published by the American Dialect Society.* 3 v., Norwood and New Haven, 1896–[1912].

AMERICAN PHILOLOGICAL ASSOCIATION. *Transactions* . . . . 43˜ v., Hartford, etc., 1871–1912. (Later volumes have title *Transactions and Proceedings.*)

ARNOLD, MATTHEW. *The Literary Influence of Academies.* In *Essays in Criticism,* London, 1895.

ASSER. *Life of King Alfred together with the Annals of Saint Neots* . . . . Edited . . . by William Henry Stevenson. Oxford, 1904.

AUBREY, JOHN. '*Brief Lives,*' *chiefly of Contemporaries, set down . . . between . . . 1669 & 1696.* Edited by Andrew Clark. 2 v., Oxford, 1898.

AUBREY, JOHN (Editor). *Letters [from the Bodleian] written by eminent Persons in the seventeenth and eighteenth Centuries* . . . . 2 v. in 3, London, 1813.

BACON, SIR FRANCIS. *The Advancement of Learning.* Edited by William Aldis Wright . . . . 2d Ed., Oxford, 1873.

BACON, SIR FRANCIS. *The New Atlantis* . . . . Edited . . . by G. C. Moore Smith. Cambridge, 1900.

(BALE, JOHN.) *A letter from Bishop Bale to Archbishop Parker.* Communicated by H. R. Luard . . . . *Cambridge Antiquarian Communications,* III, 157–73. Cambridge, 1879.

(BANNATYNE CLUB.) *Adversaria. Notices illustrative of some of the earlier works printed for the Bannatyne Club.* [Edited by David Laing.] Edinburgh, 1867.

BARTHOLD, F. W. *Geschichte der Fruchtbringenden Gesellschaft* . . . . Berlin, 1848.

BIBLIOPHILE SOCIETY. *First [Second, etc.] Year Book.* 11 v., [Boston], [1902]–1912.

BIRCH, THOMAS. *The History of the Royal Society of London for Improving of Natural Knowledge* . . . . 4 v., London, 1756–7.

BOHN, HENRY G. *Appendix relating to the Books of Literary and Scientific Societies.* (Vol. 6 of William Thomas Lowndes' *Bibliographer's Manual of English Literature.*) London, 1864.

BOSTON BROWNING SOCIETY. *Papers . . . 1886–1897.* New York, 1900.

BOSWELL, JAMES. *Life of Johnson* . . . . Edited by George Birkbeck Hill. 6 v., Oxford, 1887.

BOWKER, R. R. *Publications of Societies; a Provisional List of the Publications of American Scientific, Literary, and other Societies* . . . . New York, 1899.

BOYLE, ROBERT. *Works.* To which is prefixed the Life of the Author. A new Edition. 6 v., London, 1772.

BRABROOK, EDWARD WILLIAM. *On the Fellows of the Society of Antiquaries who have held the Office of Director. Archaeologia,* LXII, 59–80, 1910.

BRITISH ACADEMY. *Proceedings . . . , 1903–1904.* London, n. d.

BRITISH MUSEUM. *Catalogue of Printed Books; Academies, Part I* [complete in this part]. London, 1885. *Supplement.* London, 1900.

BROWNING SOCIETY. *Papers* . . . . Nos. 1–13 [No. 6 not issued], in 3 v., London, 1881–91.

BURTON, JOHN HILL. *The Book-Hunter Etc.* New York, 1883.

Caedmon's Metrical Paraphrase of Parts of the Holy Scriptures
. . . . [Edited by] Benjamin Thorpe. Society of Antiquaries, 1832.

(CAMDEN, WILLIAM.) *Gulielmi Camdeni et Illustrium Virorum Epistolae* . . . . Praemittitur G. Camdeni Vita, Scriptore Thoma Smitho . . . . Londini, 1691.

CAMPBELL, JOHN, LORD. *The Lives of the Lord Chancellors and Keepers of the Great Seal of England* . . . . 8 v., London, 1846–69.

CAREW, RICHARD. *The Survey of Cornwall* . . . . With the Life of the Author . . . [by Pierre des Maizeaux]. London, 1723.

CHALMERS, GEORGE. *The Life of Thomas Ruddiman* . . . . London, 1794.

CHAMBERLAYNE, EDWARD. *Angliae Notitiae or The Present State of England* . . . . Continued by his Son, John Chamberlayne . . . . 21st Ed., London, 1704.

CHATTERTON, THOMAS. *Poetical Works*. With an Essay on the Rowley Poems by W. W. Skeat. 2 v., London, 1875.

(CLERK, SIR JOHN.) *Memoirs of the Life of Sir John Clerk of Penecuik* . . . . Edited . . . by John M. Gray. Scottish History Society, 1892.

COWLEY, ABRAHAM. *Essays, Plays and Sundry Verses*. The text edited by A. R. Waller. Cambridge, 1906.

[CROKER, THOMAS CROFTON.] *Remarks on an Article inserted in the Papers of the Shakespeare Society*. [1849].

CUST, LIONEL, and SIDNEY COLVIN. *History of the Society of the Dilettanti*. London, 1898.

(DEFOE, DANIEL.) *Earlier Life and chief earlier Works*. Edited by Henry Morley. London, 1889.

DELEPIERRE, OCTAVE. *Analyse des Travaux de la Société des Philobiblon de Londres* . . . . Londres, 1862.

DIBDIN, THOMAS FROGNALL. *The Bibliographical Decameron* . . . . 3 v., London, 1817.

DIBDIN, THOMAS FROGNALL. *Reminiscences of a Literary Life*. 2 v., London, 1836.

DIRCKS, H. *A Biographical Memoir of Samuel Hartlib*. London, n. d.

DRYDEN, JOHN. *Works* . . . . Illustrated with notes . . . and a life of the author by Sir Walter Scott. Revised and corrected by George Saintsbury. 18 v., Edinburgh, 1882–93.

[DUNCAN, WILLIAM JAMES, Editor.] *Notices and Documents illustrative of the Literary History of Glasgow during the greater Part of the Last Century.* Maitland Club, 1831.

(EDINBURGH SHAKSPEARE CLUB.) *Rules and Regulations of the Edinburgh Shakspeare Club and Library, Instituted MDCCCXX* . . . . Edinburgh, 1826.

ELLIS, SIR HENRY (Editor). *Original Letters of Eminent Literary Men of the Sixteenth, Seventeenth, and Eighteenth Centuries.* Camden Society, 1843.

English Dialect Dictionary (The). Founded on the Publications of the English Dialect Society and on . . . material never before published. Edited by Joseph Wright. 6 v., London, 1898–1905.

EVELYN, JOHN. *Memoirs . . . comprising his Diary, from 1641 to 1705–6, and a Selection of his Familiar Letters* . . . . Edited . . . by William Bray. 5 v., London, 1827.

FITZMAURICE, LORD EDMOND. *The Life of Sir William Petty, 1623–1687* . . . . London, 1895.

FLETCHER, JEFFERSON B. *Areopagus and Pleiade. Journal of English and Germanic Philology,* II, 429–53. Bloomington, [1898].

FLÜGEL, EWALD. *Die älteste englische Akademie. Anglia,* XXXII, 261–8. Halle a. S., 1909.

FORBES, JAMES DAVID. *Opening Address, 1862.* In *Proceedings of the Royal Society of Edinburgh,* V, 2–34, 1866.

(FURNIVALL, FREDERICK JAMES.) *Frederick James Furnivall, a Volume of Personal Record.* Oxford, 1911.

FURNIVALL, FREDERICK JAMES. *The "Co." of Pigsbrook & Co.* [London, 1881.]

[GOUGH, RICHARD.] *A List of the Members of the Society of Antiquaries of London, from their Revival in 1717, to June 19, 1796.* London, 1798.

[GOUGH, RICHARD.] *An Historical Account of the Origin and Establishment of the Society of Antiquaries. Archaeologia,* I, i–xxxix. London, 1777.

GOSSE, EDMUND. *Jeremy Taylor.* London, 1904.

GRAHAM, HENRY GREY. *Scottish Men of Letters in the Eighteenth Century.* London, 1901.

GRIFFIN, APPLETON PRENTISS CLARK. *Bibliography of American Historical Societies . . . .* 2d Ed., [Vol. II of *Annual Report of the American Historical Association for 1905*]. Washington, 1907.

GROWOLL, A. *American Book Clubs; their Beginnings and History, and a Bibliography of their Publications.* New York, 1897.

HALLIWELL-PHILLIPPS, JAMES ORCHARD. [*Published Correspondence with Robert Browning, President of the New Shakspere Society.* 1881.]

HAMMOND, ELEANOR PRESCOTT. *Chaucer; a Bibliographical Manual . . . .* New York, 1908.

HEARNE, THOMAS. *A Collection of Curious Discourses written by Eminent Antiquaries upon several Heads in our English Antiquities . . . .* 2d Ed., 2 v., London, 1775.

HEARNE, THOMAS. *Remarks and Collections.* Edited by C. E. Doble, [Vols. 4–5 by D. W. Rannie, and Vols. 6–8 under the Superintendence of the Committee of the Oxford Historical Society]. 8 v., Oxford Historical Society, 1885–1907.

HIBBERT, SAMUEL, and DAVID LAING. *Account of the Progress of the Society of the Antiquaries of Scotland, from 1784 to 1830. Archaeologia Scotica,* III, App., v–xxxi, 1831.

HICKES, GEORGE. *Linguarum Vet[erum] Septentrionalium Thesaurus Grammatico-Criticus et Archaeologicus . . . .* 2 v., Oxoniae, 1705. (For title page of Vol. 2, see Humphrey Wanley, *Antiquae Literaturae Septentrionalis Liber Alter.*)

HUME, ABRAHAM. *The Learned Societies and Printing Clubs of the United Kingdom . . . .* Compiled from official Documents. With a Supplement . . . by A. I. Evans. London, 1853.

HUNTER, JOSEPH. *An Account of the Scheme for erecting a Royal Academy in England in the Reign of King James the First. Archaeologia,* XXXII, 132–49, 1847.

[INNES, COSMO.] *Memoir of Thomas Thomson.* Edinburgh, 1854.

JOHNSON, SAMUEL. *Works.* 9 v., Oxford, 1825.

JUNIUS, FRANCISCUS. *Etymologicum Anglicanum.* Ex Autographo descripsit & Accessionibus permultis Auctum edidit Edwardus Lye . . . . Praemittuntur Vita Auctoris [Auctore Johanne Georgio Graevio] . . . . Oxonii, 1713.

KEMBLE, JOHN M. *Letter to Francisque Michel.* In Michel's *Bibliotheque Anglo-Saxonne.* Paris, 1837; pp. 1–63.

KENNETT, WHITE. [*The Life of Mr. Somner.*] In William Somner's *A Treatise of Gavelkind, both Name and Thing* . . . . 2d Ed., 1726.

KERR, ROBERT. *Memoirs of the Life, Writings, and Correspondence of William Smellie* . . . . 2 v., Edinburgh, 1811.

LAING, DAVID. *Anniversary Address on the State of the Society of Antiquaries of Scotland, from 1831 to 1860. Archaeologia Scotica,* V, 1–36, 1890.

LELAND, JOHN. *The laboryouse journey and serche of John Leylande, for Englandes antiquitees . . . With declaracyons enlarged: by Johan Bale* . . . . [Colophon] Emprented at London by Johan Bale. Anno. M. D. XLIX.

LEWIS, LADY THERESA. *Lives of the Friends and Contemporaries of Lord Chancellor Clarendon* . . . . 3 v., London, 1852.

LITERARY AND PHILOSOPHICAL SOCIETY OF MANCHESTER. *Memoirs* . . . [First Series]. 5 v. in 7, Warrington, 1785–1802.

LOCKHART, JOHN GIBSON. *Memoirs of the Life of Sir Walter Scott.* 5 v., Boston, 1902.

LOWE, ROBERT W. *A Bibliographical Account of English Theatrical Literature* . . . . London, 1888.

McCOSH, JAMES. *The Scottish Philosophy . . . from Hutcheson to Hamilton.* New York, 1875.

MACKENZIE, HENRY. *Report of the Committee of the Highland Society of Scotland appointed to inquire into the Nature and Authenticity of the Poems of Ossian* . . . . Edinburgh, 1805.

MACRAY, WILLIAM DUNN. *Annals of the Bodleian Library, Oxford, A. D. 1598–A. D. 1867* . . . . London, 1868.

[MAIDMENT, JAMES.] *Notices relative to the Bannatyne Club . . . including Critiques on some of its Publications.* Edinburgh, 1836.

(MAITLAND CLUB.) *Catalogue of the Works printed for the Maitland Club . . . with Lists of the Members and Rules of the Club.* Printed for the Maitland Club, 1836.

MARRIOT, J. A. R. *The Life and Times of Lucius Cary, Viscount Falkland.* London, 1907.

MARTIN, JOHN. *A bibliographical Catalogue of Books privately printed . . . .* London, 1834. (Second Edition, 1854.)

MATTHEWS, BRANDER. *Bookbindings old and new . . . . With an Account of the Grolier Club of New York.* New York, 1895.

MODERN LANGUAGE ASSOCIATION OF AMERICA. *Transactions,* 7 v., Baltimore, 1886–92. (Vols. 4–7 have title *Publications.*)

MODERN LANGUAGE ASSOCIATION OF AMERICA. *Publications . . . . New Series.* 20 v., Baltimore, 1893–1912.

MONROE, B. S. *An English Academy. Modern Philology,* VIII, 107–122. Chicago, 1910.

MONROE, WILL S. *Comenius and the Beginnings of Educational Reform.* New York, 1900.

MOORE, WILLIAM. *The Gentlemen's Society at Spalding, with Notices of the Researches and Labours of the earliest Lincoln-shire Antiquaries.* In *Memoirs communicated to the Annual Meeting of the Archaeological Institute of Great Britain and Ireland held at Lincoln, July, 1848;* 82–9. London, 1850.

MUNK, WILLIAM. *The Roll of the Royal College of Physicians of London . . . .* 3 v., London, 1878.

NEW SHAKSPERE SOCIETY. *Transactions, 1874–[1892].* 14 nos.. London, [1875]–1892.

[NICHOLS, JOHN.] *An Account of the Gentlemen's Society at Spalding.* Being an Introduction to the *Reliquae Galeanae.* [Nichols's *Bibliotheca Topographica Britannica,* No. XX.] London, 1784.

NICHOLS, JOHN. *Biographical Memoirs of the late Isaac Reed, Esq. Gentleman's Magazine,* LXXVII, 80–2, 1807.

NICHOLS, JOHN. *Literary Anecdotes of the Eighteenth Century . . . .* 9 v., London, 1812–15.

NICHOLS, JOHN GOUGH. *A Descriptive Catalogue of the Works of the Camden Society . . . .* Camden Society, 1862.

NICOLSON, WILLIAM. *Letters on Various Subjects . . . to and from William Nicolson . . . .* [Edited by] John Nichols. London, 1809.

OLDYS, WILLIAM. *Life of Sir Walter Ralegh.* In Sir Walter Ralegh's *History of the World . . . .* 2 v., London, 1736, I, iii–ccxxxii.

PARKER, JAMES. *The Early History of Oxford, 727–1100 . . . .* Oxford Historical Society, 1885.

(PARKER, MATTHEW.) *Correspondence . . . , comprising Letters written by and to him, from 1535 to . . . 1575.* Edited . . . by John Bruce and Thomas Thomason Perowne. Parker Society, 1853.

(PATON, GEORGE.) *Letters from Thomas Percy, John Callander, David Herd, and others, to George Paton.* Edinburgh, 1830.

PEPYS, SAMUEL. *Diary . . . .* Edited . . . by Henry B. Wheatley. 9 v., London, 1893–9.

PERCY, THOMAS. *Reliques of Ancient English Poetry . . . .* Edited . . . by Henry B. Wheatley. 3 v., London, 1886.

(PERCY, THOMAS.) *Bishop Percy's Folio Manuscript. Ballads and Romances.* Edited by John W. Hales and Frederick J. Furnivall. 4 v., London, 1867–8.

PETHERAM, JOHN. *An Historical Sketch of the Progress and Present State of Anglo-Saxon Literature in England . . . .* London, 1840.

PHILOLOGICAL SOCIETY. *Proceedings . . . .* [*1842–1853.*] 6 v., London, 1854.

PHILOLOGICAL SOCIETY. *Transactions . . . .* 26 v., London, etc., [1856]–1913.

PRIOR, SIR JAMES. *Life of Edmond Malone . . . .* London, 1850.

QUARITCH, BERNARD. *Account of the Great Learned Societies and Associations, and of the Chief Printing Clubs of Great Britain and Ireland . . . .* [Sette of Odd Volumes, *Miscellanies,* No. 14.] London, 1886.

RITCHIE, THOMAS EDWARD. *An Account of the Life and Writings of David Hume.* London, 1807.

ROBERTSON, D. MACLAREN. *A History of the French Academy, 1635[4]–1910 . . . .* New York [1910].

Roxburghe Ballads (The). [Vols. 1–3 edited by William Chappell, and 4–9 by Joseph Woodfall Ebsworth.] 8 v. in 9, Hertford, 1888–97 [–99].

ROXBURGHE CLUB. *Chronological List of Members; Catalogue of Books; Rules and Regulations*. London, 1855.

(ROXBURGHE CLUB.) *Roxburghe Revels, and other relative Papers; including Answers to the Attack on the Memory of the late Joseph Haslewood* .... Edinburgh, 1837.

ROYAL HISTORICAL SOCIETY. *Transactions, New Series.* 20 v., London, 1884–[1906].

(ROYAL IRISH ACADEMY.) *Charter and Statutes of the Royal Irish Academy for Promoting the Study of Science, Polite Literature, and Antiquities.* Dublin, 1786.

ROYAL IRISH ACADEMY. *Transactions* .... 32 v., Dublin, 1788–1904.

(ROYAL SOCIETY OF EDINBURGH.) *History of the Society.* In *Transactions of the Royal Society of Edinburgh*, I, 3–22, 1788.

ROYAL SOCIETY OF LITERATURE. *Transactions* .... Vol. I, Pt. I, London, 1827.

(ROYAL SOCIETY OF LONDON.) *Philosophical Transactions of the Royal Society* .... Abridged by Charles Hutton, George Shaw, and Richard Pearson. 18 v., London, 1809.

(ROYAL SOCIETY OF LONDON.) *The Record of the Royal Society of London.* Third Edition, entirely revised and rearranged. London, 1912.

SAUNDERS, BAILEY. *The Life and Letters of James Macpherson* .... London, 1894.

SCOTT, SIR WALTER. *Familiar Letters.* [Edited by David Douglas.] 2 v., Boston, 1894.

SCOTT, SIR WALTER. *Journal* .... From the original Manuscript at Abbotsford. [Edited by David Douglas.] 2 v., Edinburgh, 1890.

SCOTT, SIR WALTER. *Minstrelsy of the Scottish Border.* Edited by T. F. Henderson. 4 v., Edinburgh, 1902.

[SCOTT, SIR WALTER.] [*Review of*] *Trials, and other Proceedings, in Matters Criminal, before the High Court of*

Justiciary in Scotland. Selected . . . by Robert Pitcairn . . . . *Quarterly Review*, XLIV, 438–75. London, 1831.

Shakespeare Societies of America: Their Methods and Work. Shakespeareana, II, 480–8, 1885.

SHAKESPEARE SOCIETY. *Papers* . . . . 4 v., London, 1844–9.

SHEFFIELD SHAKESPEARE CLUB. *Proceedings . . . from its Commencement, in 1819, to January, 1829* . . . . Sheffield, 1829.

SHELLEY SOCIETY. *Note-Book* . . . . Edited by the Honorary Secretaries. Part I, being the First Part of Volume I [all published]. London, 1888.

SKEAT, WALTER W. *The Chaucer Canon. With a Discussion of the Works associated with the Name of Geoffrey Chaucer* . . . . Oxford, 1900.

SKEAT, WALTER W., Editor. *Chaucerian and other Pieces.* Oxford, 1897.

SMALL, JOHN. [*Memoir of David Laing.*] In *Select Remains of the Ancient Popular and Romance Poetry of Scotland, collected and edited by David Laing.* Re-edited . . . by John Small. Edinburgh, 1885. (*Memorial Introduction*, v–xxviii.)

SMELLIE, WILLIAM. *An Historical Account of the Society of the Antiquaries of Scotland.* In *Transactions of the Society of the Antiquaries of Scotland*, I, iii–xxxiii, 1792.

SMITH, R. ANGUS. *A Centenary of Science in Manchester* . . . . London, 1883.

SMITH, THOMAS. *Vita D. Roberti Cottoni* . . . . In [Christian Gryphius's] *Vitae Selectae quorundam eruditissimorum ac illustrium Virorum*, 434–536. Vratislaviae, 1711. (Reprinted from Smith's *Catalogus Librorum Manuscriptorum Bibliothecae Cottonianae* . . . . 1696.)

(SOCIETY OF ANTIQUARIES OF LONDON.) *Archaeologia or Miscellaneous Tracts relating to Antiquity.* Published by the Society of Antiquaries of London. 62 v., London and Oxford, 1770–1911.

SOCIETY OF THE ANTIQUARIES OF SCOTLAND. *Transactions* . . . . 5 v., Edinburgh, 1792–1890. (Vols. 2–5 have title *Archaeologia Scotica or Transactions.*)

SOMNER, WILLIAM. *Dictionarium Saxonico-Latino-Anglicum ... Acceserunt Aelfrici Abbatis Grammatica Latino-Saxonica, cum Glossario ....* Oxonii, 1659.

SPELMAN, SIR HENRY. *English Works ... published in his Life-Time; together with his posthumous Works relating to the Laws and Antiquities of England ....* 2d Ed., London, 1727.

SPINGARN, J. E., Editor. *Critical Essays of the Seventeenth Century.* 3 v., Oxford, 1908–9.

SPRAT, THOMAS. *The History of the Royal Society of London for the Improving of Natural Knowledge.* London, 1667.

STEEVES, HARRISON ROSS. *'The Athenian Virtuosi' and 'The Athenian Society.' Modern Language Review,* VII, 358–71, 1912.

STEVENSON, THOMAS GEORGE. *Notices of David Laing ... To which is added a Chronological List of the various Publications which were issued under his editorial Superintendence from ... 1815 to ... 1878 inclusive.* Edinburgh, 1878.

STEWART, DUGALD. *Collected Works ....* Edited by Sir William Hamilton. 10 v., Edinburgh, 1854–8.

STEWART, DUGALD. *Account of the Life and Writings of Adam Smith.* In *Essays on Philosophical Subjects by ... Adam Smith.* London, 1795.

STEWART, DUGALD. *Account of the Life and Writings of Thomas Reid ....* Edinburgh, 1803.

STEWART, DUGALD. *Account of the Life and Writings of William Robertson ....* London, 1801.

STOW, JOHN. *The Annales, or Generall Chronicle of England. Begun first by Maister Iohn Stow, and after him continued and augmented ... unto the Ende of this present Yeere, 1614, by Edmond Howes ....* Londini, 1615.

STRANG, JOHN. *Glasgow and its Clubs ....* Glasgow, 1856.

STRYPE, JOHN. *History of the Life and Acts of ... Edmund Grindal ... to which is added an Appendix of original Manuscripts ....* Oxford, 1821.

STRYPE, JOHN. *The Life and Acts of Matthew Parker ....* 3 v., Oxford, 1821.

[STUART, JOHN.] *Notices of the Spalding Club. With the*

Annual Reports, List of Members and Works printed for the Club, 1839–71. Edinburgh, 1871.

STUKELEY, WILLIAM. *Family Memoirs . . . and the antiquarian and other Correspondence of William Stukeley, Roger and Samuel Gale, etc.* 3 v., Surtees Society, 1882–7.

SWINBURNE, ALGERNON CHARLES. *A Stuly of Shakespeare.* London, 1880.

TAYLOR, GEORGE. *A Memoir of Robert Surtees . . . .* A new Edition, with annotations by . . . James Raine. Surtees Society, [1852].

[TEDDER, HENRY RICHARD.] *Learned Societies.* In *Encyclopaedia Britannica . . . .* 11th Ed., XXV, 309–19. Cambridge, 1911.

TERRY, CHARLES SANDFORD. *A Catalogue of the Publications of Scottish Historical and kindred Clubs and Societies, 1780–1908 . . . .* Glasgow, 1909.

[THOMPSON, J. DAVID, Editor.] *Handbook of Learned Societies and Institutions: America.* Washington, Carnegie Institution, 1908.

THYNNE, FRANCIS. *Animaduersions vppon the Annotacions and Corrections of some Imperfections of Impressiones of Chaucers Workes . . . reprinted in . . . 1598 . . . .* Newly edited . . . by G. H. Kingsley . . . . Revis'd Edition by F. J. Furnivall . . . . Early English Text Society, 186[7]5.

TIMBS, JOHN. *Club Life of London . . . during the 17th, 18th, and 19th Centuries.* 2 v., London, 1866.

TYTLER, ALEXANDER FRASER. *Memoirs of the Life and Writings of Henry Home of Kames . . . .* 2d Ed., 3 v., Edinburgh, 1814.

VOCKERODT, GOTHFRED. *Exercitationes Academicae: sive Commentatio Eruditorum Societatibus . . . .* Gothae, 1704.

WANLEY, HUMPHREY. *Antiquae Literaturae Septentrionalis Liber Alter. 'Seu . . . Librorum vett. septentrionalium . . . Catalogus historico-criticus . . . .* Oxoniae, 1705. (Second volume of Hickes's *Thesaurus.*)

WARNER, GEORGE F. *Catalogue of the Manuscripts and Muniments of Alleyn's College of God's Gift at Dulwich.* [London], 1881.

WARTON, THOMAS. *Poetical Works* . . . . Fifth Edition . . . together with Memoirs of his Life and Writings, and Notes . . . by Richard Mant. 2 v., Oxford, 1802.

WATSON, FOSTER. *Scholars and Scholarship, 1600–60.* In *Cambridge History of English Literature*, VII, 304–24, 1911.

WELD, CHARLES RICHARD. *A History of the Royal Society, with Memoirs of the Presidents.* Compiled from authentic Documents . . . . 2 v., London, 1848.

WHEATLEY, HENRY B. *How to Form a Library.* 2d Ed., New York, 1886. (Chapter VII, *Publishing Societies*, 184–216.)

WHEATLEY, HENRY B. *Notes on the Life of John Payne Collier; with a complete List of his Works, and an Account of such Shakespeare Documents as are believed to be spurious.* London, 1884. (Reprinted from *The Bibliographer*, 1883–4).

WHITE, R. M. [and JOHN EARLE]. *The Ormulum, with the Notes and Glossary of R. M. White.* Edited by Robert Holt. 2 v., Oxford, 1878. (*Preface*, including a valuable account of Anglo-Saxon scholarship, i–liii.)

WOOD, ANTHONY À. *Athenae Oxonienses* . . . . A new Edition, with Additions and a continuation by Philip Bliss . . . . 5 v., London, 1813–20.

WORDSWORTH SOCIETY. *Transactions* . . . . 8 Nos., [*1882–7*].

(WORDSWORTH SOCIETY.) *Wordsworthiana, a Selection from Papers read to the Wordsworth Society.* Edited by William Knight. London, 1889.

WORTHINGTON, JOHN. *Diary and Correspondence* . . . . Edited by James Crossley [and Richard Copley Christie]. 2 v. in 3, Chetham Society, 1847–86.

WRIGHT, THOMAS. *Biographica Britannica Literaria, or Biography of literary Characters of Great Britain and Ireland arranged in chronological Order.* 2 v., London, 1842–6. (All published.)

WÜLCKER, RICHARD. *Grundriss zur Geschichte der angelsächsischen Litteratur mit einer Übersicht der angelsächsischen Sprachwissenschaft.* Leipzig, 1885.

Year-Book of the Scientific and Learned Societies of Great Britain and Ireland . . . . 28 v., London, 1884–1911.

INDEX

17